FIRST BOREDOM, THEN FEAR

By the same author

Introducing Literary Studies
A Linguistic History of English Poetry
The Look of It: A Theory of Visual Form in English Poetry
John Milton: A Complete Critical Guide
Milton's Paradise Lost: An Open Guide
Roman Jakobson: Life, Language, Art
Silence and Sound: Theories of Poetics from the Eighteenth Century
The State of Theory
Stylistics

Also published by Peter Owen

Lucky Him: The Life of Kingsley Amis

FIRST BOREDOM, THEN FEAR

The Life of Philip Larkin

Richard Bradford

Peter Owen
London and Chester Springs

PETER OWEN PUBLISHERS
73 Kenway Road, London SW5 0RE

Peter Owen books are distributed in the USA by
Dufour Editions Inc., Chester Springs, PA 19425-0007

First published in Great Britain 2005
© Richard Bradford 2005

ISBN 0 7206 1147 4

A catalogue record for this book is available from the British Library.

Printed and bound in Bodmin, Cornwall
by MPG Books Ltd

For Helen and Gerard Burns
and Amy

Acknowledgements

Particular thanks are due to Rosemary Savage for the time she gave to this project in the summer of 2004. Michelle Martin has also provided valuable assistance. Amy Burns, as usual, has been patient and tolerant. I apologize for any omissions with regard to copyright material and will be pleased to incorporate missing acknowledgements in future editions.

Contents

Illustrations

Introduction

The photograph of Philip Larkin which most people, fans and begrudgers alike, would select as by far the most Larkinesque has him sitting at the side of the road at Coldstream on the Scottish border. It's 1962, he's wearing a check tweed jacket and plain cloth tie and staring intently at the camera. One suspects that the ghost of a smile is beginning to form, a blend of self-directed irony and self-satisfaction. It is perfect, 'like something almost being said'. He looks like one of his poems, but, best of all, the photograph has him off-centre, seated as he is on the side of a low stone obelisk which bears a single word beneath St George's shield: 'ENGLAND'.

Five years earlier Charles Tomlinson had written that Larkin's 'narrowness suits the English perfectly'. 'They recognise their own abysmal suburban landscapes, skilfully caught ... The stepped down version of human possibilities ... the joke that hesitates just on this side of nihilism, are national vices.' Whether Larkin had Tomlinson in mind when he posed for the photograph will remain a point for speculation – it is possible, because Monica Jones, the photographer, later reported that Larkin took time to urinate over the sign before posing for the shot – but the image was certainly prescient. After Tomlinson there was a good deal of complicit grumbling, with Larkin savoured by radicals and internationalists as an easy target. Terms such as 'philistine', 'parochial', 'suburban' or more sympathetically 'wistful', 'sad' and 'circumspect' would follow him to the grave, with Englishness as their accompanying subtext.

Even Seamus Heaney, whose admiration for Larkin as a fellow poet was unconditional, found it necessary almost to apologize on his behalf for a state of mind over which Larkin had no control.

> He is . . . the insular English man, responding to the tones of his own clan, ill at ease when out of his environment. He is a poet indeed of a composed and tempered English nationalism, and his voice is the not untrue, not unkind voice of post-war England, where the cloth cap and the royal crown have both lost their potent symbolism. (*Preoccupations: Selected Prose, 1968–78*, p.167)

The accumulation of reflective, qualifying sub-clauses – 'not untrue, not unkind' – indicates Heaney's wish to excuse Larkin from what might otherwise be taken as an accusation: he *is* an Englishman but, well, he's not the worst sort. Others were less charitable.

According to Tom Paulin, Larkin might seem to speak for 'the English male, middle class, professional, outwardly confident, controlled and in control', which Paulin implies is bad enough, but this demeanour masks deeper repressions and complexes. Larkin 'writhes with anxiety inside that sealed bunker which is the English ethic of privacy', a collective mood of loss and failure, the end of Empire. In Paulin's view even Larkin's reluctance to get married partakes of this psychological fear of losing sovereignty. Larkin's political counterpart is Norman Tebbit. 'Larkin's snarl, his populism and his calculated philistinism all speak for Tebbit's England and for that gnarled and angry puritanism which is so deeply ingrained in the culture' (*Times Literary Supplement*, 20–26 July 1990, pp. 779–80). The hint that there is a connection between England's national decline and sexual disappointment, both apparently evident in Larkin's verse, became something of a cliché. (Note Heaney's reference to a 'lost . . . potent symbolism'.) Neil Corcoran: 'Larkin's idea of England is as deeply and intimately wounded by such post-imperial withdrawals [*sic*] as some of the personae of his poems are wounded by sexual impotence' (*English Poetry Since 1940*, p. 87).

Had a commentator proposed a similar interrelationship between a particular, if presumed, state of mind and a national condition with regard to an Irish, Scottish or Welsh writer he or she would probably have been accused of racism or condescension. But for some time open season has been declared on the type of Englishness that Larkin is perceived to represent. In a 1959 essay Larkin offered an admiring appraisal of John Betjeman, and there are parallels between their work. Both valued a sense of place, and while Betjeman's idyllic blend of suburbia and countryside was recognizably Home Counties, Larkin's shabbier provincial locations carried the same air of contented tenancy. But in 1964, the year *The Whitsun Weddings* was published, Betjeman had become as much a lovable curiosity as a serious literary presence – his England could be filed under the same category of willed antiquarianism as Stratford-upon-Avon. Larkin, however, had become associated with a more antagonistic, far less tolerable brand of Englishness.

The movement became a Movement following the publication of three anthologies of contemporary verse, edited by Robert Conquest, D.J. Enright and G.S. Fraser, in 1955–6; Larkin's work featured in all three. At the time the Movement was disliked mainly because it favoured accessibility and craftsmanship over the experimentalism of the Modernists and the neo-Romantics of the 1940s; and aesthetic conservatism in the twentieth century always guaranteed accusations of treachery. Since the 1950s, Movement writing has been regarded as a more complex network of ideological, political and cultural doctrines, as Blake Morrison's comprehensive but by no means impartial study (1980) demonstrates. If one wonders how Heaney and Paulin felt licensed virtually to accuse Larkin of Englishness, Morrison offers a kind of theoretical subtext: Anti-modernism is complicit with political conservatism; the use of England as the locative fabric of writing is a version of colonialism; provincialism, and its handmaiden nostalgia, could at a stretch be associated with racism.

All of the criticism of Larkin cited so far was produced either during his life or in the seven years following his death in 1985. But when Thwaite's edition of the *Letters* was published in 1992 and Motion's biography came out a year later Larkin's enemies seized upon these new disclosures with a frenzy hardly witnessed since the McCarthy era.

The letters themselves provided a number of fascinating examples of what had hitherto been regarded only as potential inclinations evidenced by Larkin's poems. He complained to Amis in 1943, for example, that 'all women are stupid beings' and remarked in 1983 that he'd recently accompanied Monica to a hospital 'staffed ENTIRELY by wogs, cheerful and incompetent' (31 July). His views on politics and class seemed to be pithily captured in a ditty he shared again with Amis. 'I want to see them starving, / The so-called working class, / Their wages yearly halving, / Their women stewing grass . . .' For recreation he apparently found time for pornography, preferably with a hint of sado-masochism: '. . . I mean like WATCHING SCHOOLGIRLS SUCK EACH OTHER OFF WHILE YOU WHIP THEM.'

Tom Paulin had had his suspicions confirmed but managed to curb his elation. He found the letters to be 'a distressing and in many ways revolting compilation which imperfectly reveals and conceals the sewer under the national monument Larkin became' (*Times Literary Supplement*, 7 November 1992). So there. One suspects that Paulin's metaphor lodged in Andrew Motion's mind because a sanitized version of it resurfaced in the preface to his biography of Larkin little more than a year later. Motion wrote of 'the beautiful flowers of his poetry . . . growing on long stalks out of pretty dismal ground'.

Others disagreed with Motion's maintenance of a separation between the man and his art. Lisa Jardine of the English Department, Queen Mary and Westfield, University of London, stated that while they would not go quite so far as to ban the study of Larkin his poems would be removed from the core curriculum and dealt with only to disclose 'the beliefs which lie behind them' – presumably according them a status similar, say, to *Mein Kampf* in a course on political philosophy. How, asked Jardine, could Larkin continue to be presented as a 'humane' writer when the student who consults the *Letters* is met with 'a steady stream of obscenity, throwaway derogatory remarks about women and arrogant disdain for those of different skin colour or nationality?' (*Guardian*, 8 December 1992). How indeed. One feels confident that parents throughout Britain remained grateful for Professor Jardine's concern regarding the innocent, fragile sensibilities of their undergraduate offspring.

Jardine was not alone. Otherwise sane and judicious critics seemed almost overnight to take on the role of arbiters of public morality. Peter Ackroyd judged Larkin to be 'essentially a minor poet who acquired a large reputation'. Bryan Appleyard: 'a minor poet raised to undeserved monumentality'. James Wood: 'a minor registrar of disappointment, a bureaucrat of frustration'. Apart from their exhaustive use of a single adjective these registrars of Larkin's minority had one other thing in common. They did not bother to ground their judgements in anything resembling evaluation. Larkin's poetry had not changed, and since none of these figures had previously claimed membership of the anti-Larkin camp of Tomlinson, Paulin et al. one can only assume that after reading the letters they had decided that Larkin was a bad man and as a consequence his work no longer deserved approbation.

A number of Larkin fans protested against the general consensus that Larkin *post mortem* should be sent to his birthplace, Coventry. The *Guardian* received a surprising number of pro-Larkin letters. One correspondent offered to eat all his copies of Larkin's poetry if Jardine could find explicit expressions of racism or misogyny in any of them. Another pointed out that evidence could be found of T.S. Eliot's anti-Semitism, D.H. Lawrence's racism and Evelyn Waugh's contempt for the working classes, yet their works were still taught and respected. These were versions of the old art-for-art's-sake maxim, and in an interview shortly after the publication of his biography of Larkin a year later Andrew Motion joined in, stating that 'the vast majority of Larkin's work magnificently floats free of its surrounding material'.

The defensive strategy of the pro-Larkinists, that a writer's prejudices are separable from and irrelevant to their literary achievement, is charitable but both demonstrably invalid and impossible to maintain. To treat poems as pure artefacts is formalism gone mad – try reading Yeats's 'Easter 1916' without involving thoughts on the actual Easter Rising and Yeats's experience of it – and to cite only those elements of a writer's life which we believe best correspond with his stature as an artist takes us back to the worst aspects of Victorianism.

The *Letters* did inestimable damage to our understanding and appreciation of Larkin not because of their content but because of the intellectual environment in which they were received. The pro- and anti-Larkinists reflected a widespread, almost obligatory mindset, and while they seemed to disagree radically they shared a number of fundamental inclinations. One group argued that we should either ignore the appalling characteristics of Larkin the man or treat him as we might an immensely talented but embarrassing old relative whose life and work involved the white, middle-class threnody of decline. The other maintained that his characteristics contaminated and consequently invalidated his writing. No one, however, seemed inclined or able to tackle two fundamental and related questions. Can we claim to know the real Philip Larkin? He played different roles for different people. The personae selected for particular scrutiny and condemnation are, post-1992, the ones which accord with the image of him as a loathsome archetype of Englishness. There are many others, and all are curious combinations of candour, exaggeration and self-parody. Just as significantly, why should we assume that our appreciation of his poems will be tarnished by our knowledge of Larkin as alien from our, in Martin Amis's words, 'newer, cleaner, braver, saner world'.

Not once during the debate surrounding the *Letters* and Motion's biography was it pointed out that virtually all indications that Larkin was a misogynistic, intolerant racist occur in his letters to Colin Gunner and Kingsley Amis. From the 1940s when they first corresponded Amis and Larkin had evolved an epistolary style that was exclusive to their letters to each other. These letters drifted between farce, caricature and self-parody. Essentially they became exaggerated versions of themselves and mimicked their own and other people's linguistic habits and attitudes. By the late 1950s this private blending of satire and role playing had acquired a straight-faced, public counterpart. Both men in interviews, essays and various *ex cathedra* comments on their work contributed to images of themselves, and the press played along. Eventually their public personae became a feature of their letters. In 1982 Larkin told Amis that he was standing down from the Arts Council Advisory Panel and why:

> – not my cup of piss. Just sitting there while lady novelists shoot their mouths off. Fey Weldon wyyoaarch Margaret Foster (Forster?) yuuuuk And Chas Os. Sittin and grinning and fixing it all up afterwards the way he wants it. I agree with you that it should all be scrapped. No subsidies for Gay Sweatshirt or the Runcorn Socialist Workers Peoples Poetry Workshop. Or wogs like Salmagundi [Salman Rushdie] or whatever his name is. (23 February)

Case proved? Well, not quite. If this passage were cited as evidence of Larkin's irredeemable prejudices against women writers, blacks, gays and probably culture in general one might point out the interesting contrasts between these statements and his letters to Barbara Pym, his friend, to whose work he gave sincere and unqualified praise, his frequent promotion again in the *Letters* of Louis Armstrong as an artist in his own right irrespective of his race and colour and his honest, almost indifferent reflections on his personal inclinations towards homosexuality. In the letter to Amis he was not telling lies about his opinions – he had become convinced that the Arts Council was becoming less concerned with the aesthetic quality of the work it sponsored and more attuned to the fashionable causes which underpinned it. Also he was aware that Amis shared these views and had three years earlier given a speech to the Conservative Party Conference on this very topic just prior to Mrs Thatcher's election as prime minister. The language of Larkin's letter to Amis would indeed be offensive to most people, but when Larkin wrote it it was not intended to be read by anyone else. He was turning himself into a caricature of one of the figures that he and his friend had become, particularly among the polarized anti-Thatcherite left.

Certainly his poems, even the more autobiographical ones left unpublished until Thwaite's collection, contained nothing that could be treated as the promotion of blatantly racist or misogynistic opinions. But if we read the letters alongside the poems we experience a continuous sense of the former as the day-to-day habitual fabric which would be distilled into the latter. For example, 'Vers de Société' involves Larkin's customary switch of registers between his private thoughts and his public persona. He has been asked round to dinner by a distinguished university colleague, and he alters the wording of the letter in accordance with his feelings about the prospect.

> My *wife and I have asked a crowd of craps*
> *To come and waste their time and ours: perhaps*
> *You'd care to join us?* In a pig's arse, friend.

Thereafter the poem becomes the occasion for reflections on how such gatherings prompt him to reflect on how life is largely a catalogue of equally pointless routines, variously customized to reinforce the illusion that something might matter.

If we read a letter to Kingsley Amis written a year after the poem we find the same voice, the same presence. He even uses the phrase 'in a pig's arse I did' for Amis's benefit after telling him of a letter he had just received from his once girlfriend Winifred Bradshaw (neé Arnott). Like the poem the letter switches between different versions of Larkin. There is transparent sincerity, thanking Amis for enquiries about his ailing mother, shifting to a farcical self-caricature regarding his own thoughts on illness and death and back again to a genuine note of friendship as Larkin signs off with a best wishes to Amis and his wife Jane Howard and 'Let's meet soon'.

Contra Motion I shall argue that to pretend his work 'floats free of its surrounding material' undermines a proper understanding of Larkin both as a writer and as a man. Anyone who has read 'Sunny Prestatyn', particularly if that person is male, is attended by twin feelings of empathy and guilt. The 'girl on the poster' in the swimsuit is advertising the seaside resort and her image has been defaced.

> Huge tits and a fissured crotch
> Were scored well in, and the space
> Between her legs held scrawls
> That set her fairly astride
> A tuberous cock and balls

The most troubling aspect of the poem is not so much its mood of quiet indifference as an implied sense of approval. The original image of the girl 'In tautened white satin' was visited by what it provoked, aggressive male sexuality. As art, 'Sunny Prestatyn' is excellent. It combines a superb control of language with an incautiously honest demonstration of male uncontrol. How then is our estimation of it as a poem affected by the knowledge that Larkin very much enjoyed pornography and was as concerned with the words accompanying the images as with the pictures themselves? Indeed less than a year before the poem was finished he had written to his occasional pornography supplier Robert Conquest that the author of a piece in *Swish* should be recommended for the Somerset Maugham Award and had done so with only a degree of irony. Feminists and psychoanalytic critics would have a field day, of course, but for less sanctimonious readers the poem becomes even more intriguing as a poem. Larkin has always been celebrated as a writer whose verbal craftsmanship grafted significance on to the mundane and caused informality of speech to carry a muted elegance – a Dutch Master of modern verse and life. The mental image of him reading a particularly gratifying edition of *Swish* while the plan for 'Sunny Prestatyn' forms in his mind is neither prurient nor aesthetically reductive. It is like watching an artist at work and, more unusually, like sharing the spaces that divide up the components of his life.

The writers who so vigorously condemned Larkin were motivated by a combination of impulses – predominantly envy and political self-righteousness – but for all of them the factor that underpinned their outbursts was aesthetic prejudice. Larkin is one of the most superbly talented practitioners of English verse. Moreover he is a traditionalist who undermines the long-standing preoccupation of the literary and academic establishment that without innovation writing is hidebound, indebted to the past. Larkin employs metre, rhyme and stanzaic formulae in a manner that often surpasses the skills of his most esteemed Renaissance predecessors. At the same time his artistry is coterminous with his voice, his presence. He is original in that he overturns key assumptions of Modernism, demonstrating that formal conservatism can coexist with stunning, often perplexing urgency and transparency. And for this reason he is loathed. Academics hate him because he is not self-indulgent. He makes language work for him and the reader, not for them: 'there's not much to *say* about my work. When you've read a poem, that's it, it's all quite clear what it means' (*Required Writing*, pp. 53–4). For other creative writers he is regarded with a mixture of respect and contempt: to acknowledge quite how good he is would invite comparisons with their own work – so better to dismiss him as, at worst, a racist and, at best, a pitiable eccentric.

Larkin as a man was imperfect, but he treated his prejudices and peculiarities with detached circumspection and sometimes shared them, self-mockingly, self-destructively, with a number of his closest friends. What follows will show that he divided up his life, cautiously, fastidiously, so that some people knew him well but none completely. It was only in his poems that the parts began to resemble the whole.

Part 1

Home and Oxford

1

Not the Place's Fault

If a particular muse had been in charge of matters for 1922 it would probably have been Thalia, who specialized in comedy. This was the year Modernism reached its apex. Joyce published *Ulysses* and Eliot *The Waste Land*. Yeats's *Later Poems* came out, as did Woolf's *Jacob's Room*, Lawrence's *Aaron's Rod* and Edith Sitwell's *Façade*. Richmal Crompton's *Just William* did not quite have the same impact, but her story of a cheeky lad with a cutting sense of humour and a robust disrespect for pretension was prescient since two others were born the same year. They would meet two decades later, become a double act and along with maybe a dozen others would set about dismantling the myths that had underpinned the Modernist project. One was Kingsley Amis and the other was Philip Larkin.

Philip Larkin was born on 9 August 1922 to Eva Emilie Larkin (née Day) and her husband Sydney in Coventry, Warwickshire, the geographical centre of England. Philip's sister Catherine, known to all as Kitty, was ten years old. His Christian name was chosen by his father after the sixteenth-century poet Sir Philip Sidney whom he regarded as England's first major literary presence, not least because his reputation as a poet and critic was interwoven – at least in Larkin senior's view – with his status as patriot and military hero who died fighting the Spanish. Philip's middle name, Arthur, while carrying similarly heroic resonance, was in truth an acknowledgement of Eva's side of the family, specifically her brother. He was a healthy enough child, weighing in at over 10 lb as a consequence of Eva's pregnancy running to almost ten months. His thick luxuriant black hair would even by his late teens be showing signs of retreat, and by the age of ten his eyesight was diagnosed as poor. He required and would for the rest of his life continue to wear spectacles. From his earliest articulated utterances until his thirties his speech would be afflicted by a slight but noticeable stammer. These facts are straightforward. The others which make up the fabric of his childhood and home life have become by their very nature more nebulous and intractable.

Larkin usually recalled his childhood with a mixture of feigned forgetfulness and irritation at being obliged, through fame, to speak of it at all. In one poem, however, he says very much. 'Best Society' begins:

When I was a child, I thought,
Casually, that solitude
Never needed to be sought.
Something everybody had
Like nakedness, it lay at hand,
Not specially right or specially wrong.
A plentiful and obvious thing
Not at all hard to understand.

Larkin was twenty-nine when he wrote this, and he goes on to state that the adulthood of 'after twenty' has caused him to realize that solitude now involves effort; other people and the burden of being sociable have to be dealt with. Only then can he properly appreciate their avoidance: 'I lock my door . . . Once more / Uncontradicting solitude / Supports me on its giant palm.' In 1951 Larkin was still a relatively obscure poet, but his speaking presence anticipates the figure we would come to know – a man for whom the mundane, the dreary and the mildly depressing were inspirational. The poem is fascinating because it raises questions about the kind of solitude which Larkin claims to have experienced as a child. He was never isolated or maltreated by his parents, and he had a standard retinue of school friends. It was not that he was using childhood, as Wordsworth had done, as a conceit, a vehicle for creative misremembering; not quite. When he wrote the poem his father had been dead for three and a half years, enough time to reflect and take stock of the past as something genuinely irrecoverable. He could now look at his childhood and adolescence with dispassionate sincerity, and what he found was difficult to describe, one might even say bizarre. It was not so much that he remembered solitude, more that the act of remembering caused him to doubt that he could ever really have been a participant in that curious assembly known as the Larkin family.

On the face of things the Larkins embodied the stereotype of provincial, lower-middle-class ordinariness, but Sydney was a figure who regularly disrupted expectations. He was descended from four generations of small businessmen – tailors, coachmakers, cobblers and finally shopkeepers – based in Lichfield. At Lichfield Grammar School he proved impressive enough to secure a place at the more esteemed King Edward VI High School in Birmingham where he continued to shine as an exemplar of self-discipline, raw intelligence and commitment. He left school aged eighteen in 1902, and his first job was as a junior clerk in Birmingham City Treasury. For the next five years he successfully completed a series of part-time courses in accountancy at Birmingham University, sufficient to earn him promotion to Chief Audit Accountant in 1911. In 1913 he moved further up the ladder of local government finance and was appointed Assistant Borough

Accountant in Doncaster, and six years after that he moved back to the West Midlands to become Deputy Treasurer of Coventry City Council. In 1922 he applied successfully for the position of Treasurer, where he would remain until his death in 1947.

Sydney Larkin is never mentioned in 'Best Society', but for Philip he patrolled the poem's genesis as a spectral presence, felt but not acknowledged. Significantly the same effect informs the extant accounts and records of Sydney's life. His obituaries, for example, praise his studious efficiency and dedication to the duties of local authority administration, but they read like encyclopaedia entries for some obscure twelfth-century cleric of whose personality virtually nothing is known – except that in Sydney's case the omissions were deliberate. The war had been over for little more than two years, and his family had to be thought of. He had during the thirties been an ardent and vocal supporter of fascism, particularly its German manifestation.

There are accounts in Sydney's notebooks, preserved by Philip, of how he perceived himself as a necessary and ruthless agent of efficiency in his work in local government. For example, the 'clauses inserted by my suggestion in the Doncaster Corporation Act of 1915' have 'completely reformed the system of short term loans and brought into effect a consolidated system of taxes'. And at Coventry he had created a template of 'financial legislation . . . for many years the best in the country'. The style and temper of these accounts carry echoes of Mr Pooter, but the Grossmiths would have required a much darker sense of humour to have created someone like Sydney Larkin. On the mantelpiece in the house where Philip grew up stood a 12-inch statue of Hitler which, when a button was pressed, would do a passable imitation of a Nazi salute. Sydney had acquired this on one of his many trips to Germany during the late 1920s and 1930s; he had attended at least two Nuremberg rallies. Sydney's notebooks include no direct references to Nazi Germany as the inspiration for his approach to local authority administration and accounting – or at least those which Philip retained do not – but the parallels were clear enough to everyone who knew him. In the mid-1930s he corresponded regularly with Hjalmar Schacht, the German Economics Minister. Schacht is credited with rescuing the German economy from the cycle of depression and inflation carried over from the 1929 slump, and Sydney was keen to impose a similar model upon Coventry. He was also by all accounts the only city Treasurer in Britain whose office was decorated with Nazi regalia, causing it to resemble the by then familiar newsreel of the Führer's headquarters. Even up to the declaration of war in 1939 these remained in place, only to be removed reluctantly and at the insistence of Sydney's superiors in City Hall.

He could not have claimed – as after the war did many of the British Union of Fascists, the so-called Blackshirts – that his affiliations were fuelled by a personal experience of poverty. Nor could he have pretended that his preoccupation with Germany was grounded exclusively in the pursuit of economic efficiency: by the mid-1930s Nazi economics had become one strand of an all-encompassing ideology, including, of course, savagely pragmatic anti-Semitism. (At the Nuremberg rally of 1935, two laws were announced: one forbidding any form of sexual contact between non-Jews and Jews, the other depriving Jews of basic civil rights. Sydney was there.) Yet strangely he possessed a personality which while less than amiable was difficult to stereotype. He was an avid reader of contemporary and near contemporary literature, with a keen taste for Hardy, Bennett, Wilde, Butler and Shaw. By the time Philip was born he had acquired complete collections of their works alongside an impressive selection of other contemporaneous authors. More significantly, he knew and admired the poetry of Ezra Pound and of T.S. Eliot, had read Joyce's *Ulysses* and enjoyed the stories of Katherine Mansfield. Literary Modernism was not a particularly widespread interest among local authority figures in the West Midlands, but Sydney's enthusiasm gives some credence to the claim that there was a natural affinity between the fascist notion of disciplined elitism and the view held by some Modernists and their followers that accessibility involved populist degradation.

The author who fascinated Sydney most of all was D.H. Lawrence, and the parallels between them are intriguing. Both were self-made men in that they evolved mindsets and ideological viewpoints which unshackled them completely from the formative influences of their respective backgrounds. Above all they shared a belief in the power and supremacy of the individual. This was not the liberal-humanist notion of the freedom of the individual but a more exclusive model of individualism as an ability to detach oneself from the weary excesses of collective thinking and consensus – such as a belief in God, attendance to the idealism of democracy or deference to such abstractions as generosity or compassion. In *Aaron's Rod*, for example, Lilly, one of the principal characters, argues for the reintroduction of 'a proper and healthy and energetic slavery', plus a programme of extermination for the worst of the lower orders and for the rest an instilling of respect for a natural aristocracy. The novel was published a few months before Philip's birth in 1922. Whether Sydney purchased his copy at this time is not known, but its subsequent influence upon his son makes one wonder. Sydney had to an extent modelled his life upon what would become Lilly's thesis (which, incidentally, Lawrence treats with respectful objectivity), but Philip's arrival gave him the opportunity to create an embodiment of it from the raw material of a new male, human being.

Philip was not of course the exclusive product of Sydney. Sydney met Eva Day when both of them were on holiday in Rhyl during the summer of

1906. She was twenty, he twenty-two, and their backgrounds were similar. Her father had been a minor civil servant – excise officer and then pensions administrator – in Epping, Essex. She had been to grammar school, and when they met she was a junior school teacher.

The story of their first encounter, as passed on to Philip, resembles an extract from Arnold Bennett's *Clayhanger* series. They found themselves sheltering from the rain in a hut overlooking the beach, exchanged pleasantries, and Sydney became intrigued when Eva continued to read her book. Obviously this was a woman for whom literature demanded attention, more so than the potentially unsettling situation of sharing a hut with a male stranger. He introduced himself, persuaded her to meet him again, and within three days they were engaged. It sounds romantic, in a very English, Edwardian kind of way, but in truth it was a moment of misunderstanding that would have miserable consequences. Eva was attracted by Sydney's confidence and impetuosity. She had never met anyone quite so exciting before, yet at the same time his apparent commitment to a respectable, secure career reminded her of home. For Sydney she was a manageable version of the new independent woman: educated, moderately cultured but not overambitious. These early impressions were sustained by circumstances. Sydney explained that marriage would only be possible when he had a better-paid job, and, because of the distance between Essex and Birmingham, they met for relatively brief periods and exchanged letters. During the five years between their first meeting and their marriage in 1911 Sydney would have no idea that his fiancée was in truth a nervous, jittery individual who craved support, and Eva had no evidence to foresee a life with a monomaniac who would interpret such cravings as evidence of weakness and failure.

Larkin mentions his parents' first meeting only once in his published work. 'To the Sea', written in 1969, is a curious poem. It is a catalogue of images of a seaside town drawn randomly from the past – part remembered, part imagined – and the perceived present. It could be anywhere on the English or Welsh coast. Larkin has been there before, as a child: 'happy at being on my own, / I searched the sand for famous cricketers'. The fact that 'my parents . . . first became known' in this place is a brief aside, their presence of little apparent significance among the crowded retinue of happy children, bathers, chocolate papers, rusting soup tins and families trekking back to cars as the day concludes. They met there, of that he is certain, but the consequences of the meeting seem to be obscured by matters of questionable significance. What happened after they met is not mentioned; best left unsaid. The poem is Larkin at his most transparent; elegance is mixed with listlessness, not much is said but a great deal is magnificently inferred.

When Philip was born they lived at 2 Poultney Street in a suburb of Coventry. It was a council house but not the type to be mythologized in histories of the Labour movement. Poultney Street had been built by Coventry Corporation as an investment to provide housing for the skilled workforce of the locality. For the Larkins it was a temporary residence until Sydney found something that befitted his status as Treasurer. This would be 'Penvorn', Manor Road, closer to the city centre. They moved in when Philip was five, and the house would be the locus for his memories of childhood and adolescence. It was almost new and its combination of Tudor and Gothic features gave it an incongruously sinister aspect, fully reflected by life within.

Sydney Larkin had six brothers, of whom at least four lived in the vicinity, but Larkin cannot recall meeting any of them until he was obliged to stay with his uncle Arthur during the Blitz in 1940. His one maternal uncle, another Arthur, lived in Essex and never visited the family. Apart from there being no relatives to speak of, Philip's parents appeared to have no friends. Penvorn was occasionally visited by people from Sydney's office, but these were not social calls.

When they met, Eva's nervousness presented itself as a tolerable eccentricity. Sydney treated her fear of thunderstorms and anxious concern for unforeseen trivialities as superficial elements of her otherwise reliable character. By the time Philip was born his authoritarian, sometimes short-tempered manner had exacerbated Eva's jittery tendencies, turning her into an involuntary recluse. And one might easily forget that there was a fourth member of the Penvorn household, Catherine (Kitty); one might because through no fault of her own she had become in Sydney's view an appendage to Eva. She was born in 1912, and after that Sydney put child production on hold. He wanted a boy, a version of himself, and he was willing to wait until the family had reached an appropriate level of financial security until he tried again.

Sydney ran the household in the same way that he presided over the finances of the City Corporation, and Eva and Kitty became more like possessions than sharers. He was a member of the local chess club – he had always treated chess as an invigorating form of intellectual exercise – he went for long cycle rides, gave papers to the Coventry Literary and Philosophical Society, mostly on contemporary writers, and became a respected after-dinner speaker. This aspect of his life was essentially his own. Eva and Kitty would accompany him to Shakespeare performances in nearby Stratford and to concerts in Coventry but more for appearance's sake than as a genuine reflection of a family with shared cultural interests. Eva became more and more reluctant to do anything but stay at home, attend to a schedule of duties planned by Sydney and look after the children. This active–passive imbalance was a feature of most lower-middle-class marriages of the time, but with Eva and Sydney Larkin the conventionalism of their relationship intensified their personality traits. The only figure upon whom Eva could rely for advice or encouragement, let alone sympathy, was an autodidact for whom anxiety meant weakness.

Larkin made few public statements about his childhood. The most detailed is probably an article called 'Not the Place's Fault' (1959), an almost nostalgic recollection of his early schooldays and hobbies and of day-to-day life in Coventry in the early 1930s. His parents are hardly mentioned at all. In 1986 he was interviewed by Melvyn Bragg for the *South Bank Show* and the most curious thing about his reflections on childhood is the way in which he appears to want to explain or allude to something in particular without ever saying what this is. He states that children 'don't control their destinies'; they have no choice regarding what they can do and where they live. Then he shifts from the general to the personal. 'This isn't to say I didn't have nice friends I visited and played with and so on, or that my parents weren't perfectly kind to me', but he has also found other people's accounts of their childhoods to be more exciting than his. His 'seemed to have a fairly insulated quality that looking back I can't quite account for'. 'Can't quite' is a suitably ambiguous term, but 'would rather not' is closer to the truth. A more honest account can be found in his notebooks, written in the early 1950s and never intended for publication. Sydney, according to Larkin, treated Kitty as 'little better than a mental defective', all the more irritating because of her apparent reluctance to find a husband and leave home. Sydney himself had a mind that was 'dominating, active and keen', but he seemed to find difficulties with other human beings. He had no friends, 'he worked all day and shut himself away reading in the evening'.

The notebooks are remarkably candid and at the same time perverse. Rarely, if ever, does he allow his own feelings or his memories of them to intrude upon the catalogue of facts. They read like a physician's report upon the dreadful circumstances surrounding an untimely death, and in his summing up he maintains this mood of cool objectivity. His parents' marriage has left him with two certainties: 'that human beings should not live together; and that children should be taken from their parents at an early age'. It is intriguing to read this alongside the poem celebrating solitude, 'Best Society', written around the same time. It becomes apparent that the speaker of the poem, who laments the loss of the unasked-for solitude of childhood and recognizes that he prefers it to the efforts of adult companionability, is in fact a compendium of recollections and recognitions, not least of which is Larkin's growing acceptance that, temperamentally, he has an enormous amount in common with Sydney. More significantly he has decided to design his life in a way that abates these affinities. In the third stanza he reaches the conclusion that the more agreeable aspects of humanity are manifest only when provoked by the presence of others – lovers, friends, family: 'in short, / Our virtues are all social; if / Deprived of solitude, you chafe / It's clear you're not the virtuous sort'. So after he has locked his door and retreated from the company of others ' . . . there cautiously / Unfolds, emerges, what I am'. Or, rather, what I prefer.

The short poem 'To My Wife' was written in 1951, the same year as 'Best Society'. It is a depressing piece uttered by a man who perceives his marriage and subsequent existence as a kind of living suicide; a single decision has systematically eliminated all others. It 'shuts up that peacock-fan / The future was . . . for your face I have exchanged all faces'; 'No future now.' Motion suggests that it was prompted by his feelings for Winifred Arnott, then his fiancée, but if it was a grisly projection of the consequences of commitment it was grounded as much upon second-hand experience as hypothesis. It is a savagely economical account of his parents' marriage and could indeed have been uttered by his father. In the notebooks Larkin writes of how Sydney's 'personality had imposed that taut ungenerous defeated pattern of life on the family, and it was only to be expected that it would make them miserable and that their misery would react on him'. Something very similar informs the last three lines of the poem spoken by the man to his wife:

> Now you become my boredom and my failure
> Another way of suffering, a risk,
> A heavier-than-air hypostasis.

For the figure in the poem, and Sydney, it is too late, but Larkin still has a choice. In the notebooks he writes of how his parents' marriage has 'remained in my mind as something I mustn't *under any circumstances* risk encountering again'.

Irrespective of our innate dispositions some aspect of our adult personality will be a consequence of our experiences in childhood. The problem arises, however, when we attempt to estimate exactly how and to what extent we are formed by our past, because memories of childhood are a contradiction in terms. We might recollect events that occurred when we were twelve, but for the adult mind their effects involve as much a process of reconstruction as remembering. For Larkin this juggling act was further complicated by his having effectively inhabited two separate childhood worlds. One involved the family home and the presence of Sydney, while the other was comprised partly of his state of mind and partly of the people and events that he knew outside the home.

Despite the fact that Sydney was an agnostic he had Philip christened in Coventry Cathedral: the grandeur of the place offered a suitable starting point for an envisioned successful future. More pragmatically he made sure that his son was enrolled for King Henry VIII School. KHS, as it was known, was the best grammar school in the region (the fact that it was named after a dictatorial psychopath obsessed with male offspring was purely coincidental). The then headmaster, A.A.C. Burton, ran the place more like a public school, introducing a streaming system which ensured that bright pupils could be spotted early and introduced to Latin, a basic Oxbridge entrance requirement. Indeed Burton employed only teachers with first-class degrees from Oxford or Cambridge.

Larkin enrolled at the KHS Junior School aged eight in 1930. The school was about ten minutes' walk from Manor Road, and most significantly it represented Larkin's first real encounter with life outside Penvorn. Previously he had been educated at home. Eva's experience as a primary school teacher came in handy here, and Kitty, ten years Philip's senior, was used as a kind of junior assistant, reading to him and encouraging him to write and draw. So when Philip, accompanied by Eva, set out on an August morning in 1930 he was about to experience something unprecedented: never before had he encountered so many people of the same age and size gathered in the same place. Larkin adjusted surprisingly well both to this and to the equally unfamiliar experience of collective schooling. His academic performance was adequate, and although the stammer he had acquired as an infant made him anxious about speaking in class it seems to have been treated with commendable tolerance by his teachers and peers. No one made fun of him; it was simply part of his physical make-up, like the colour of his hair.

During the three years at Junior School he met and became friends with James (Jim) Sutton, a friendship that would endure for the following two decades (and then cease, without apparent cause). After his move to Senior School in 1933 he met Colin Gunner and Noel 'Josh' Hughes. As the four of them reached their early teens Gunner and Sutton in particular would operate as foils, points of correspondence and contrast for Larkin's own attempts to establish an identity beyond the stifling atmosphere of Manor Road. Gunner was the imaginative joker. He would do imitations of teachers, and more significantly he encouraged Larkin to participate in a kind of surreal, mildly anarchistic version of the Famous Five's adventures. If a particular teacher irritated them they would create around him an unpleasant personal history, such as 'that the repellent-looking dwarf who stumped the town wearing a black cricket cap was in fact his father'. On one occasion during the period of the Munich Crisis in 1938 the two sixteen-year-olds imitated newspaper sellers and ran alongside a stationary train in Coventry station yelling 'War Declared!' They had become fantasists in order to contemplate the effects, particularly on the expressions of the passengers, caused by their interferences with fact.

For Gunner these exercises were an extension of his ebullient personality, but for Larkin they were rehearsals for something more ambitious. By 1936 he had begun to write short stories and make plans for longer pieces of fiction. These veered between pseudo-fictional sketches anchored to the real events and people of Larkin's immediate experience and self-conscious excursions into the unknown, such as murder mysteries involving famous saxophonists and Chinese detectives. He would recollect that during the late 1930s he 'wrote ceaselessly', and by 1938 he began to supplement his attempts at fiction with verse, his range of styles and subjects being equally eclectic: nature poetry of a descriptive, pre-Romantic temper along with interrogative, subjective considerations of the nature of existence, influenced by a random selection of literary thinkers from Keats to Aldous Huxley.

While Gunner had played a peripheral role in all this Sutton was more of a stabilizing presence. The Suttons lived on the other side of town from the Larkins, and Philip from about twelve onwards became a regular visitor to their house in Beechwood Avenue. Jim's father, Ernest, was a successful building contractor and had built and partly designed the house himself. It contrasted sharply with Penvorn, making concessions to a suburban version of Modernism. The rooms admitted generous amounts of natural light and opened via French windows to a large garden complete with tennis court. Not only did the shape of the building show Larkin that home life could be different; he also found that Sutton's parents were the antithesis of his own. During the summer they would have regular garden parties, and all year round occasional visitors would take a drink, stay on and match the agreeable appearance of the house with the sound of relaxed companionability. Larkin liked his visits but knew also that this enjoyment was double-edged; not false but weighted by the fact that the place and the people were made all the more fascinating by his knowledge of their alternative.

By their teens the temperamental affinities which first drew them together had been supplemented by a precocious intellectual and aesthetic partnership. They discovered jazz, graduating from the anglicized mediocrity of Billy Cotton and Teddy Foster to the real thing of the USA – Louis Armstrong, Pee Wee Russell, Bix Beiderbecke, Sidney Bechet. Much later Larkin would raise the possibility that his early love for jazz had influenced his poetry. Jazz lyrics scanned and rhymed: it was his first private, pleasurable encounter with something that resembled poetry outside the dreary obligations of having to study it at school. By about fifteen Larkin, prompted by his father, had started reading D.H. Lawrence. Larkin in turn introduced Sutton to him, and the two of them would argue over the qualities and embedded messages of his work. Sutton was more interested in the visual arts and preferred the unemotional detachment of the French post-Impressionists to the loaded turmoil of Lawrence. Sutton would eventually go to art school, but he recognized that his friend's aesthetic inclinations were verbal and encouraged him to write.

Nothing survives of the prose fiction written during his late teens, but the poems are intriguing. Six appeared in the school magazine, *The Coventrian*, in 1938–9 while others remained unpublished until after Larkin's death. They are, as one would expect of a well-read late adolescent, a patchwork of resonances and borrowings. Snatches of the contemplative–symbolic mood of late T.S. Eliot occasionally interrupt the more pervasive presence of Auden. Just to remind us that this poet is still a schoolboy we sometimes encounter awe-laden locutions from a Shakespeare-to-Tennyson miscellany – 'footsteps cold . . . o'er wood and wold', etc. But despite the chaotic potential of all this learned shoplifting the young Larkin proves himself to be a skilled technician. It is easy enough to spot the acquisitions, but he fits them together well, if not quite seamlessly. At KHS he would have been taught to recognize and name the devices of poetry, and when we read these early attempts at writing it we sense the apprentice trying them out, almost self-consciously. Enjambment, for instance, crops up with studied decorum – rarely more than twice in a poem and executed so as to create a polite *contra rejet*. For example,

> I do not think we shall be
> Troubled . . .

With thanks to Milton.

The most consistent and puzzling feature of these early poems is their anonymity. All manner of themes and inferences are tried out – predominantly isolation, embedded significance, loss – but there is not a recognizably individual presence behind the performance. Certainly most young writers are often difficult to locate among the fabric of debts to their eminent forebears or contemporaries, but with Larkin it seems almost to be a deliberate act of disappearance. This, given his circumstances, was understandable and consistent with many of his other personal traits.

By the age of sixteen he had begun to dress in a self-confidently unconventional manner. Daringly bright waistcoats and bow ties would set themselves off against his expensive, well-polished brogues and country tweed suits. One would assume that he was translating his new-found taste for European *fin de siècle* culture into a fashion statement. As well as offering poems to *The Coventrian* he would submit letters and diatribes on all manner of subjects (the state of the cricket pitch, the existence of God, etc.) and became an enthusiastic participant and organizer for sessions of the school debating society. His stammer was as pronounced and unhidden as his bow ties. It would be too easy to classify all of this as merely performance – the standard repertoire of hormone-fuelled late adolescence – because in most instances such rites of passage are involuntary, a necessary state in the process of growing up. It is only in retrospect, having reached maturity, that we are granted an impartial, often embarrassed, perspective upon our activities. There is, however, evidence to suggest that Larkin was engaged in a bizarre process of conscious self-scrutiny; he was watching himself.

Alongside the actual writing of the poems of the late 1930s he played the roles of publisher and critic. He arranged them into collections, with separate titles. These he would literally sew together as booklets with self-illustrated title pages. In one called *Poems* he inserted a foreword, offering a disarmingly honest description and evaluation of the contents ('silly, private, careless or just ordinarily bad,' for example). If this was a kind of formalized dialogue between the poetic voice and its real-life counterpart, a less restrained version of the latter made its presence felt with longhand comments in the margins adjacent to the poems themselves: 'Bollocks', 'another bucket of shit'.

Between 1937 and 1940 he produced five novels, 250,000–300,000 words of prose fiction, moving between the fantasist crime thriller pieces to more conventional, naturalistic accounts of contemporary life; the latter would, however, involve individuals and situations that were purposively distanced from Larkin's own world. Each would be destroyed almost immediately after completion; it was as if the process of writing was an addictive but self-defeating process. Significantly, he also kept a pocket diary in which he would record events in Penvorn and at school with brief, dispassionate comments such as 'Mop [mother] in bad form. Pop [father] better', 'awful day', 'pretty awful week'. Although the pocket diary was not a commentary upon the fiction, a parallel can be seen between their relationship and his dialogue with the poems. He was deploying different types of writing in a chameleonesque manner, the one consistent feature of this being the determined exclusion of anything resembling himself or his circumstances from the literary output. It is a truism that good literature is never exclusively grounded in autobiography, but at the other end of the spectrum ruthless adherence to self-negation is equally damaging. So why was Larkin doing this? Certainly he had literary ambitions, but he was unable to resolve an innate paradox in his early attempts to realize them. In one sense writing literature enabled Larkin to suspend engagement with immediate reality, an escape route from Penvorn, but in his meticulous separation of the world he knew and inhabited from its creative counterpart he was denying himself access to a more pragmatic long-term prospect, the desired elsewhere of actually becoming a writer. In 1940, aged eighteen, he wrote to Sutton regarding his latest 'very advanced and modern' novel: 'I shall try to have it published by Hogarth Press . . .' Within a few weeks he had burnt it.

The cause of Larkin's self-destructive relationship with his early writing is easy enough to locate: Sydney. The image of Sydney as the frightening autocrat, one that he himself did little to dispel, is slightly misleading when it comes to his relationship with Philip. If he had attempted, stereotypically, to create in his only son a more successful version of himself, then at least Philip would have had something to rebel against or retreat from. But instead Sydney behaved more like a Renaissance patron, infinitely flexible and encouraging. Despite having an autodidact's distaste for popular culture he fully supported Philip's new interest in jazz. He paid for a subscription to the radical jazz magazine *Down Beat*, bought him a drum kit and saxophone and made sure that money was always available for the purchase of the latest American records or for visits, usually with Sutton, to performances by British bands in Coventry. With literature, Sydney choreographed a game of cat and mouse. He began by encouraging an interest in respectable nineteenth- and twentieth-century writing, figures who had earned esteem within the conservative purview of English literary culture, but he made sure that his son was always finding fault lines and contrasts. Christina Rossetti's poetry would be promoted alongside Housman's; the novels of Bennett, Hardy and J.C. and T.F. Powys would show how England could be a different place for different people. And with a magician's sleight of hand Sydney had also begun to open doors to a different literary world, beginning with Lawrence, leading to James Joyce, T.S. Eliot and Ezra Pound and including the left-leaning, radical and very contemporaneous presences of Auden, Upward, Isherwood and Spender.

Sydney's calculating tutelage ranged far beyond music and literature. In the summer of 1936 he arranged for his fourteen-year-old son to accompany him on one of his frequent visits to Germany. Most of these involved what were euphemistically referred to as his business interests – in truth, his connections with Nazism – but on this occasion he insisted that the trip would be a holiday, an opportunity for father and son to savour the social and cultural delights of a resurgent nation. Wernigerode, in Saxony-Anhalt, seemed the perfect spot: a medieval city of half-timbered houses, overlooked by a Romantic ducal castle and flanked by the Harz mountains. This idyllic reminder of Germany's fascinating history was of course, like everywhere else, draped with motifs of the present. Apart from the ubiquitous swastika, the Nazi poster campaign was in full flow, involving vivid representations of a muscular, confident ideology along with grotesque caricatures of Jews as the archetypes of greed and deception. Their real-life counterparts had by then been obliged to signal their presence with Star of David armbands.

Sydney had made no secret of his political beliefs, but he had treated Eva and Kitty as his intellectual inferiors and hence unworthy of any attempts at indoctrination. Philip, however, was showing a degree of precocity that seemed adequate enough for this stage in the character-formation process. Germany and its people, irrespective of what they actually represented, were so demonstrably different, so exciting in comparison with the West Midlands, that surely this experience would encourage a more involved interest. He repeated the exercise the following year, this time involving Bavaria, home of the German stereotypes of lederhosen, beer halls, oompah bands and fairy-tale castles; it was also the region which most enthusiastically associated itself with Hitler and his beliefs.

The visits are the episodes of Larkin's life over which he drew a calculatedly impenetrable veil. His school friends were aware of them of course, but, given Sydney's widely known affiliations, no one was surprised and a diplomatic acceptance was maintained. Much later, when fame had opened up his life to public scrutiny, Larkin chose the wise option of dissimulating candour, claiming that his enduring memory was of confusion and mild embarrassment: he did not share his father's enthusiasm for participating in beer-hall folk singing and he could not speak German. His statement that the trips were probably responsible for his infamous 'hatred of abroad' exploited the largely self-cultivated mythology of the Movement. It is rather like Byron claiming, albeit conversely, that his affection for the sun-drenched vistas of Greece was prompted by the cold, damp misery of his Scottish childhood: the facts hang together but one knows that a fair amount has been left out.

What exactly passed between father and son and the overall effect of related events upon the latter are open entirely to speculation; even his closest friend Kingsley Amis knew only of evasive, amusing anecdotes on Larkin's problems with the German language. All that can be observed is that Larkin's childhood and teenage years were touched with a hint of the surreal. The commonplace and predictable features of provincial lower-middle-class existence were present in abundance yet peculiarly configured and informed.

Potted histories of twentieth-century European culture and politics will tell us that in the 1920s and 1930s there was an incursion of radical and unprecedented techniques in music, painting and writing and that fascism announced itself as the disturbing antithesis to that other recent monolith-in-power, communism. Common sense will interject that while such phenomena existed their direct impact upon, say, Middle England – at least with the latter until 1939 – was minimal. But not in the case of Philip Larkin, and one begins to understand why his early attempts at literary writing, while disclosing precocious assimilative skills, were generically perverse, addressed to putative extremes of the human condition but about nothing in particular. The contrasts and bizarre dichotomies of day-to-day life seemed to amount to something beyond fiction.

There is a famous cartoon that Larkin drew in 1939 just before his departure for Oxford and for the amusement of Sutton. His father, seated, is reading a newspaper announcing the outbreak of war and he comments that 'the British Government has started this war . . . Hitler has done all he can for peace . . . well I hope that we get smashed to Hades . . .', followed by some Lawrentian reflections on the end of a false civilization as we know it, etc. His mother, 'Mop', is knitting. 'Oh do you think so,' she answers, and adds, 'I wonder what we ought to have for lunch tomorrow . . . well, I hope Hitler falls on a banana skin . . . by the way I only washed four shirts today.' Kitty, standing, is more concerned with her account of her visit to Munich (she replaced Philip on Sydney's final journey) and how George the 'Storm Trooper' was asking after her despite her being too tired to attend the dance. Philip himself is seated, his face a dark shade of something, probably a mixture of rage and confusion. He seems apparently unable to speak or, with a pen prominently detached from paper, write.

The cartoon is an impressive piece of work. Apart from disclosing a talent for visual caricature it shows us that the seventeen-year-old Larkin had a fine ear for the inadvertent comedy of dialogue, of the ways in which, with a small amount of adjustment and some tactically astute juxtapositions, people and their relationships with each other can be made both vivid and hilarious via speech. It also prompts the question of why Larkin did not see potential interfaces between his undoubted literary ambitions and this inherent talent. The easiest answer would probably be that for a seventeen-year-old, alive to the adolescent attractions of Modernism, writing like a provincial version of Evelyn Waugh (whose work he had read) was an unattractively conservative, downmarket option. Just as significant and more obstructive was the fact that, as yet, the material from which such realist black comedy could be drawn was exclusively his own, immediate experience. Sydney, who took trips to Munich with as much joyous insouciance as his colleagues savoured the annual delights of Yarmouth and Llandudno, was, literally, beyond parody: He was also very much, too much, part of Larkin's existence.

Within a week or two of the cartoon he wrote Sutton a letter informing him that 'half my days are spent in a black, surging, twitching, boiling HATE!!!' He does not inform his friend of the cause or direction of this feeling, but Sutton knew him well enough to read between the lines. Larkin was subject to a strange panorama of conditions and their attendant emotional registers. He did not hate his father or any other member of his family, and his feeling was not self-directed in any conventional manner; rather the upper-case monosyllable was his way of killing a sentence that would otherwise have continued as a sequence of adverbs indicating frustration and confusion.

Sydney was by even the most generous measure a bizarre and unsettling individual. He was immensely learned, and he followed enthusiastically, and indeed judgementally, the twists and turns of contemporaneous cultural radicalism in a way that would put Bloomsburyites to shame. Yet he was a self-educated West Midlands local authority official – T.S. Eliot at his best could not have invented him. He loved England – its landscape, its architecture, its, as he saw it, esteemed past – yet he saw the hideous spectre of Nazi Germany as something even more venerable, a lesson for an empire in decline. Larkin's maintenance of a degree of composure during those years is commendable.

In the summer of 1938, the year after his two visits to Germany, he sat for a standard retinue of subjects in the School Certificate – the equivalent of what would become O levels and GCSEs – and gained only one A grade, in English, with Ds and Es distributed liberally through his other six subjects. In normal circumstances this would have prompted the school to offer polite discouragement regarding entry to the sixth form – his D in Latin presaged a poor chance for Oxbridge consideration. However, Burton the headmaster was aware that the results were, for whatever reason, incongruous with Larkin's inherent intelligence and potential and allowed him to proceed. L.W. Kingsland, head of English, recognized that this would be the most promising subject for university entry. In March 1940 Larkin took the train to Oxford to sit for the entrance examinations to read English at St John's College, the only Oxbridge college with which his school had connections. He passed and in June won distinctions in English and History for the Higher School Certificate. In October he would for the first time begin to spend lengthy periods away from his family.

2

Oxford and Amis

Much of Larkin's life involved either making do with the routine and mundane or anticipating disappointment. A precedent for this had already been set with his bizarre family existence, and Oxford established a sense of continuity. Larkin arrived on 9 October 1940, little more than a decade after Waugh's *Decline and Fall* had presented the place as an agreeable combination of decadence and absurdity. Now it appeared as though doleful farce had taken a hand.

The traditional academic calendar had been replaced by a random, capricious timetable, with undergraduates beginning, graduating or deferring the completion of their degrees according to the demands of military service. The undergraduate population of St John's College now rarely rose above seventy, and all had to take rooms in the Front Quad. The New Quad was occupied by civil servants whose 'secret' work involved the administration of the white fish and potato ration, earning St John's, one of the richest and most prestigious colleges, the nickname of Fish and Chips.

The Blitz had not yet begun – it would a few months later and, terrifyingly for Larkin, soon involve Coventry – but it was generally assumed that the *Luftwaffe* would at some point shift their bombers to urban centres, including morale-sapping raids on the glittering prizes of Oxford and Cambridge. Consequently St John's, like the rest of the colleges, had taken on the uniform of expectation. Fire buckets, extinguishers and sandbags decorated the staircases and quads, and the mullioned windows had tape on the glass and blackout curtains on the frames. Each undergraduate had to do an all-night 'fire-watching' stint every ten days or so. Most teaching was done by dons ranked too old, infirm or inappropriate for civil or military service. The glamour and elitist self-confidence of the city appeared to have been absorbed by a fabric of ominous dreariness. But some things did not change, such as the place's distillation of the British class system into the undergraduate population. The majority of Larkin's new peers were from public schools, and for them Oxford was a continuation of the customs and routines of a life spent mostly away from the family home. Larkin, although reasonably secure regarding his intellectual abilities, was visited by various registers of anxiety. 'Public schoolboys terrified me. The dons terrified me. So did the scouts.'

He dealt with this in a number of ways, initially by spending his first few months almost exclusively in the company of friends from Coventry. He shared rooms at St John's with Noel Hughes with whom he had co-authored in September 1940 'Last Will and Testament', a parodic goodbye-note poem to the masters at KHS. Ernest Roe and Frank Smith, also from KHS, were respectively at Exeter and Hertford Colleges. His close friend Jim Sutton had gone to the Slade School of Art in London, but just before Larkin's arrival all Slade students had, for the duration of the war, been moved to Oxford. This sense of extended provincialism would eventually be embodied in John Kemp, the hero of *Jill*, except that Kemp had no friends at all and was made to feel even more isolated by being dropped a class from middle to working. And unlike Kemp Larkin in his early months made an attempt to create a bohemian self-image. Before leaving Coventry he had acquired, with Sydney's approval, an unusual and dazzling variety of clothes: cord trousers ranging in colour through green, purple and red, waistcoats of slightly contrasting brightness, most notably yellow, and a selection of flamboyantly patterned bow ties. Sometimes he wore a slouch brimmed hat, and his red cerise trousers soon earned fame as allegedly the only pair in Oxford. Larkin did his best to supplement his blink-inducing appearance by cultivating the verbal mannerisms of a wit, rehearsing clever and sardonic observations on the dons and the curriculum; both, he noted, favouring the ancient and the obscure. His stammer presented problems here, of course, and he took up pipe-smoking as a non-verbal means of diverting attention from his frequent mid-sentence truncations. Who or what he imagined he was creating are given some indication in the dozen or so poems, most unpublished in his lifetime, that he wrote in his first eighteen months in Oxford. Many of these are promising, precocious pieces. Or they would be if they did not also give the impression of being manuscript drafts written by someone else, most obviously Auden.

'Ultimatum' (June 1940) was Larkin's first published poem and reads like a thesaurus of Auden's phrasings and metrical orchestrations. The 'Auden Generation' (aka the 'Pylon Poets') had yet to attain the status of an enduring cliché, but the fact that the *Listener*'s sagacious literary editor, J.R. Ackerley, had accepted Larkin's poem indicates that their radical edge had within a decade become a fashionable idiom. The one intriguing difference between Auden's contemporaneous verse and Larkin's rehearsals of it is that while the former offers a stark impression of civilized Europe moving towards a fascist-inspired apocalypse Larkin maintains a studied avoidance of any particular frame of reference. They are like poems written by an Auden afflicted with aphasia, and it is likely that Ackerley's decision to publish

'Ultimatum' was influenced as much by external events as by the piece itself. It resonates with suggestions of collective anxiety and uncertainty leavened with an image stolen shamelessly from Auden's 'Look Stranger'.

> For on our island is no railway station,
> There are no tickets for the Vale of Peace . . .

Read as a text in its own right it is an exercise in Modernist-licensed discontinuity, intimating much but saying nothing, but before it arrived at the *Listener*'s office the battle for France was entering its disastrous final phase and by the time Ackerley came to look at it Dunkirk had turned Britain into an island from which there were indeed 'no tickets for the Vale of Peace'. 'Ultimatum' was a lucky break, its shambolic obscurity given apparent coherence by Hitler's military successes. In Oxford it lent credibility to Larkin's cultivated self-image; he looked like a poet, albeit of *fin de siècle* vintage, and now he had been published.

Tutorials were done in twos, and Larkin's partner was a man called Norman Iles. Iles was the Oxford variation on Gunner, a cross between a *Brideshead* throwback and a self-promoting vandal. Larkin frequently found himself alone in tutorials; Iles attended when he felt like it. He hardly ever went to lectures and he earned an unenviable reputation as a burglar: he stole coal, jam, beer and other rationed consumables from everywhere in college, including the rooms of his fellow undergraduates. Despite all of this Larkin got on well enough with Iles. It was not a close friendship, but one incident would make it a very memorable one.

Larkin had been in Oxford for two-thirds of his first academic year, and at the beginning of summer term 1941 Iles pointed out to him on the Porters' Lodge list of freshmen the name of a man he had met the previous year when both had tried, unsuccessfully, for Cambridge scholarships. According to Larkin Iles noted enigmatically that this chap 'was a hell of a good man . . . who could shoot guns'. Later that afternoon, 5 May, Larkin found out what he meant. Iles pointed his right hand, pistol style, at 'a fair haired young man' emerging from the corner staircase of the Front Quad and did a passable imitation of a shot. The stranger clutched his chest and half collapsed against the piled-up laundry bags. After introductions Kingsley Amis offered them his own recently practised pistol-shot performance, supplemented with ricochet and echoes. Larkin's account of this ends with the comment: 'I stood silent. For the first time in my life I felt myself in the presence of a talent greater than my own' (*Required Writing*, p.20). There is of course more than a hint of sarcasm in this. Larkin wrote it twenty years after the event, reflecting perhaps on how the time he had spent with Amis in Oxford was rather like a living parody of serious young writers honing their skills and exploring their ideas. Their friendship would be important; each would significantly affect the development of the other's work, and as individuals they would be two of the most influential figures in the history of post-war British literature. But Wordsworth and Coleridge they were not.

Amis's 'talent' for sound-effects and imitations is part of the mythology of those years. What is rarely mentioned is that in Oxford at the time practically everyone else was doing this. Another St John's freshman of 1941, Edward du Cann, later to become one of Mrs Thatcher's cabinet ministers, was celebrated for his 'set piece' reproduction of a Soviet propaganda film 'full of small arms fire and shell noises'. Larkin and Amis traded imitations of senior English Faculty dons. Amis would offer a version of Lord David Cecil's effeminate, upper-middle-class drawl, celebrating the delights of 'Chauthah . . . Dvyden . . . Theckthypyum' in return for Larkin's rendition of J.R.R. Tolkein's semi-audible mumble which added an extra layer of impenetrability to his special subject, Anglo-Saxon. Impersonation enabled Larkin to suspend completely his stammer and played a small part in his gradual removal of the affliction from normal speech.

Larkin and Amis helped to found a group called 'The Seven', the other five being Jimmy Willcox, Philip Brown, Nick Russel, David Williams and Norman Iles, all St John's undergraduates. Ostensibly the model for this circle was the early eighteenth-century Scriblerus Club comprising among others Pope, Swift, Gay and Arbuthnot and whose object was to 'ridicule all false tastes in learning' and by implication uphold their meritable counterparts. Such lofty antecedents soon gave way to a less purposive opportunity to meet at least once a week, tell jokes, share cigarettes, get drunk and maybe discuss contemporary literature. Sometimes they would pass round a poem that one of them had written and talk honestly about its various qualities and short-comings, at least until the drink began to take hold.

This combination of high culture and disorganized indulgence accurately reflects the nature of Amis's and Larkin's friendship. The two of them would spend long periods, usually in Amis's rooms, listening to jazz records, often prancing around in an attempt to embody the rhythms and improvisational nuances of the piece. In the Victoria Arms in Walton Street Larkin could sometimes be persuaded to do a twelve-bar blues number on the battered piano, and 'if there were no outsiders present' Amis would join in with lyrics borrowed from their records. Larkin's recollections of his time with Amis in Oxford often carry a slight but tangible note of envy and resentment, and there was sufficient cause for this. It was as though they were two versions of the same character created by a novelist who was uncertain about which would make it to the final draft.

Their backgrounds were remarkably similar. Amis had been educated at the City of London School, the metropolitan equivalent of KHS, and for each of them school was a treasured alternative to their relationships with their respective fathers. Amis's father, William, could have been Sydney Larkin rewritten as a more tractable, easy-going presence. Both were hard-working self-made office men, and both were agnostics. William had once been a Liberal who had turned into an arch-Tory after the Great War, an affiliation strengthened by the General Strike and the emergence of the Labour Party as a serious contender for power. Amis responded by espousing radical causes that were antithetical to his father's or, as he put it later, by 'becoming a bloody little fool of a leftie'. When Amis and Larkin talked with each other of their backgrounds and families it must have seemed to the latter as if his new friend had drawn the longer, more generous straw. At every turn it appeared as though some omnipotent wordsmith was having fun with two parallel scripts, choosing to reframe Amis's as suburban comedy and Larkin's as provincial Gothic. Amis, when he arrived in Oxford, was an enthusiastic communist, proudly exhibiting a polemicist's knowledge of the works of Marx and Lenin, but even then he admitted that his commitment was acquired partly as a way of irritating his father, a means of asserting his independence. He had become a radical among lower-middle-class Tories. How, wondered Larkin, would he too have acquired a similar, albeit immature sense of a separate identity? By declaring his loyalty to Stalin? Sydney would probably have relished the challenge – the polarities of European fanaticism embodied in father and son.

And then there was jazz. 'Our heroes', wrote Amis, 'were the white Chicagoans, Count Basie's band, Bix Beiderbecke, Sidney Bechet, Henry Allen, Fats Waller, early Armstrong, and early Ellington . . . and our heroines were Bessie Smith, Billie Holliday, Rosetta Howard . . . and Cleo Brown.' These enthusiasms were not unique to Larkin and Amis – every undergraduate not prematurely middle-aged was a jazz fan – but what was striking for the two new friends was the weird contrast between how they had acquired their tastes. Amis told of how his father regarded Duke Ellington records as evocative of dark-skinned savages dancing round a pot of human remains and much classical music, without the human voice, as a form of grandiose self-indulgence. Amis senior preferred Gilbert and Sullivan. So again Amis made sure that his early encounters with Mozart, Haydn, Schubert and, particularly, American jazz were accompanied by a learned polemic. His love for music, jazz and classical, became transparent and unflagging, but it was inspired by his early instinct to rebel against anything his father espoused. Sydney encouraged and promoted all the activities that in the Amis household functioned as symbols of youthful dissent. Classical concerts in Coventry were standard fare, and Larkin ended up with his own drum kit and annual subscription to *Down Beat*. Amis's parents enjoyed middle-market contemporary fiction; women novelists such as Ursula

Bloom, Norah C. James and Ann Bridge being his mother's favourites, William preferring the detective writing of Austin Freeman, Francis Greerson and John Rhode. At Amis's school the likes of Auden, MacNeice and Eliot were coat-trailed by masters and pupils as examples of something almost dangerous. How different from Penvorn where Modernism was perfunctory, de rigueur. The literary, political and cultural affiliations that Amis used as a means of projecting himself into an impertinent adulthood appeared for Larkin to have been anticipated and pre-empted by his father.

It would be wrong to assume, as some have, that Amis, particularly at the beginning of their friendship, became a substitute for Gunner or even Iles. Certainly his taste for caricature and practical jokes amused Larkin, but more and more each found in the other dimensions of their own personality either more fully developed or comfortably contained.

They talked a lot about literature, and Amis later claimed that Larkin 'was always the senior partner . . . the stronger personality, always much better read'. This was true in that Larkin knew a lot more about contemporary writing than his friend. He encouraged Amis's slight interest in Auden and introduced him to the idiosyncratic fiction of Flann O'Brien and Henry Green. He also recommended to him Julian Hall's *The Senior Commoner*, a humourless exploration of class difference, isolation and repressed sexuality. This would influence Amis's first novel, *The Legacy*, completed after the war and unpublished. *The Legacy* was like none of the works that would sustain his career as a novelist. It was introspective, lacked narrative energy, contained nothing resembling wit, and in an intriguing, rather paradoxical way it reflected the nature of Amis's early friendship with Larkin. Amis's presence encouraged, even licensed Larkin's taste for visiting upon respectable culture a blend of the satirical and the obscene as a valve for his frustrations and uncertainties regarding his serious literary ambitions. At the same time Larkin's learning and sophistication offered Amis a stabilizing counterbalance for his own addiction to irresponsible humour.

According to Amis, Larkin would write obscene clerihews about the college dons, and they collaborated on a record cover involving 'Bill Wordsworth and his Hot Six': 'Wordsworth (tmb) with "Lord" Byron (tpt), Percy Shelley (sop), Johnny Keats (alto and clt), Sam "Tea" Coleridge (pno), Jimmy Hogg (bs), Bob Southey (ds) . . .' During their discussion of other people's poems, including those of friends from 'The Seven', they considered having two rubber stamps made, reading 'What does this mean?' and 'What makes you think I care?' Larkin later commented, enigmatically, that there would be 'one for each of us', and we will never know which question best reflects the attitude of either himself or his friend. They even evolved a private, ritualistic habit of speech in which, to save time, any idea or person they regarded as pompous, boring or pretentious would be attached without connectives to an obscenity: Spenser bum, piss William Empson, Robert Graves shag. This mildly juvenile practice survived in their letters until Larkin's death. Despite being much more shy than Amis and less inclined to turn his taste for mockery and caricature into a public performance, Larkin could be far more cynical. He wrote a parody of Keats's 'La Belle Dame Sans Merci' which included the sensitive Romantic's confession that

> And this is why I shag alone
> Ere half my creeping days are done
> The wind coughs sharply in the stone
> . . . There is no sun.

Amis's copy of Keats's *Poems* contained a comment by Larkin on that famous moment of ethereal unification and transcendence in *The Eve of St Agnes*: 'YOU MEAN HE FUCKED HER.' It was as though both were in private able to enjoy breaking down the institutionalized borders between comic irreverence and high culture, while in their attempts to produce proper literature they deferred to the humourless conventions of the latter.

Around the same time as this Amis had taken on, for a term in 1942, the editorship of the University Labour Club *Bulletin*, and in the spring issue he included two of Larkin's poems called 'Observation' and 'Disintegration', the titles of which bespeak their intense, self-focused moods.

In early 1942 they collaborated in what Amis later called a series of 'obscene and soft-porn fairy stories'. One was entitled 'The Jolly Prince and the Distempered Ghost' and was a parody of the sometimes dreary medieval narratives that were a compulsory element of the Oxford curriculum. It involved a ghostly presence whose insubstantiality is belied by his constant habit of farting. Another, called 'I Would Do Anything for You', was about two beautiful lesbians who discover in their Oxford flat a collection of jazz records left there by the previous, male, occupant. Scrupulously these records are listed, and they are the ones which both Amis and Larkin had read about but never heard. This is an intriguing evocation of circumstantial and psychological pessimism. If the man had returned to the flat to reclaim his property he would have found women to whom he was attracted but who would never feel anything similar for him. The records, similarly observed but not experienced by the authors, testify to their own anticipation of failure – although for Larkin, much less attractive and confident than his co-author, the symbolism would have been more cutting. The story, combining in one figure characteristics of each of them, would remain a token of their early friendship: Amis refers to 'IWDAFY' on at least six occasions in his letters to Larkin during the 1940s and 1950s.

The sense of stoical gloom that underpins the story would re-emerge in

Larkin's first published novel, *Jill*, four years later. It is a novel that is addressed to his own ever-present sense of vulnerability. The element of mildly pornographic irresponsibility and the sheer fun that had attended his collaboration with Amis had disappeared. It was only when he began to write his late-1940s poems that the assertive, sardonic spark of the latter began to show itself.

Although Amis described Larkin as the 'senior partner' in their friendship, this is more a tribute to the latter's learning than an accurate reflection of their conventions of exchange. For Larkin their co-authored stories involved a degree of self-mockery. He had become a devotee of the psychologist John Layard, whose theories of sexuality, identity and socio-cultural enclosure found parallels in the fiction of D.H. Lawrence, whose work Larkin also admired. Amis summed up his own view of Layard and Larkin's preoccupation with his ideas as 'all that piss about liar's quinsy', and he loathed D.H. Lawrence. Lawrence, in Amis's opinion, was a psycho-sexual evangelist masquerading as a literary writer. Amis always believed that whatever else literature might be it should not become the vehicle for an explanation of the human condition. Amis and Larkin did not argue about this, because Amis simply forbade from their exchanges anything which in his view was spurious, intellectually pretentious and consequently boring, and Lawrence was top of the list.

So while their stories might appear to be the products of similarly disposed *farceurs*, they grew out of the unevenness of their relationship. For Larkin they provided some relief from the harsh and unsettling world of self-examination that constituted his early writing. Amis, as Larkin has stated, did not really have another world; he 'lived in a zone of the most perfectly refined pure humour'.

The relationship formed between Larkin and Amis in the year before the latter left Oxford for military service is fascinating principally because we fail to appreciate its immense significance. It would be a decade before each of them had served their apprenticeships as writers and begun to produce prestigious work, and this process was informed, instigated, by their friendship. The reason why we do not recognize the influence of one upon the other is because it was involuntary. Few if any writers would be willing to concede that the essential character of their work, its success, was due to an accident for which they were only partially responsible.

The most widely quoted and returned to account of Larkin's Oxford years, particularly 1941–2, is his introduction to the reprint of *Jill* written more than twenty years later. For some reason, which Larkin does not bother to explain, Amis holds centre stage. The other characters – Noel Hughes, Iles, his tutor Gavin Bone, his other close friend Bruce Montgomery – feature as a graciously acknowledged cast of extras. Amis takes precedence, but

Larkin makes sure that we do not get the wrong impression. After telling of his friend's abilities to render everyone incapable with laughter he adds: 'This is not to say that Kingsley dominated us. Indeed to some extent he suffered the familiar humorist's fate of being unable to get anyone to take him seriously at all.' This must come close to a record for breadth of implication generated by economy of words. Virtually everyone who read it, in 1964, would see not the undergraduate *farceur* but the bestselling novelist. Moreover, those who had followed Amis's work would see a writer whose claims to be taken seriously had been regularly undermined by a solid core of reviewers who treated his apparent addiction to comedy as his Achilles' heel, the characteristic that denied him admission to the rank of proper novelists. Certainly Amis was a far more talented joker and imitator than virtually anyone else in Oxford, but to imply, as Larkin does, that this was an accurate anticipation of his literary presence is a calculated distortion of fact. Larkin does this as much as a private means of repackaging the past as a snide gesture towards the public reputation of his friend.

Among his friends, Amis, at the time, seemed to Larkin the least likely to succeed as a literary artist. Before he met Amis Larkin had, albeit tentatively, begun to cultivate a friendship with Bruce Montgomery. Montgomery was already a legendary figure in Oxford: composer, painter and author of two novels and a monolithic tome entitled *Romanticism and the World Crisis* (all at the time unpublished). His background, looks and behaviour were those of a lazy, idiosyncratic sybarite – a talented version of Sebastian Flyte. Also he presented himself in his dress and manner as potentially bisexual. Larkin was fascinated and influenced. In 1942, for example, he began to make hesitant sexual advances towards Philip Brown, a medical student with whom he had shared rooms in 1941 and a co-member of 'The Seven'. Brown later confessed to being more puzzled than offended by this, given that Larkin himself appeared to be trying to recreate himself as a version of Montgomery. He was attempting to build a world around himself where any form of unorthodoxy and radicalism – sexuality included – indicated artistic promise. Amis, the boozy, talented jester, seemed to belong in a completely different sort of drama.

Part 2

Life and Fictions

3

Brunette and *Jill*

Aside from the pseudo-erotic pieces co-written with Amis, Larkin's own literary output during his undergraduate years can best be described as outlandish. It is comprised principally of two pieces of fiction, *Trouble at Willow Gables* and *Michaelmas Term at St Bride's*, and a verse sequence called *Sugar and Spice: A Sheaf of Poems*. The work is fascinating in its own right but even more so because all of it is written by a figure invented by Larkin, one Brunette Coleman. It would be tempting to treat the two novels – the first set in a girl's boarding school, the second involving some of the same characters a few years later in Oxford at a version of Somerville College – as a blend of mild pornography and self-parody: women's sexuality, specifically lesbianism, appears to be the predominant theme, and it would of course have been both satisfying and a compensation for his own sexual immaturity for Larkin to have set his own most lurid fantasies against his imaginative and technical skills as a writer. However, on closer scrutiny it becomes evident that he had involved himself in something far more strategic and complex than an exercise in vicarious gratification.

In *Trouble at Willow Gables* the style shifts between three registers: cautious indifference, archly overwritten symbolism with a hint of Lawrence and prose that appears to disclose its writer's involuntary feelings of sexual excitement.

Chapter 1 begins with such spare unobtrusive passages as 'The postman surveyed the tall façade as he began to walk round the lawn. It had originally been an eighteenth-century house, but an enterprising nineteenth-century educationalist had altered it extensively . . .' Later as the narrator introduces us to the characters so her style, for she is Brunette Coleman, alters, and we find that she begins to exchange her classic third-person mode as the text's choreographer for a far more intuitive, impressionistic stance. For example:

> As the sun declined, the sky grew more vast and more remote, until it was a great bowl, azure in the east where a thin shaving of moon drifted, and copper green, crimson, and gold in the west, where the sun burnt farther and farther away . . . Preparation and supper had been disposed of, and one by one, starting with the lowest the various forms had gone up to bed. (p. 79)

Soon after this contemplation of a night laden with unstated significance we are provided with a precise description of one of the principal characters going to bed.

> Sitting on her bed in the fourth form dormitory, Myfanwy peeled off one black stocking after another, miserably remembering her harsh words to Marie . . . Dejectedly she slipped out of her knickers and vest, laying them carefully on a chair. She was rather surprised to find herself quite naked, and as the green curtains were nearly fully drawn, she remained standing before the mirror for a few moments, studying the lissom lines of her brown body. (p. 80)

The novel is written by someone who is evidently unable to prevent their own emotional and instinctive impulses from interfering with the act of composition. A precedent for this had been set with Joyce's narrator of *A Portrait of the Artist as a Young Man*, but that had been a single innovative process coterminous with one novel. Larkin achieved something more elaborate and curious because *Michaelmas Term at St Bride's* and the poems in *Sugar and Spice* disclose via their various flaws and idiosyncrasies further dimensions of the character of Brunette. Along with the literary pieces Larkin/Brunette also produced two *ex cathedra* works, a short autobiography called 'Ante Meridian' and what amounts to Brunette's creative manifesto, 'What Are We Writing For? An Essay'. The latter disposes of any inclination to regard Brunette as a figure of absurdist fantasy. It is a meticulously researched paper on the sub-genre of early twentieth-century boarding-school fiction to which Brunette's two novels are, she implicitly contends, a radical contribution: the setting is a school or even the similarly enclosed educational institution of the ancient university, and the subject is sexuality and its influence upon the passage from adolescence to early maturity. If *Essays in Criticism* had been founded in 1940 this paper might well have been taken seriously by its editor F.W. Bateson.

The autobiography is extraordinary in that Brunette's manner changes yet again: this time to puzzled transparency as she attempts to make sense of her childhood and background. Larkin's achievement is considerable because not only does he offer meticulous reproductions of four very different modes of writing, he maintains throughout an authentic image of a particular woman adapting her own presence of mind to each.

Even B.S. Johnson did not attempt to turn writing against itself, to use its various accidents and stratagems as a means of creating a human being that stands outside it. The question is, why did Larkin commit himself to this peculiar task?

Amis's sarcastic dismissal of Layard was accepted by Larkin as a precondition of their friendship. It soon became evident to him that Amis's cynicism regarding psychoanalysis, Lawrentian ideas or anything else that dropped beneath his established mean of rationalism, coherence and common sense was an invitation to put up or shut up, so for the sake of convenience he chose the latter. In truth, however, Larkin became if not exactly a devotee of Layard then someone who treated his eclectic, inconsistent theories as counterpoints to his own. He was particularly intrigued by Layard's thesis that the social emancipation of women in the late nineteenth and early twentieth centuries was significant not just as a socio-political phenomenon but as a means by which gender difference would now involve a more open dialogue. He wrote enthusiastically to Sutton of a lecture that Layard had given in Oxford in June 1941:

> As he saw it . . . women should be the priestesses of the unconscious and help men to regain all the vision they have lost . . . What women must do is – as they are in the unconscious, rubbing shoulders with all those archetypes and symbols that man so needs – is bring them up and give them to men. (16 June)

He added that 'How this is to be done, he [Layard] didn't really know.' Nor did Larkin, but the lecture had become the moment of inspiration for Brunette Coleman. She is Layard's 'priestess of the unconscious'. In classic Freudian theory – of which Larkin knew the basics – the unconscious was a sub-system of drives and instincts which would only be released into the conscious world via dreams, slips of the tongue, fantasies or, crucially, writing. Brunette became for him a working model of the interplay between conscious and unconscious states because, given that he had invented her, he was both in full control of the latter and the arbiter of how much of this would be released through her various writings. This sophisticated version of Frankenstein's creation enabled him to pretend that he was exploring Layard's hypothesis while at the same time using her as a release mechanism for two other more pressing concerns: literary ambition and sexual frustration.

The most engrossing passage of Brunette's mini autobiography – at least for those with some knowledge of Larkin's childhood – is her recollections of her own childhood home in Cornwall.

> The front door was never shut – I believe because it *would* not – and during all our stay there nothing was ever stolen. Or perhaps things *were* stolen, and we simply did not notice . . . None of the clocks ticked. All the drawers and bureaus and chests were always left open, and nothing of importance was ever kept in them . . . except one, which I found full

of *snake skins*. What they were there for I do not know even now . . .
In fact only three rooms in the house were ever used: the kitchen, my
mother's room and my father's room. The last two were almost always
locked and I scarcely remember even getting a glimpse into them. (p. 240)

The passage enacts the thesis of Freud's 'Creative Writers and Day
Dreaming'. She is telling a form of the truth as she recollects it. In doing so
she becomes concerned with events and occurrences and equally reluctant
to expand upon their implicitly odd, even sinister significance. Penvorn must
have been in Larkin's mind as he, via Brunette, wrote this.

He pretended to his friends that Brunette was a joke, but in truth she
was a rehearsal for what he knew he would give proper time to after graduation. She enabled him to invent a writer, to stand outside this presence,
sometimes allying her with his own inclinations – sexual and familial – and
sometimes watching her operate as a figure attempting to reconcile what
she was with what she put on the page. Within a year of completing the
strange fabric of texts that created Brunette he would begin his first serious
attempt at fiction. There would be parallels, in that the principal figure
would be a fantasist, not unlike the creator of Brunette, for whom life
and fiction involve fragile, nebulous borders. Brunette was the preamble for
Jill.

Considering the amount of time and effort given over to the creation of
Brunette and her literary constellation it is extraordinary that he had any
in reserve for other activities, such as his final examinations in June 1943.
Throughout the spring and early summer he complained regularly to his
friends that he was, variously, unprepared for finals, unsuited to academic
study *per se* and indifferent to the nature of his degree. To Norman Iles he
wrote that 'There's so much to be learnt – and of course the best thing to
have is a "genuine love of literature". I haven't got one . . .' (7 April 1943).
For Iles he predicted 'a Second if I'm lucky', for Sutton 'a Third, at most a
Second' (12 April) and for his parents 'a Third or lower' (4 April). His
pessimism was genuine in that he was aware that he had spent too long doing
other things to make the best of his innate talents as a literary scrutineer –
perversely Brunette's 'What Are We Writing For?' discloses the analytical
talents of its, and her, creator. When, in mid-July, he ascended the steps of
the Sheldonian Theatre to look for his name on the degree lists he was well
prepared to be ranked as mediocre or worse, and the combination of surprise
and elation was all the more priceless when he found that he had a First. For
once the Larkin family shared an unalloyed feeling of happiness. Eva and
Sydney attended his graduation ceremony in late July, and afterwards the
three of them went to lunch with Diana Gollancz and Bruce Montgomery.
He spent the rest of the summer in Coventry with occasional visits to

friends still in Oxford, and it is during this period that he exchanged experiments with Brunette for plans for a piece of fiction that might be taken seriously by publishers. At the end of *Michaelmas Term at St Bride's* there is a curious passage in which one of the two principal characters, Pat, informs the other, Marie, that the 'story' in which they had both been involved is 'over now' and that reality beckons. The specifics of this non-fictional world involve a bar-room full of young men, some of whom she has met before and others not. Members of 'The Seven' would probably have recognized versions of themselves. 'Teddy' is, no doubt, Edward du Cann, and one man, Bruce Montgomery, is even referred to as author of *The Case of the Gilded Fly*, as indeed he was. Not only had Larkin introduced his fictional character to some of his actual acquaintance, he further guaranteed the authenticity of this world by basing it upon a real event. On 5 June 1943 he wrote to Iles:

> We went drinking last night with Bruce Montgomery, Philip and two freshmen and Lt Colin Strang and Kingsley did The Man in the Pub and The Man in the Train etc. etc. . . .

As Marie pushes ajar the Smoke Room door she witnesses them, including 'a fair haired second-lieutenant talking about a man in a train': 'Marie shut the door hastily. If this was reality, she decided, she would rather keep in the story.'

So also concludes Larkin's period in a world inhabited and created by someone else. He had allowed Marie to return to it, but he was moving elsewhere. He wrote to Sutton a couple of months later, 'I am writing a story called (provisionally) "Jill"' (20 August 1943).

At the end of the Introduction to the 1963 reissue of *Jill* Larkin wrote that 'It will, I hope, still qualify for the indulgence traditionally extended for juvenilia.' It has, in that most critics have treated it with benevolent restraint. In truth, it is a shambolic piece of work, and had R.A. Caton not published serious literature to provide his pornography list with a shroud of respectability it would probably never have got into print. As is the case with a number of novels which lack coherence or direction the critical scrutineer might be tempted to elevate *Jill* to the status of a commendable, if botched, attempt at pseudo-Modernism. John Kemp, the main character, fails to engage the interest or sympathy of anyone inside or outside the novel, so perhaps his real function is that of an embodied device, the means by which the fictional text folds into itself and contemplates its own status as fiction. He invents a separate life for himself involving the creation of a younger sister, Jill, a process which begins with him writing letters to and from her in which he presents himself as the witty, confident figure he aspires to be but for some unexplained reason finds himself unable to become in real life. This spirals into a private fantasy, with Jill becoming the subject of an extended short story and then the author of her own diary. Soon after that he encounters a real Jill (or rather Gillian) who spoils the fantasy by proving to be not quite what he expects and certainly not, as he hopes, interested in him.

The problems with this model of *Jill* as an exercise in dynamic self-referentiality is that while it is credible – Larkin had not as yet turned his back upon Modernism – the facts surrounding the evolution of the novel offer a very different and more mundane account of how and why he wrote it.

Apart from a small number of poems, practically everything that Larkin had written before starting *Jill* was not intended for publication. In 1943 he wrote to Sutton and Amis (10 and 20 August respectively) of how, out of a batch of half-completed short stories, something more intriguing was emerging, confiding in Sutton that 'it could lengthen into a novel, if I could ever do it'. He gives them a brief description of the plot of *Jill*, enthuses about it, but having raised the question of why this new idea might be the one to get him into print leaves it unanswered. One is further puzzled by two other letters to his friends, each written the same day (30 September). For Sutton: 'Novel about Oxford? Oh yes, usual stuff. Ten a penny. Young hero. Intelligent, sensitive, bit of a poet. Cheap introspection. Patches of sheer beauty. First love, local colour – scraps of "varsity life", homosexuality, rags and the rest of it. Disappears into luminous future . . .' The young hero was originally to be based on Larkin himself, but in the letter to Amis he discloses difficulties with this. 'I really and truly wish that it wasn't based in Oxford,' he writes, goes on to list people and locations which he and Amis know and adds that ongoing and recent reality are continually interfering with the imaginative impulse. 'I am constantly conducting a defensive battle against these things with one hand while trying to carry on with the story with the other.'

In the novel itself his attempts to distance himself from John Kemp read like an alibi offered by the accused. Kemp's working-class background, his childhood in Huddlesford, a Lancashire industrial town, and, worst of all, his parents are assembled from second-hand stereotypes. He tells in the introduction of how he and Norman Iles had invented a 'Yorkshire Scholar' when amusing each other on trips to and from tutorials by conversing in music-hall versions of northern working-class speech. However, a more revealing example occurs in a letter to Amis (14 July 1942) in which he places himself, with his own classless accent unaltered, in an imaginary exchange with two Leeds University undergraduates.

Me: Of course, the fundamental quality of Russell. [Pee Wee Russell, the jazz musician]
1st Scholar: E-e-ehhh! Dust mean Professor Russell of Awld English Philologee?

He prefaces this with the comment that he and Amis were lucky not to have ended up in the University of Leeds, but within a year this joke had rebounded. Kemp's parents' speech habits are not quite as excessively provincial as the scholars', but they nevertheless come close to sounding like a parody of Elizabeth Gaskell's *North and South*. Joe Kemp: 'You ain't talkin' to a man with backward ideas . . . I want to do t'best by the lad as I can.' Clearly John Kemp had to lose his accent. If he had introduced himself to his new Oxford acquaintances with something like 'Ma name's Kemp and a'm from 'uddlesford', the entire novel would have collapsed into a farcical sequel to *Jude the Obscure*. Without explaining how Kemp has acquired a different, classless accent from that of his parents Larkin provided him with one and immediately faced another problem. In the episodes involving Kemp's pre-Oxford life his parents' vocal habits vividly announce their region and status, and to avoid either the question of how their son seems to have received lessons from a voice coach or a repetition of the ludicrous exchange with the Leeds scholars Kemp in these passages says very little and mostly in monosyllables.

It would have been apparent to Larkin that his dressing up of Kemp as a working-class northerner was unconvincing, but he kept at it because it was his only hedge against his increasing and uneasy awareness that he was indeed writing about himself. He wrote to Amis that 'John Kemp is getting rather clever, but that's because he is growing like me, a tendency I shall sternly redress in the third draft' (12 October 1943). He was referring here to Kemp's imaginative cunning, evidenced in his preparation of the false letters to and from Jill. But he did not redress the tendency and a month later he reported to Amis that 'the diary and the short story he writes . . . may have to be cut out. A little twerp like John Kemp couldn't think of anything so perverse' (8 November 1943). He could not because nowhere else in the novel does he indicate anything resembling literary talent or ambition; again the problem originates in Larkin's attempt to separate himself from his character. In the end, however, Kemp's inventions become a key element of the novel, and he became even more like his creator than Larkin had envisaged. The diaries and the short story are a cannibalized version of *Trouble at Willow Gables*. Jill's boarding school is called Willow Gables, many of the characters from the original manuscript are there too and only the mildly pornographic material is left out. More significantly he disclosed to Amis that, with regard to this transference, 'Brunette Coleman, who wrote "Trouble at Willow Gables" is helping me' (20 August 1943), and throughout his account to Amis on the progress of the novel Brunette is indeed always there helping him. This might seem to be a joke, but in truth it is an acknowledgement by Larkin that he had effectively lost control of the balance between invention and autobiography.

Brunette was based partly on Diana Gollancz, at the time Larkin's closest woman friend. They had met during his final undergraduate year, and he had kept in touch with her during 1943–4 when writing *Jill*. She was an art student at the Slade, daughter of the publisher Victor Gollancz and given to the mixture of moneyed flirtatiousness and bohemianism with which Waugh's novels had drenched the image of Oxford between the wars. There could hardly have been a better model for the author *manquée* of Larkin's erotic fantasies, and when he refers to Brunette in the Amis letters as his helpmate in the planning of *Jill*, fantasy was yet again bleeding into fact: Diana read and commentated on Kemp's letter and diaries. Brunette could not of course feature as herself in Larkin's first attempt at publishable fiction, but her real counterpart could, and Diana becomes Elizabeth Dowling. She, like Diana, is self-consciously and proudly attractive to men and dresses in a way that enhances both her erotic and artistic self-image.

Apart from Kemp's eventual obsession with the real Jill, Elizabeth provides the novel's one moment of almost unbridled sexuality. She is advising Kemp on how to wear his newly acquired bow tie (blue silk with white spots, one taste he shared with his author), and as they move closer together and make physical contact Kemp begins to feel a 'flaring theoretical lust'. Elizabeth's expression indicates that she wants him to touch her. 'He saw in a second that she expected him to do this, that she was waiting for it.' This is an economical version of a more extended dance of mutual attraction between Larkin and Diana. He reported to Amis that he had heard that 'Diana Gollancz thinks very highly of me and would like to get into the same bed that I do . . . she waits for me to make the advances.' In the letter he cannot quite make up his mind about whether he will respond to Diana's apparent attraction to him (actually his account is touched by vain optimism and in the end nothing happened between them), while in the novel he expands on this by having Kemp's narrator helpfully explain the curious notion of 'flaring theoretical lust': 'A horrible embarrassment tingled and shuddered inside him, that what he had imagined to be his most secret feeling was almost cynically common.' This carries echoes of Layard and Lawrence in its disgust at the mechanized, habitual aspect of sexual desire having displaced its idealized, primitive alliance with the life of the spirit. Such matters might at the time have engaged Larkin's higher thinking, but in truth his uncertainty regarding Diana, which clearly inspired the episode in the novel, was based more upon sexual inexperience and lack of confidence than Lawrentian theorizing.

Larkin's anxiety about separating himself from Kemp might appear to be driven by the standard elevation of imaginative and intellectual sophistication over a dependence upon given facts. In fact his fears were far more rudimentary. Kemp was a version of him – he had come to accept that – but now he had to decide the extent to which his creation would improve upon or embody those aspects of himself that caused him most discomfort.

After informing Amis of the sexual potential in his friendship with Diana he adds in the same letter that he only mentions this 'as a vague answer to your weekly Rabelaisianism'. What he means is that Amis had over the previous eighteen months kept him regularly informed of his prodigious sex life. Amis, then stationed at Catterick, North Yorkshire, was having an affair with a married woman whose husband was serving overseas and in his spare moments had seduced three other young women of the area. Larkin was fascinated and amused by Amis's stories and, when comparing them with his own attempts to initiate something resembling a relationship, envious and disappointed. He had made tentative and ultimately unsuccessful advances to Margaret Flannery and Hilary Allen of the University English Club, both involving a mixture of uncertainty and, on his part, nerves. He had arrived for a date with another undergraduate, having prepared his strategies carefully, including the presentation of a bunch of flowers. She had disrupted his calculated sequence of charm and chat by opening the door too early, causing him to present her with the bouquet and, fearing an attack of the stammers, depart hastily down the road. On one occasion he had attempted to kiss a woman when both were savouring the romantic ambience of a shared punt on the Cherwell. 'I'd sooner not, thanks,' she had said, as if he'd offered her another drink. He reported to Sutton that 'Women (university) repel me inconceivably . . . they are shits' (20 November 1941). In truth, they did not, and on the whole the ones he knew were not. It was just that while he felt sexually attracted to them he did not have Amis's enviable combination of charm, wit and looks. As a compensation, of sorts, he theorized about sex with the assistance of Lawrence and Layard. Kemp was born out of this cheerless meshing of sexual vacuity and unspecified ambition. When he informed Amis that he was thinking of cutting out Kemp's creation of the diaries and the short story, Larkin was actually addressing his own confused and intermingled notions of fantasy and creativity.

From 1940 onwards he had kept Sutton regularly informed of his thoughts about Lawrence, whose entire works in print he was reading again and again and in which he was finding a web of speculations which might explain if not compensate for his own feelings about sexuality. For example: 'We drew strength and life from Lawrence's works, and I don't think one can do any more from any book' (21 December 1942). 'WHY conventional critics don't admit DHL into the holy of holies as a prose writer alone never ceases to baffle me' (16 March 1943). 'When Lawrence says "only the mind tries to drive my soul and body into uncleanness" by creating rules in the soul's judgments, he means surely that beauty is untangible and unreliable' (4 April, 1943). What attracted Larkin most to Lawrence was his ability to break down the established borders between speculative, theoretical discourse and literary writing. His novels did not simply record and enact elements of the human condition; they informed representation with ideas, even solutions. Larkin: 'Imitation is absurd. Perhaps plots are the thing – someone [Lawrence] with a lively penis kicking a hole in society . . .' (6 July 1942). If Larkin could similarly integrate his literary ambitions and sexual uncertainties in a novel then he might at least realize the former while offering himself a more secure perception of the latter. It was no accident that Sutton was the first to hear of plans for Gillian: 'he [Kemp] begins to construct a complicated sexless daydream about an imaginary sister who serves as a nucleus for a dream-life. Then he meets a girl who is exactly like this imaginary sister (the sister-aspect having by now changed into a rather more emotional relationship) and the rest of the story in action and in a long dream, serves to disillusion him completely' (10 August 1943).

The contrast between the Sutton letters and those to Amis during the same period is hilarious. Often the subjects are the same – sex and literature particularly – but the Lawrentian high-mindedness of the Sutton correspondence is exchanged for Amis with something closer to Rochester. 'My flogging chart [daily record of masturbation] reads 2.3. My writing, when it happens, is the only happy thing . . . I don't fuckin' drink, I don't fuckin' smoke . . . I don't fuckin' fuck women – I might as well be fuckin' dead' (14 July 1942); perhaps not quite what Lawrence meant when he reflected on the mind's role in driving soul and body into uncleanness. Larkin is honest enough about his own failures to attract women and concentrates on his friend's reports of doing little else. Sometimes Amis would amuse Larkin by reporting conversations with his lovers, with pseudo stage directions, partly as a rehearsal for the use of dialogue in fiction (Amis actually transcribed some of these, almost verbatim, for his first, unpublished, novel 'Who Else Is Rank'), and all the time their exchanges shifted the emphasis from the pragmatic theorizing of the Sutton letters to celebrations of ribaldry. When he informed Amis, a week after Sutton, of his plans for *Jill* his synopsis was far more tough and succinct – 'a young man who invents a younger sister and falls in love with her' – and in case Amis suspects some intellectual complexity he adds the tone-lowering reference to Brunette. Amis's subsequent enquiries on the progress of the book, particularly the invention of Gillian, were obviously consistent with this mood because Larkin answers on 19 October 1943 that 'No, he [Kemp] doesn't "slap a length on her, ole boy".'

In *Jill* Kemp's rejection of Elizabeth Dowling was a sign of Larkin's commitment to a Lawrentian prototype for the novel, and earlier in the book there is another passage that reinforces this and which is laden with enough clues to make its private resonance very clear. Kemp has just arrived in Oxford and is meeting the group of people who will variously intimidate, attract and irritate him during the remainder of the story. Kemp feels excluded from the conversation, which at one point turns to an absent Julian who has recently volunteered for the Royal Corps of Signals.

> 'That's right. In the Signals.'
> 'Oh I see. I thought there was something in it.'
> 'You bet.'
> 'Aren't the Signals dangerous then?' Elizabeth asked . . .
> 'Is that what you mean?'
> 'Can't be if Julian –'

Apart from reinforcing Kemp's feeling of exclusion the exchange seems oddly redundant, but one reader at least would have recognized its significance. During 1942 Amis was deemed fit for military service and advised by his friend Norman Manning to choose the Signals, the safest of all active service regiments given that they operated mainly behind the front line. Amis's and Larkin's acquaintances in Oxford frequently made amused but by no means pejorative references to shrewd young Kingsley finding the best option. The exchange is followed by an even more enigmatic one involving Elizabeth and a recollection of having met Julian 'in Town' when they went to see a show. Patrick adds that 'what Lizzie means . . . is that he [Julian] . . .' '*Shut* up!' says Elizabeth. It is intriguing that on 26 October 1943 Amis had written to Larkin of his trip to London also involving a show, and sex, with his married lover. And the lover's name? Elizabeth Simpson. In their correspondence Amis always refers to her as Betty, but Larkin for no obvious reason insists on calling her Lizzie, and the passage involving Julian (Amis) is the only moment in the novel when Elizabeth Dowling is given the same abbreviated version of her Christian name.

Julian is never again mentioned, and for the ordinary reader the episode appears as a gratuitous, peripheral moment in the text, which further strengthens its significance as a token, private register. In a crude sense he is signalling to Amis that he will not feature in the novel, but more significantly he is attempting to make a choice between those dimensions of his personality that would inform the book and those that would be excluded. Dowling is certainly based upon Diana Gollancz, and Larkin's linking of her with Amis/Julian anticipates the moment when Kemp spurns her gaudy attractions. In both instances he is detaching Kemp from the world of bad behaviour, bravado and (rationed) decadence that he, Amis and others such as 'The Seven' had shared. Kemp and the fictional world that was inseparable from his presence would owe allegiance to Larkin's Lawrentian inclinations. The letters to Sutton and Amis show that he could effectively separate his boozy, scurrilous, cynical persona from its more elevated literary–intellectual counterpart. The latter would be the controlling hand in the construction of *Jill*, and the ideas of Lawrence would be its guiding principles.

It is significant that while Sutton serves as his sounding board for Lawrentian theorizing – part of his planning procedure for *Jill* – he never once mentions Lawrence in his letters to Amis. It was not that Larkin was intimidated by his friend or afraid to argue his case. He, too, had doubts regarding the validity of Lawrence's spiritual–aesthetic philosophy, but for the time being he needed for pragmatic purposes to decide upon what kind of method and thesis would underpin his first serious attempt at fiction. He did not, however, recognize that while we can and do alter our persona according to circumstance this activity has self-determined limitations, and that to systematically exclude from his writing the element of his personality that had a natural affinity with Amis was suicidal. He was pretending, at least as an author, that part of him did not exist. He treated Lawrence as his guide, substitute and mentor in a process of self-immolation. There is another curious episode later in the story which indicates the catastrophic effect of this upon the book as a whole.

When Kemp hears of the German air raid on Huddlesford he is unable to determine if his parents are still alive and hurries north to find out. This is an almost verbatim account of what happened to Larkin in November 1940 after the first massive raid on Coventry. Noel Hughes accompanied his friend to Coventry after the bombing – he, too, had no certain knowledge of his parents' fate. Apart from his sense of relief at eventually finding that both their families were unharmed, Hughes's enduring memory of the trip is of the sad spectacle of Larkin when together they reached the latter's home in Manor Road. The house was intact but empty, and it soon became evident to Hughes that Larkin's feeling of panic had been intensified by his sense that he seemed a stranger outside his own childhood home. He did not know who to ask about whether his parents were safe or where they were because he had obviously never spoken to any of his neighbours and neither, it seemed, had his mother or father. Larkin returned to Oxford that same evening, still with no news of his family, to find a telegram from his father informing him that all were safe and variously located in the homes of relatives and, in Sydney's case, a colleague.

For Larkin the experience was at once terrifying and horribly enlightening. For the first time he saw from the outside the fact that his family had formed a weird, isolated colony of their own or, rather, of Sydney's making. They had disappeared, and no one, at least in the immediate vicinity, appeared to have noticed. The effect of this registers in the novel in a distorted but tangible way. The narrator shows us through the eyes of Kemp the smouldering ruins of Huddlesford, and it is described not only as physically altered but alien. In the town centre he comes across Fred, whom he vaguely remembers from school. Fred does not know whether Kemp's area has been hit – he is from another part of town – but what is curious, even for the reader who knows nothing of Larkin's own experience, is that thereafter during his anxious trip to his own street and on his arrival at the house, which like Larkin's is intact but empty, Kemp neither meets nor speaks to anyone else.

Evidence that his own complex experience in Coventry was in his mind as he created Kemp's is further provided by the contrast, indeed the apparent inconsistency, between Kemp's feelings before and after reaching the house. On the journey north he can think only of his parents' 'goodness', of how things about them which once irritated him had now become 'emblems of their most lovable qualities'. 'Any attempts at a personal life he had made seemed merely a tangle of hypocritical selfishness: really he was theirs, dependent on them for ever.' Unlike Larkin Kemp learns before he returns to Oxford that his family is safe: his father has left a note on the front door. This is a subtle alteration because it accentuates Kemp's sudden feeling of detachment from his childhood environment – he learns of his parents' safety without actually meeting them – and this enables him, on the journey back, to reflect on what this means: 'it seems symbolic, a kind of annulling of his childhood'.

> The thought excited him. It was as if he had been told: all the past is cancelled: all the suffering connected with that town, all your childhood, is wiped out. Now there is a fresh start for you: you are no longer governed by what has gone before. (p. 219)

Within hours Kemp has moved from being 'dependent upon [his parents] for ever' to having all of his past 'cancelled', 'no longer governed by what has gone before'. Neither Kemp nor the narrator indicates how or why exactly this change has occurred. Moreover, the reference to 'all the suffering' of his childhood being wiped out is entirely inconsistent with the rest of the novel. The Kemps did not have much money, but his childhood was not in any conventional sense unhappy. Larkin's three years in Oxford, up to the time he began *Jill* in 1943, had involved him in various attempts to evolve a personality, absorb himself into a fabric of beliefs and individualistic perceptions of things which would in some way erase his sense of having been assembled by his father. Sydney had not made his son in his own image, not quite, but his separation of the family from much of the world in which they lived had resulted in Larkin perceiving his childhood as a vacuum.

It is therefore not unreasonable to assume that Kemp's meditations on the visit to Huddlesford reflected Larkin's own after Coventry, and for Larkin himself the parallels between both and Lawrence's *Sons and Lovers* would have been striking – Larkin had read Murry's 1931 biography of Lawrence and was fully aware that the novel was autobiographical. The passage following Kemp's determination to cancel his past as he returns to Oxford and the closing paragraphs of Lawrence's novel are remarkably similar: both men are setting out upon a journey which, wherever it leads, will separate them for ever from what has gone before.

But there was a significant difference. Lawrence, through Morel, had made calculating use of his past, and by the end of the novel his reliance upon it had reached a natural conclusion. Despite Kemp's confident claim to have similarly relinquished this dependency Larkin knew different, and the concluding section, following Kemp's return to Oxford, is moving, in the same way that one might be moved by the spectacle of a self-consciously incompetent actor who insists on completing his audition. Kemp's failure to meet Jill, exchanged for an intimate encounter with the college fountain, is bad enough, but his consequent bout of bronchial pneumonia causes his parents to visit him in Oxford. So much for his 'fresh start'. It is all too dreary to elicit much sympathy from the reader, but one should not treat it as Larkin's anticipation of the drab verisimilitude of Sillitoe et al. It is, instead, Larkin's own admission of failure. Once he had decided that Kemp would not, like himself, rely upon literary ambition as a means of absorbing his anxieties and certainties, Kemp was, both as a character and the vortex for the novel, fatally flawed. He had no future and would never unshackle himself from his past. Novels frequently conclude with their author's *alter ego* variously disillusioned, humiliated, facing intellectual or social oblivion, even dead, but *Jill* has a claim to uniqueness in that there can be few, if any, in which the hero's unenviable state reflects his author's disappointment with the novel.

4

A Girl in Winter

The writing and rewriting of *Jill* had taken up most of Larkin's time during the summer and autumn of 1943. Occasionally he visited Oxford to meet old friends and, reluctantly, applied for jobs. His interview for the Civil Service, in August, was unsuccessful, and Larkin told Sutton that this was partly his intention. He claimed to have informed the panel that he would be happy to offer them his services if they provided him with a decent livelihood to pursue his true vocation as a writer. Something must have impressed them, however, because his name and details were passed on to the department of the War Office which ran the counter-intelligence and code-breaking establishment at Bletchley Park, near Oxford. Since recent disclosures of what actually went on there – particularly the breaking of the German Enigma Code – Bletchley has achieved legendary status, and, while little if any of this was made known to Larkin at his interview on 14 September, he offered Amis a parodic account of how the Admiralty official had intimated that the work was vital to the war effort. 'Of course, yah're workin' against the clock all the tahm . . . one day orf everah seven . . . one week everah three months . . . Christmas, Eastah, Bank Holiday – they don't exist . . .' (16 September 1943). Again he was deemed unsuitable for the job.

In October he applied for the post of Librarian in the public library at Wellington, Shropshire, was interviewed on 13 November and given the job. Reporting this to Sutton he states that he is 'not very proud of the fact . . .[I] spend most of my time handing out tripey novels to morons' (13 December 1943). In fact he is remembered by people who used the library during his two years there as courteous, helpful and willing to make use of the inter-library loan service for anyone whose interests extended beyond the somewhat limited stock. 'The books in the library are mostly very poor, but there is a copy of "Aaron's Rod", "Bliss", "The Garden Party" and "Crome Yellow", all of which make me feel at home. I can't imagine how they got there. There's no poetry later than Housman' (Letter to Sutton, 13 December 1943). Wellington was one of the more disappointing towns of Housman's favourite county. Red-brick Victorian and Edwardian buildings cast a dismal shadow over what remained of its more engaging pre-nineteenth-century architecture. Larkin found a bedsit in an ill-heated Victorian house about five minutes' walk from the library. He shared a small kitchen and bathroom with two other residents, and his landlady, Miss Jones, would not allow him to play his jazz records. Social life, at least for strangers, was generally non-existent, and Larkin compensated by making regular train journeys to visit Bruce Montgomery in nearby Shrewsbury.

Montgomery had been teaching at Shrewsbury School for more than a year, and his presence there was one of the reasons why Larkin had applied for the job. Montgomery had always enjoyed alcohol as a stimulant to easy acquaintance, but during their encounters Larkin took the lead, probably as an antidote to the general sense of dullness that seemed to him to embrace the locality. Accounts of their wild nights in Shrewsbury include Larkin interrupting their conversation on the way back from the pub by falling sideways over a garden wall, passing out on the train and missing his stop at Wellington and one night, after eight pints of local bitter, attempting to break into a shop. The most famous involved an evening when the two of them attended the school's literary society, after several hours on the town. Larkin found that his bladder was demanding more of his attention than the debate and, given that he did not, characteristically, wish to draw attention to himself by leaving the room and estimating that his heavy overcoat and several layers of winter clothing were sufficiently absorbent, he decided to urinate *in situ*.

When sober the two friends discussed and advised each other on their respective writings. Montgomery was particularly helpful with the final draft of *Jill*, which Larkin completed in spring 1944. To an extent their partnership resembled Amis's and Larkin's in Oxford before the former departed for wartime service, with one significant difference. Amis had willingly played foil to Larkin's creative fantasies and caricatures, even co-authoring one of them, but Montgomery was already a published and respected novelist – albeit in the sub-genre of crime fiction – and had a network of useful contacts. Montgomery was sufficiently impressed by *Jill* to recommend it to Charles Williams of Oxford University Press who, if he shared Montgomery's opinion, would forward it to T.S. Eliot at Faber. He didn't and returned it to Montgomery who next tried Gollancz. They, too, rejected it. J.A. Caton's Fortune Press was Larkin's last hope, and eventually in late summer 1944 Caton replied with contractual impositions – including no royalties to the author – which confirmed Larkin's suspicion that Caton made his money from pornography while acting as little more than a vanity publisher for 'serious' writers. This suspicion was challenged, however, when in October Caton wrote to Larkin to ask if he would care to submit a volume of poems for consideration. He did, and the collection, *The North Ship*, appeared three months before the novel in 1945.

Most of the poems of *The North Ship* were written between late 1942 and summer 1944, alongside *Jill* and Larkin's first attempts at *Jill*'s successor A

Girl in Winter. Most critical assessments of *The North Ship* cite an authorial subtext provided by Larkin in the introduction to the 1966 reissue. In early 1943, in Oxford, he met the poet Vernon Watkins whose admiration for W.B Yeats was apparently infectious. Larkin: 'I spent the next three years trying to write like Yeats, not because I liked his personality or understood his ideas but out of infatuation with his music (to use the word I think Vernon used).' Typically Larkin combines apologetic candour with evasion in that he does not comment on what else he was attempting to do, let alone what the poems might disclose. Certainly the poems incorporate a Yeatsian affiliation to aspects of the natural world. Yeats in his later verse integrated this with his own mystical, symbolic infrastructure, but Larkin appears to be using the particulars of landscape and nature as a backdrop for something more nebulous and depressing. The weather is generally miserable, and if the time is not indicated as wintry dusk or dawn it might as well be, since forthcoming days and nights are shrouded with unremitting gloom. The imagery is potentially symbolic – water, stars, sky, ice, rain, wind, faces and hands abound – but its potential is never realized or specified.

In 1965, in the wake of Larkin's first decade of eminence, the Fortune Press threatened to reissue *The North Ship*, and Larkin wrote to his Faber editor Charles Monteith that 'they are such complete rubbish . . . that I am just as unwilling to have two editions in print as I am to have one' (16 June). (Faber were bidding to take over the copyright.) In a letter to Norman Iles in 1944 he compares his personal characteristics with his friend's: 'You aim at increased positiveness of character while I aim at increased negativeness, a kind of infinite recession in the face of the world' (16 April 1944). It would be difficult to find a more accurate prefatory piece for *The North Ship*, and in the same letter he provides an enlightening account of how he has attuned his state of mind to his theory of writing:

> I feel that myself and my character are nothing except insofar as they contribute to the creation of literature – that is almost the only thing that interests me now. To increase one's value as a pure instrument is what I am trying to do: I conceive the creative process as depending on an intricate arrangement of little mirrors inside one and by continual care and assiduity and practice these mirrors can be cleaned and polished, so that in the end artistic perception is a whole time and not a part time thing.

This serves as a very adequate explanation of why the poems of *The North Ship* are so bad, particularly when aligned with his celebration of 'increased negativeness' and 'infinite recession'.

Apart from himself and his writing Larkin's frame of reference was severely limited. He found the world cheerless and often depressing and, as a self-proclaimed instrument for literary transparency, he did not attempt to improve on this by making the poems themselves more engaging, let alone agreeable, than their emotive underpinnings. There is of course a long tradition of beautifully executed poems about melancholia which succeed because the poet generally has a clear perception of its cause. This might remain undisclosed, but its pervasive presence will prompt the reader to reach for clues. With *The North Ship*, however, the promptings require close and diligent scrutiny and remain in the end indiscernible. They coalesce around the presence of a figure other than the speaker who stalks from poem to poem and is certainly female. For example:

> 'Your lips that lift at mine' ('Is it for now or for always')
> 'And if she were to admit / The world weaved by her feet' ('The Dancer')
> 'Within the dream you said: Let us kiss then, / In this room, this bed'
> ('Within the dream you said')
> 'Love, we must part now: do not let it be / Calamitous and bitter'
>   ('Love, we must part now')
> 'Last night you came / Unbidden, in a dream . . .' ('Morning has spread again')

Beyond her existence as a pronoun little more is disclosed of this figure, which, on Larkin's part, is involuntarily candid. His experience of 'love' (mentioned nine times in separate poems) and its attendant, embodied causes was that of the sophisticated but endlessly frustrated adolescent, and the dreary atmospherics of the whole collection suddenly seem more appropriate.

During early spring 1944 Larkin found himself forming a friendship with one of the library borrowers to whom five years later he would propose marriage. Ruth Bowman was intelligent, interested in high- and low-brow literature and impressed by the cautious, learned Oxford graduate who ran the library, and she was sixteen years old. Larkin never commented on what first attracted him to Ruth. She was short, although not petite, wore spectacles and while not distractingly pretty was not unattractive either. Motion contends that she reminded him of himself. 'Her apprehensive, short-sighted face mirrored his own self doubt and potential self disgust' (p. 118). It might be true that Larkin's sense of an alliance between his physical shortcomings and temperamental inhibitions caused him to feel unthreatened by Ruth, but there was more to it than that. He was, when they met, a man whose existence was comprised as much of invented hypotheses as of endured experience, and she became a channel between the two states. It was not that he saw her as a living model for further writing, at least not at the beginning. She embodied a pervasive element of work complete and in progress. She did not intimidate him, as Diana Gollancz and her fictional counterpart Elizabeth Dowling had done with their erotic sophistication. She carried the same attractions that Jill had done for Kemp, but Larkin did not have to contend with Kemp's experience of an unwelcoming competitive context; this was dull provincial England and Ruth was not part of the high-living set, up from London. Most significantly she was innocent, inexperienced and very real, a perfect replacement for the ill-defined presence who in *The North Ship* seems as threatening as she is attractive and for whom 'fear' might easily be substituted for 'love'. Ruth lived in the town, in modest circumstances. Her father had died when she was eleven and, encouraged by her grandfather who had been assistant editor of the local newspaper, she had ambitions to read English at university – she eventually went to the University of London. Larkin at first acted as a kind of informal tutor, advising her on what to read and locating books not otherwise available. Their courtship developed out of this. They were observed walking in the town, reciting poetry to each other, and Ruth was advised by her teachers to be less arrogant and rebellious, tendencies which, as gossip suggested, Larkin had inculcated. When Larkin was first invited to her home for a meal his diffidence had registered for Ruth's mother as something more unsettling and sinister: he was 'arty', an intellectual, a type known to cause heartbreak and personal catastrophe, at least in the opinion of the English lower middle classes of the 1940s. Ruth's mother was attuned to local unease about this man who had encouraged the reading of Lawrence, Huxley, Joyce and other unsuitable authors.

Much later, after Larkin had achieved literary fame, Ruth Bowman reflected on their relationship as something that at the time had confused her. He could be unpatronizingly erudite, share her taste for literature and bring to it his own tendentious breadth of reading. And he could make her laugh. He adapted his Oxford-practised talents to caricatures of local dignitaries. His stammer, always present in the library, fell away when they were alone and together. But she was never certain of when this exclusively caring and entertaining presence would be exchanged for a mood of withdrawn introspection, a sadness he never explained. She knew of his ongoing publications and was, as she put it, 'star struck', but what he did not tell her was that she had become part of the weirdly fatalistic interweaving of his life and his writing.

In June 1946 Larkin applied for and got the post of Sub-Librarian at University College, Leicester. He was at the time halfway through a correspondence course which would eventually qualify him as a member of the Library Association, and he persuaded the Leicester selection board that his commitment to the profession was genuine; he claimed that the war had delayed his full-time training and his job at Wellington operated as a practical introduction. His reasons for the move were various. Obviously a city and an academic environment were more attractive than a rural backwater, and there was a degree of truth in his presentation to the interview board. He was finding more and more that the way in which libraries worked suited his temperament and to an extent operated as a fitting compensation for many aspects of his non-working life. The relationship between writing and everything else might have seemed capriciously unreliable, but in libraries books were obliged to know their place and librarians maintained order.

Ruth Bowman knew that the job and his life in Wellington had been temporary contingencies, but in a letter she wrote to him the day after he left she seems uncertain of what exactly the move would mean for each of them. Alongside customary lamentations on how she would miss their day-to-day companionship she indicates a fear that something more significant has changed: ' . . . how can I battle my way through life . . . without you?' She concludes that they 'mustn't let the mere fact that we do not live in the same town come between us irrevocably' (4 September 1946). The letter gives the impression that it was written in response to one from Larkin, suddenly announcing a momentous change of circumstances; which is puzzling since one assumes that they had talked of the move over the four months since his interview in June. A year earlier Ruth had been accepted by King's College, London, to read English, and her elevation from schoolgirl to independent woman was reflected in their relationship. They had started having sex and, particularly during Larkin's visits to London, had behaved like a mature couple, attending the theatre and cinema, visiting the National Gallery and the Tate and going out for meals. Over the period between 1946 and 1948 Ruth accompanied Larkin on what seemed to be a tour of his enthusiasms. In summer 1947 they had spent a week in Oxford, and shortly afterwards Larkin had taken her to Eastwood, where he had shown her the D.H. Lawrence family home and they had wandered through the locality looking for the likeliest original settings for their fictional counterparts. A year after that they had gone to Hardy country. Larkin had exchanged Yeats for Hardy as his poetic mentor, read the novels along with the poems, and during their visit they had repeated the Nottinghamshire exercise, trudging avidly between the landmarks around Dorchester.

Given these continuities and apparent signs of commitment, her anxieties about his move to Leicester appear unfounded, but it is possible that the longer she knew him the more she began to detect a chameleonesque dimension to his personality. It was not that he was misleading her, at least not in the conventional sense, rather that he was dividing up his life into components, some of which he shared with her but often only obliquely. This is indicated in his renewed friendship with Amis. Larkin introduced Ruth to Amis in January 1946, and they met on several occasions after that, up to and following Amis's marriage to Hilary Bardwell. Much later Ruth informed Motion that she found Amis to be a divisive presence, often displaying a tendency to draw Larkin away from her and towards his own self-image of boozy debauchee. She didn't know the half of it.

From 1945 when Larkin first informed Amis of her presence he, Larkin, referred to Ruth either as the 'schoolcaptain' or 'Misruth'. In effect she became a real version of the fantasies he had shared with Amis and used in the Brunette writings and *Jill*. He was watching her grow up, and he shared with his friend some of the questionable pleasures derived from this blend of involvement and voyeurism. He does not change facts for Amis, but he adapts them to a mood and a setting that had since 1945 become their exclusive terrain. His anecdotes include an account of a step-cousin 'who used to watch misruth undressing' (24 September 1946). This turns out to be Ruth's cousin Isobel who, Larkin implies, causes Ruth to fear that when she is away at university 'Miss Isobel and I would instantly get into the same bed' (12 July 1946). Jane Exall, a friend of Ruth's, would later be presented as the 'bosomy English Rose' of his 1962 poem 'Wild Oats'. At the time he wrote of her to his friend as inspiring men 'to want to FUCK HER UP TO THE NECK' (30 September 1946). Larkin's presentation of himself to Amis as a lecherous bon viveur was one feature of a letter-writing style that had evolved between them since the war, a pun-laden discourse in which their opinions on literature, details of their private lives and ambitions, resentments and invectives on life in general became an exclusive and usually hilarious dialogue, sometimes accompanied by photographs or sketches.

One letter in particular is intriguing. On 26 February 1947 he informs Amis of how his relationship with 'misruth' was going through one of its occasional bouts of uncertainty. He wonders about the benefits or otherwise of sex with Jane Exall and reflects that in the end 'a pock is a pock'. Would the effort of getting Jane into bed be worth it when this 'wouldn't be nearly so nice in reality as it is in my imagination WHEN I'M TOSSING MYSELF'? So, he asks, why doesn't he just put up with 'what is to hand', in this case figuratively, and 'resign myself to misruth'? There is no evidence that Larkin kept copies of all of his letters, but it is almost certain that he did with this one, given that it reads as a prose version of the poem he would write thirteen years later, 'Wild Oats'. For instance, in the poem Ruth is referred to as 'her friend in specs I could talk to', the one he 'took out', despite the attraction of Jane, the bosomy rose. In the letter Ruth and he 'got on . . . because we are really quite alike', she being less attractive, less a reminder of his own inadequacies and in whose company he could 'start thinking about something else' – something other than sex.

He had ceased any kind of contact with Ruth when he wrote the poem, and while one might be tempted to treat it as insensitive, confessional would be more apt. The poem tells us much, principally that the figure he felt himself becoming in the late 1940s would soon be the abiding influence for its public, literary counterpart. In his most celebrated poems he uses the artefact in much the same way that he used his letters. There is a confidential openness interweaved with mundane, sometimes embarrassing, personal detail, and then the focus will shift abruptly to a reflection on general significance or, just as likely, prevailing insignificance.

In 1948 Larkin produced something that can only be described as a hybrid, somewhere between a letter and a poem. It nods self-consciously towards the poetic by being broken into non-metrical free verse lines whose length and rhythm appear to reflect units of speech and thought – its closest formal counterpart would probably be Eliot's *Four Quartets*. Just as significantly it involves a distorted echo of the letters in that although the topics are those he regularly shared with Sutton and Amis – literary ambitions, off-hand comments on people and places and so on – here they are addressed to no one in particular. While library archives bulge with manuscript first drafts that would eventually mutate into canonized poems, this document is unique because of its peculiar, multiple identity. Its formal laxity – something he had never tried before and never would again – was as much a token gesture as a concession to radicalism. It was a framing device, a means by which for the first time ever he placed private, confidential material and concomitant reflections in a literary context. Within two years he would take this a stage further by beginning to compose poems in which content was stripped of its personal particulars, so that the speaker became at once anonymous and confidential and far more comfortable within secure poetic structures.

It is interesting to compare the following passage from this unnamed transcript with a poem written a decade later, 'Letter to a Friend about Girls':

> Then when I visit my friends in Oxford
> Their lives seem happier and more successful than mine:
> Kingsley in particular seems to live at the centre of gratified desire.
> But when my desire is for the past or for immortality
> Who can gratify that?
> (Larkin Archive, Brynmor Jones Library [BJL], Notebook 5)

It echoes passages in letters to Amis where Larkin conceded his lack of success with women and his general sense of failure, but the letters always deflected the self-pity of such concessions via their farcical, self-parodic manner. This, however, is unadorned, brutally transparent, and a version of it reappears in the poem, which begins:

> After comparing lives with you for years
> I see how I've been losing: all the while
> I've met a different gauge of girl from yours.

It goes on to list incidents that Amis had indeed disclosed in his letters, involving girls 'In train, tutorial or telephone booth'. Amis's world is one 'where all nonsense is annulled / And beauty is accepted slang for yes', and Amis seems not to have noticed his, Larkin's, where the women are either unattractive, shy or bound by moral principles – 'anyhow, none give in'.

The texts are very similar, except that in the poem the 'friend' and the speaker remain unidentified and placed at one remove from a real letter to a real friend by being bound into elegantly constructed stanzas. The pseudo-poem was transitional, albeit unwittingly. It was up to that point Larkin's only real attempt to place himself within a literary text without projecting his feelings and sensibilities into various states of fictional disguise or symbolic obfuscation. Eventually in his best poems he would achieve a balance between candour and impersonal craftsmanship, make himself mischievously present and private. But during the period between *Jill* and his early 1950s years in Belfast Larkin equivocated. He remained uncertain about the instincts and inclinations which made claims upon his personality and in turn governed his literary ambitions.

Originally titled *The Kingdom of Winter*, *A Girl in Winter* was conceived and completed with outstanding speed. He began it shortly after his arrival in Wellington, and its final draft was ready by the end of 1945. It is difficult to rank it as either slightly worse than *Jill* or minutely better, because they are very different books, but the margin is narrow. The central character, Katherine, is a wartime refugee from continental Europe. We never learn of her background or the means by which she ends up in England, and the novel is concerned almost exclusively with her existence in a dull Midlands town. It is in three sections. The first and third involve the present day, her job in the local library and her general feeling of detachment from her surroundings and new acquaintances. The middle part tells of her first visit to England, as a teenager before the war, the guest of the Fennels, a middle-class family who live in the locality. Robin, the son, is her age and attempts half-heartedly to seduce her. Towards the end of the third part she makes contact with him again and is further disappointed. The endearingly naïve adolescent of her memory has now become a drunken lecher. They have emotionless sex and he leaves. The end.

Being foreign and a woman were the two conditions of which Larkin had least experience, and from this it would be fair to assume that Katherine was created partly as an attempt to exorcize the figure of Kemp, who embodied many of his author's irksome fallibilities and defeats. The locations in the novel – a thinly disguised Coventry and the Warwickshire countryside – and their inhabitants were familiar, but the central character would oblige him to write about them as if they were not. He informed Sutton, soon after completing the book, that Henry Green was the contemporary novelist he now most admired (15 May 1946). In his autobiographical *Pack My Bag* (1940) Green wrote that 'Prose should be a long intimacy between strangers with no direct appeal to what both may have known. It should slowly appeal to feelings unexpressed, it should in the end draw tears out of the stone.' Larkin had certainly read *Pack My Bag*, and the enigmatic phrase 'a long intimacy between strangers' registers as an apt description of what he was attempting to achieve in *A Girl in Winter*. In the middle section, for instance, the exchanges between Robin Fennel, his sister Jane and Katherine shift between conventional dialogue, marked by inverted commas, and a mutation of this where speech-acts become amorphous paraphrases. In the latter we are never sure of the borderline between what is actually said and the thoughts accompanying the words. Green used a version of this technique, and it had first appeared in Joyce's *A Portrait of the Artist as a Young Man*. Katherine was a perfect vehicle for it because she provided the naturalistic mandate of a central figure for whom English is always an uncertain translation, and this also contributes to her role as an intermediary between in Green's words 'feelings unexpressed' and what we find on the page. As with many third-person narratives we sense an intimate although unstated relationship between the narrator and the principal character, but with Katherine this is complicated by continuous reminders that her environment and its language are alien to her. She speaks English competently enough, yet when the narrator discloses the thoughts behind the words we know that something has been lost – her feelings, if not unexpressed, are always offered to us in a language which is not hers and which distorts her precious sense of identity. The only occasions where this effect of distortion and isolation seems suspended is when Katherine, alone, encounters non-human phenomena, most prominently the landscape.

> There was a tang of damp wood from the fences. After a time she leant on a stile and watched a tiny stream running along a ditch, over a bed of white sand; she stooped and flicked her hand in it, finding it very cold. She noticed a small frog in the grass, struck to immobility by her presence; when she tickled it with a straw it crawled away. There was watercress growing under the hedge. She dried her fingers on her skirt. (pp. 128–9)

This passage and many others like it are emotively transparent in that, unlike those in which she is part of a social environment, attempting to attune her ideas and feelings to people and circumstances which seem to trouble her, here she is released from the necessity of response. When *A Girl in Winter* was almost complete Larkin wrote to Sutton of how the book 'picks up where John [Kemp] left off', by which he means Kemp's feeling of isolation. Its theme is 'the relinquishing of live response to life' and he suggests that its title and the prevailing mood of winter and frozenness which informs the book are figurative, indicating a retirement from the consolations of social interaction and exchange. In the same letter he tells Sutton that he is planning a third novel in which the main character would 'pick up where Katherine left off and develop logically back to life again. In other words the north ship will come back instead of being bogged up there in a glacier' (20 September 1945). He concedes that *The North Ship* and *A Girl in Winter* were both part of the same almost involuntary process of withdrawal and isolation. In the former he had mixed a prevailing mood of discontent and melancholia with stylistic borrowings from Yeats, and in the latter he had written a novel about a communicative impasse. Their unifying theme, which they share with *Jill*, is their author's compulsive, addictive relationship with language. Kemp uses it to invent the person he wants and wants to be, Katherine is estranged by it and the poems submit themselves to its distortive capacities.

The 'life' he refers to in the Sutton letter is never defined, and we can only intuit his meaning from the fact that the third novel which he saw as a progression 'back to life' never went further than 2,000–3,000-word drafts, and by 1948 he had virtually abandoned it. It was to be a novel about an artist, a visual artist. Larkin himself was a skilled cartoonist, but Sutton was his point of inspiration, a man who was as committed to painting as a profession as Larkin was to becoming a writer. In September 1947 he wrote to Sutton that the novel comprised '44 pages now of almost complete bunk' (14 September 1947) and asked his friend for advice. Can a man teach himself to paint? When you start a picture do you know in advance what effects you want to achieve?

The novel came to nothing because his objective to move 'back to life' was effectively a further process of distancing. The visual arts theme was an extension of Katherine's brief moments of consolation when she communes non-linguistically with the natural landscape. Between 1946 and 1948 Larkin includes in almost all his letters to Sutton verbal pictures, perhaps as rehearsals for what he hoped would make up the texture of the novel. None involve contact with other people. For example:

> There was a little canvas shelter, a coke brazier with a pot slung over it, a pile of paving stones etc; on the floor by the shelter were some empty tea cans, a couple of crusts poking out of a paper bag and a few onion peelings. The scene appeared to me as a picture – there was a simplicity and solidity about it that made me give a sort of sob of pleasure and sadness. Painting must be a good way of working: no words, no drivelling 'probability' or 'construction' – only the pure vision. (24 February 1948)

This was written in the same year that Larkin finally gave up on the novel which would have had a visual artist as its controlling presence. It was effectively the end point of a downward spiral beginning with Kemp, for whom words are pure illusion and concluding, or rather not concluding, with the third novel which in the letter he sums up with a phrase resonant of B.S. Johnson or Sterne – 'no words . . . only the pure vision'. The contradiction between Larkin's addiction to language and his obsession with non-linguistic representation arose out of his unease with his self-image. Try as he might, he could not keep himself out of his writing, so he searched for a way of making his writing impersonal – pure vision.

In late 1947 he learned that his father was seriously ill, almost certainly with cancer. By Christmas his condition had worsened considerably, and at the end of February 1948 Larkin informed Sutton that 'it is all up for him, matter of weeks'. Sydney Larkin died on 26 March. Eva was in a state of shock and Larkin recognized that she looked to him, her only remaining male relative, as the principal substitute for her departed husband. He organized the funeral, a cremation, took care of the reading of the will – all to Eva – and over the next three months arranged the sale of their house in Coton End – they had moved from Penvorn two years earlier – and the purchase of a more modest one in Leicester where he would live with his mother for the next three years. His sister, now married and with a child of her own, lived half an hour away by bus in Loughborough.

Larkin loved his mother and felt responsible for her welfare, but the prospect of acting as a stand-in for Sydney brought back memories of the cartoon of the family he had drawn in 1939, with himself seated at a desk trying to work and his mother's speech bubble involving what they'd have for lunch tomorrow and how many shirts she'd ironed today; except that Sydney and Kitty were no longer in the picture. Sydney's obituaries supplemented his absence with what for Larkin was a mixture of shock, fascination and affiliation. One in particular caused him to recognize that he was becoming a version of his father, whose 'opinions, Conservative in general . . . were forthright, clear cut, consistent, disconcertingly logical, and expressed in language of crystalline clarity'. No one who knew Larkin would have disputed the parallels here, nor would they have gone against the view that 'In his own field of English literature, where incidentally his taste was impeccable, he had his favourites but no idols.' Lawrence, Yeats, Hardy, Auden, Henry Green – all had once competed for idolatry, but Larkin was beginning to recognize that modelling his work on precedents set by others was counterproductive. He had not as yet found his own idiom and perspective, but the comment that a 'preoccupation with life as a spectacle to be objectively enjoyed as akin to another of his marked characteristics – his caustic wit' was extraordinarily prescient.

Less than six weeks after his father's death Larkin proposed marriage to Ruth. Why exactly he did so will remain a matter for speculation, but the timing of the proposal, when considered in relation to other key transitional events, suggests a less than romantic motive. Sydney, he knew, had been far more influential than anyone or anything else in the formation of his character, and his death caused Larkin to take stock, to look at what, if anything, he had achieved and to consider in the light of this his plans for the future.

A *Girl in Winter* had been published in February 1947 and received a number of good reviews. The *Sunday Times* called it 'an exquisite performance and nearly faultless', and the *Church Times* looked forward to further impressive work from 'the pen of this remarkable young writer'. On the face of things his prospects as a writer were good, but Larkin knew that he had effectively written himself to a standstill. The theme which informed *Jill*, *A Girl in Winter* and the putative visual arts novel – the various effects and conditions of communicative impasse – was self-limiting. Eventually, as Larkin acknowledged, there would be 'no words . . . only the pure vision'. More revealing is the account he gave in the pseudo-poetic ramble:

> They don't come anymore, those moments –
> Moments of Vision, as Hardy called them.
> I could see astonishing pictures, splaying lines
> In all directions . . .
> Yet I believe they would return if I were free.
> So must I live alone, do nothing,
> Give nothing except in writing? Oh people do harass me.
> (Brynmor Jones Library, Notebook 5)

The question was, he knew, hypothetical. Clearly he is referring here to the 'moments' that would have impelled the visual arts novel, but he was sensible enough to recognize that the image of himself as a complete recluse, detached from all responsibility to friends and family, was in reality neither possible nor desirable. In his letters to Sutton he had sometimes pondered the question of why exactly D.H. Lawrence needed a wife, given that everything else about him seemed so radically unorthodox and self-focused. Now his own experience was providing potential answers. It is not coincidental that within a matter of months, during which the brutal reality of existence announced itself with the death of Sydney, Larkin decided that he would shift his focus away from the speculative, almost aestheticist mood of his previous writings to the opposite end of the literary spectrum – tough naturalistic fiction. In the light of this his proposal to Ruth acquires a fascinating subtext. The assumption that underpinned the speculations in his pseudo-poem was that – whether he liked it or not – the particulars of his life and his writing were causally interrelated. If he were to make a serious attempt at a different strategy for the latter then he must also take the former in a radically different direction.

When he announced the engagement to Sutton he did so in the manner of someone experimenting with a figure over whom he has complete and ultimate control but who is not quite himself. 'The engagement, to me anyway, is to give myself a sincere change of "opening out" towards some-one ... I suspect all my isolationist feelings as possibly harmful and certainly rather despicable' (8 May 1948). In the end these attempts to recreate himself, and in turn reconfigure his writings, would fail for the same reason that the creative impulses which underpinned *Jill*, *A Girl in Winter*, his early poems and the visual arts novel exhausted themselves. Both were depend-ent upon self-created falsehoods, productions by a writer he imagined himself becoming but so detached from the real Philip Larkin as to be unsustain-able. Unfortunately one of these experiments would involve someone else; his final break-up with Ruth occurred at the same time that he abandoned his attempts at gritty realistic fiction. Both had in the interim involved fluctuating twists and unsustainable turns, and while Larkin was disap-pointed Ruth endured something both more painful and puzzling. She had, unknowingly, featured as part of an exercise in turning life into fiction, and for her the distress went beyond the imaginative.

Larkin would soon discover a means by which his personality and writing could indeed commingle productively. The pseudo-poem held a clue to this, and it is fascinating to compare the above passage – his painfully candid reflection on desired separateness and loathing for other people – with the closing stanza from 'Best Society', which he wrote in 1951 shortly after his break-up with Ruth.

> Viciously, then, I lock my door.
> The gas-fire breathes. The wind outside
> Ushers in evening rain. Once more
> Uncontradicting solitude
> Supports me on its giant palm;
> And like a sea-anemone
> Or simple snail, there cautiously
> Unfolds, emerges, what I am.

The theme of both passages – the contemplation of detachment – is the same, but the jerky self-consciousness of almost writing a poem about his most private thoughts in the first is exchanged in the second for controlled artistry. There are parallels between the governing image of 'Best Society' – Larkin returning to his unimpressive, lonely bed-sitting room – and the way in which the stanza, like a room, encloses within its self-imposed conventions of octo-syllables and off-rhymes a sense of separateness, a temporary remission from everything outside and the opportunity to become what 'cautiously / Unfolds, emerges, what I am'. In 1951 he was beginning to recognize a natural affinity between what he was – including his masochistic taste for dreary bedsits – and the genre that best suited his character – accessible, coherent, orthodox verse. But first he would have a go at becoming a post-war Arnold Bennett.

5

From Naturalism to Monica

Despite his admission to Sutton of having completed forty-four pages 'of almost complete bunk' there is no evidence that the visual arts novel ever got beyond the level of theory and hypothesis. This is appropriate because his continued use of Sutton as a springboard for his speculations on what such a book might do or mean was in truth a kind of private funeral rite or ceremony of expurgation. What he did not tell Sutton, or anyone else for that matter, was that he had simultaneously begun to try out what was, for him, a completely unprecedented type of writing: naturalistic prose fiction which offered an unadorned account of the lives of ordinary people without making any claims upon significance. Workbooks discovered after the death of Monica Jones show that Larkin had been planning novels of this type since late 1945.

The first, without even a provisional title, involves three principal characters: Edward Defoe, who has spent the war as a prisoner of war; Jack Mattocks, his friend deemed unfit for military service because of a 'minor physical disability'; and Jack's sister Sheila with whom Edward has a relationship. It is more than a coincidence that this synopsis was begun shortly after Larkin's first meetings with Amis when the latter returned from Germany in August 1945. The 'glib, successful, talented' figure of Mattocks, who has succeeded as a writer in the absence of his friend, involves a self-parodic, almost apologetic nod towards a nearly identical character, named Bruno Coleman, created by Amis during 1944–5 in a half-serious attempt at fiction co-authored with his fellow Signals Officer, Frank Coles. In 'Who Else Is Rank' Amis, among other things, exacts revenge upon his Oxford contemporaries who had avoided wartime service. Amis had invented Bruno – the sarcastic gender shift from Brunette indicating his intent – during long periods in Belgium, well behind the front line, when there was little more for him to do than reflect on how he had lost four years of his literary apprenticeship while others were finishing theirs. Bruno, typically, dresses in purple corduroy with an orange silk bow tie and evinces a pretentious, sometimes camp bohemianism. His thick glasses testify to his successful avoidance of the call-up. In September 1941 Larkin failed his army medical on the grounds of very poor eyesight, a moment he celebrated with shameless relief. Mattocks and

Bruno are versions of Larkin; the latter bitterly satirical, the former mordantly apologetic. Amis returned to Britain in 1945 – relieved not to have been sent to the Pacific – and showed 'Who Else Is Rank' to Larkin. Larkin accepted that, for once, fate had treated him generously ,and his own early attempt at realism is a reply to Amis. Amis had not literally been a prisoner of war, but Larkin acknowledges that his years in the army were the equivalent of being removed from – literary – operations. Edward is based on Amis, somewhat flatteringly, since Larkin states that he had 'won the beginnings of a reputation for himself as a writer' before the army had removed him from Oxford, where he and Mattocks had met. His surname, Defoe, is another concession to Amis who even as an undergraduate professed an admiration for the hearty realism of the man who invented the English novel in the eighteenth century.

This *mélange* of characterizations – as much a reflection on his friendship with Amis as a serious plan for a book – underwent several radical revisions and redrafting over the autumn and winter of 1945–6. These also acquired titles such as *The Trap*, *Losing the Music* and *Second Thoughts*. Ruth Bowman features as a girl called Laurel while Larkin takes over from Amis as Edward Defoe. Edward on one occasion becomes the manager of a second-hand bookshop, where he meets Laurel, a schoolgirl planning to go to university who values the company of this mature, sophisticated man. This is of course a verbatim account of the early friendship between Larkin and Ruth. More unsettling, however, are Larkin's comments on these events, such as their 'uneasy friendship' being for Edward simply a hedge against the stultifying boredom of the provincial community in which all this occurs. Laurel's eventual declaration of love provokes in him a mixture of depression and panic; he imagines a life sentence involving the continuation of what they already have or don't have. The nature of these workbooks is properly disclosed when Larkin asks himself questions regarding narrative direction. At one point Edward leaves the area 'on an impulse he doesn't bother to analyse' and returns a few days later. 'But where does this all lead?' asks Larkin, and decides that Edward should commit himself to Laurel. The commonwealth of fiction is rich with books which owe some or much of their existence to actual events, but Larkin's workbooks are radically unusual in that he appeared to be using invention as means a of making decisions on the nature of his lived existence. He began to turn these into something more substantial in the summer of 1948.

No for an Answer is comprised of five draft chapters, which would have formed about a third of the novel if he had made anything of the plans in the succeeding workbooks and finished it. He did not, and although there is no obvious reason for his failure to complete the book circumstances invite speculation. Since late 1946 Amis had kept him informed of the progress of a novel that he hoped would make his name but in the end was never published. *The Legacy* is about a young unrecognized poet called Kingsley Amis, who inherits £30,000 from his father. In order to qualify for this legacy on his twenty-first birthday Kingsley must marry Stephanie Roche, a 'suitable wife' chosen by his family, and join his father's wholesale grocery firm. If, as he is tempted to do, he instead marries Jane Taylor, a 'respectable Yorkshire girl' who appreciates his poetry, he will lose his inheritance. The implausibility of the plot framework – which sounds more like something from the 1820s than the late 1940s – was one reason for its eventual rejection by Longmans, but aside from that Amis was reasonably successful at representing the moods, social mores and general dullness of lower-middle-class England just after the war. Amis sent samples of it to Larkin and although the latter had his doubts he saw potential in his friend's drafts, so much so that *The Legacy* became the principal stylistic influence for *No for an Answer*. Its substance involved yet another attempt by Larkin to reshape his experience as fiction.

What exists of the novel centres upon the relationship between Sam Wagstaff and his girlfriend Sheila Piggot and between Sam and his father Samuel. The Wagstaffs own an agricultural machinery firm on the outskirts of Birmingham – an idea probably inspired by Massey Ferguson. The most striking feature of the text is the way in which Larkin creates an atmosphere scrupulously devoid of intellectual or literary issues without implying that the characters are in any way lacking in intelligence or significance. Had the novel been completed and found a publisher – likely, since *A Girl in Winter* had recently received promising reviews – it might have subtly altered the course of post-war literary history. Braine, Barstow, Sillitoe, Storey and to a lesser degree Amis and Wain dismantled the stereotypes of class determination by showing that good writing could coexist with states of mind that had little time for high culture, but this new wave of writing did not make its presence felt until the late 1950s. Larkin with *No for an Answer* would have set the precedent ten years earlier.

By far the most impressive aspect of the existing text is the dialogue. Larkin had always been a talented impressionist, and in *Jill* we detect only a slight inclination to adapt this ability to the verbal idiosyncrasies of his fictional characters. In *No for an Answer* the text becomes energized by exchanges between characters, and the inspiration for this was a technique which Larkin and Amis had discussed since 1943 and named in their letters as pattern conversations. A successful pattern conversation would involve an exchange in which each character discloses something in their manner of speech without directly stating it. The reader recognizes the subtext but it is up to the writer to decide whether or not the other fictional characters detect it. Thus a tension, a dynamic, is achieved which is choreographed by the narrator. An early example can be found in a letter from Amis to Larkin in 1943, which was allegedly based upon an exchange that had taken place between the former and his girlfriend.

> 'It was awfully nice of you to come and see me tonight, darling, when you've got all that work to do.'
> 'Don't say that. I wanted to.' (Liar)
> 'It's been awful this week. I've missed you so much.'
> 'It hasn't been nice for me either. I've missed you too.' (Liar)
> 'You know, Bill . . . it's just like having . . . pins and needles . . .'
> 'You'll have to get used to being without me, you know.' (Bastard)
> 'Yes, I know.'
> 'Never mind, May. I shall never forget you.' (Yes I really did say that.)
> (26 October–6 November 1943)

The words in parentheses indicate the subtext, and in Amis's view a successful, fictional pattern conversation would involve an interplay between one character and the narrator which inferred this subtext and built up a triangular dynamic in which the reader, too, is involved. Hints dropped by the narrator and clues offered in the dialogue would oblige the reader to become almost a participant in the text, guessing at what lay behind speech and tying this into suspicions regarding a character's real temperament or motivation. Amis was doing his best to implement this technique in *The Legacy*, and so was Larkin.

At the end of what would have been the second chapter of *No for an Answer* Sam attempts to have sex with Sheila; she resists and slaps him in the face. Previously their exchanges had involved a degree of confidential informality suggestive, at least for Sam, of the potential for sexual intimacy. The alliance between Sam and the narrator operates subtly but effectively in that while we assume certain things about Sheila it becomes easy to forget that our perception of her is coterminous with theirs. The passage following her rejection of his advance is intriguing.

> 'I'm about sick of you. You don't want anything except what you can get. I've had about all I can stand, since you've been home; you think everyone exists just for you and for your sake.'
> 'You're talking bloody nonsense.'
> 'It's true enough.' Sheila felt a ladder climb her stocking to above her knee. 'You think you can treat me any old how. I'm a sort of permanent playmate always on hand. Well, that's all going to stop. From now on you're going to treat me properly if you want anything to do with me at all. My God, you must think I'm a fool. Well, you're wrong, d'you see?'
> Her jumper stuffed back into her skirt waist, she turned away from him,

pulling her hair angrily in the mirror.

'I don't know what you're talking about.' Sam's cross voice was shaken slightly by his thumping heart. (pp. 324–5)

While the narrator tries to maintain a level of impartiality there is an almost involuntary, compulsive emphasis upon Sheila's clothes and body: the description of her feeling 'a ladder climb her stocking to above her knee' is hopelessly erotic. In an earlier draft of the same scene the third-person description of Sam's attempt to seduce Sheila runs to about 200 words and includes passages such as 'He got his hand under her long skirt and slid it up her nyloned right leg till she was holding it tightly between her two bare thighs. His cuff caught against the edge of her girdle . . . He felt desperate to have her . . . But try as he might his hand could get no further, and when he clumsily got his knee between hers to open them she went rigid . . .' The detail is degenerately obsessive – why her 'right leg', for example? – and one detects here that his intention is commendably innovative in terms of the sexual politics of contemporary fiction writing. The aggressive verbal manner of Sheila's rejection is as surprising to the reader as it is to Sam – she has never spoken like this before – and this disrupts the complacently male-orientated alliance between Sam and his narrator. The effect is of a character establishing a degree of independence from the texture of the novel – in this case a woman character detaching herself from a verbal environment of male sexuality.

Larkin was possessed of the imaginative range and technical ability demanded of good novel writing, but this one was abandoned because he found that his radical ideas were being variously undermined and over-determined by personal, autobiographical involvement. Ruth Bowman never knew of *No for an Answer* until she was shown the typescript in 1999 prior to publication. She said that 'it must be left to literary critics to make the connection' between herself and Larkin and Sheila and Sam; 'They say nothing to me.' Certainly Larkin did his best to distance the background and mores of the fictional couple from his and Ruth's, but certain more fundamental parallels are self-evident. Both relationships seem to shift between complacency and precipitate moments of uncertainty, and if we treat Samuel as the third most significant character in the novel then the choreographed interplay between fiction and life becomes even more apparent.

The novel as it stands was begun in June 1948, six weeks after his father's death and a month after his proposal to Ruth, and abandoned in February 1949. Alongside its immediate emotional effects upon him Sydney's death registered vicariously in Larkin's novel. Samuel Wagstaff, like Sydney, is admitted to hospital with suspected gallstones, but we never learn if the early diagnosis is accurate or if he is suffering from something far more serious. The novel ends tantalizingly with Sam visiting him in a private ward. All that is left is a synopsis of what might happen next in which the following profile is offered for Samuel.

> A conservative anarchist. The craters of routine deserted by the lava of impulse . . . Tides of bitterness scarcely moving. Spends his time reading, gardening; occasionally visits works for sneering talk and dirty jokes. (p.357)

A more painfully honest description of his father by Larkin is difficult to imagine. As yet Samuel did not quite accord with this, but Larkin was clearly thinking about dropping the disguise and bringing Sydney into the novel. He also considered taking a further step towards autobiographical parallels, as his synopsis discloses: 'Operation agreed to be light but feels serious . . . the worsening illness.'

In the end he could not endure the fictional recreation of his father's recent death. Sam's relationship with Sheila is left in a similar state of uncertainty. What existed in the text involved a fabric of commitments, decisions and emotional registers that was an unsettling replica of what was happening outside it. In a letter to Sutton written soon after he had become engaged to Ruth and introduced her to his friend the resemblance between his manner and that of his synopsis for the novel is striking.

> We are sort of committed to each other by our characters, at least I think we are . . . It's odd. Really I am not sure if I want to marry at all; but when one tries to stare into the problem to seek out its exact truth one is bemused and puzzled and can't tell true from false. (18 June 1948)

Remove all first-person pronouns from the passage and the characters sound like inventions of whose true nature and future their creator is still uncertain. The closing phrase – 'can't tell true from false' – causes one to suspect that the decision he had made with Ruth in the real world was weirdly similar to the one that he had yet to make with Sheila in the novel; soon the latter would, like the former, end in mid-chapter.

In June 1950 Larkin was interviewed for the post of Sub-Librarian in the Queen's University of Belfast. He was offered the job and he accepted it. He had not informed Ruth even of his application, and when on 17 June they met in Lincoln, where she was then working as a teacher, the evening was a disaster. Over the previous two years their engagement had dwindled to the status of a token gesture, never fully revoked by him and regarded with seasoned scepticism by her. Now he went so far as to wonder if she might be willing to accompany him to Northern Ireland. She was happy enough to consider this, but as the evening wore on and drink took effect it became apparent to both of them that his application and acceptance had been a kind of undeclared act of uncoupling. But that was not quite the end of things. During the three months between his interview and his move to Belfast in September 1950 they exchanged letters regularly and met on at least four occasions. It was as though Larkin was waiting for a sign, even an order, regarding the future of their relationship; or more likely he was, by vacillating, trying to provoke one. He was successful. Ruth wrote to him in September stating that there should be no final meeting. It was over for good. Shrewdly and, given his behaviour, generously, she hoped that he 'will find yourself able to write, for I know you will never rest until you do'.

He was indeed manically able to write, but most of what he produced would never be sent to a publisher. *No for an Answer* could have formed the basis for a ground-breaking novel if it were not also a kind of sounding board for Larkin's various levels of sadness, uncertainty and dissatisfaction. For much of the text Sam and Sheila function as a reasonably happy, well-matched couple – nothing over-romantic about their relationship but nothing unsettling either – and the seduction scene (rewritten twice) features as though Larkin is searching for an excuse to end things between them. Sound familiar? In the final notebook Larkin comments that irrespective of the apparent attractiveness of a US visit for Sam there is only one reason for his departure: 'Really he is running away.' Larkin never returned to the novel again, but as Ruth concluded in her letter just before *his* departure for Belfast, 'There is really no more to say is there?'

If further confirmation were needed that *No for an Answer* involves a peculiar struggle between fiction made from life and vice versa, Larkin's letters to Sutton during 1949–50 need only be consulted. In March 1949, for example, Ruth and Larkin had gone through one of their periodic bouts of disengagement. To Sutton he wrote that 'I have given up my novel and Ruth has given up me, not seeing as you might say, any future in it. Nor do I! Therefore I am living a disagreeable life at this remnant of a home, with a general sense of being buggered up' (24 March 1949). His relationship with Ruth and the novel would be restarted, but the intriguing thing about his account of the interlude is that we, and perhaps he also, are not certain of his primary subject. Is it the novel or Ruth in which he sees no future and which is the cause of his miserable state of mind? In all probability both. Throughout this period Larkin would refer Sutton to the condition of his current 'novel' while offering no further details on this inconstant work or at least not consciously or deliberately. The mood of the letters, drifting between a distaste for his professional and personal life and an occasional moment of determination to do something about both, is a rambling version of the better-organized third-person account of the temper and existence of Sam Wagstaff. On 13 July 1949 he informed Sutton:

I feel overwhelmingly at this moment . . . that literature is a great farce and any literature in one's being should be scoured out with Keatinge's [anti-flea powder] . . . any ideas about life are almost certain to be wrong . . . I refuse to believe that there is a thing called life, that one can be in or out of touch with. There is only an endless series of events, of which our birth is one and our death another.

This is a succinct and accurate ground plan for *No for an Answer*. Apart from the narrator's very rare lapse into the figurative mode ('the sound of a distant fast train hung on the mild air, like the even breaking of a long wave', p. 300) the text is unsullied by literary reference or indulgence. It is not 'about' significances, only 'events' and their particular effects.

At one point in fragment 4 we are told this of Sam:

Many of his friends were married by this time and the others seemed to find no difficulty in having girls occasionally. He felt a little annoyed at being in neither class. The thought crossed his mind occasionally that he ought to have a serious bash at Sheila. She was the only girl he knew well, and he wasn't afraid of her. Certainly she was attractive, and although on first thoughts he could not see her agreeing he thought he might marry her if the affair was a success. He could tell her this, perhaps. (p. 285)

This is an almost exact version of the letter he sent to Sutton on their engagement in which he states that 'well, we have gone on seeing each other until the point seemed to arrive when we either had to start taking it seriously or drop it . . . nor do I want to desert the only girl who doesn't instantly frighten me away' (14 May 1948).

The novel, along with Larkin's relationship with Ruth, suddenly ceased to exist, but there was one other reason for its cessation: Amis. By the end of 1949 Amis's *The Legacy* had been rejected by Longman's and Gollancz. Doreen Marston, a reader for Collins, sent Amis a report on why she regarded the book as unpublishable. It suffered from 'redundancy and lack of conflict', it lacked anything resembling a narrative which might interest the reader, and 'there is no suspense; there is, in its place, a good deal of boredom'. Amis informed his friend of this and soon afterwards Larkin replied that he too had given up. 'Sam Wagstaff has finally gone for a Burton has he?' (Amis to Larkin, 7 March 1950).

At the same time Amis had announced to Larkin a new strategy, prompted by the negative responses to *The Legacy*. This time he would make the reader interested in the outcome – it would involve a relationship and a professional dilemma – and it would be funny. The working title, at least in the letters, was *Dixon and Christine*, and the result would eventually be

Lucky Jim. *Lucky Jim* succeeded because it dismantled and ridiculed virtually all of academia's claims upon significance, and according to Amis the idea for this first occurred to him, about a year before *The Legacy* was abandoned, on a visit to Larkin in Leicester.

> On the Saturday morning he had to go into college and took me ('hope you won't mind they're all right really') to the common room for a quick coffee. I looked round a couple of times and said to myself, 'Christ somebody ought to do something with this'. Not that it was awful – well, only a bit; it was strange and sort of *developed*, a whole mode of existence no one had got onto from the outside, like the SS in 1940, say. I would do something with it. (*Memoirs*, p. 56)

Amis wrote this in 1982 on the occasion of Larkin's sixtieth birthday. They had been friends for four decades and by then had become known respectively as the predominant novelist and poet of the 1950s' generation. Anecdotes regarding when exactly each got the idea for their best work were intriguing, amusing but hardly the cause for dispute. However, one is caused to wonder if Amis is making a claim upon territory first prospected by Larkin.

In the workbook outlines for *No for an Answer* we encounter the mysterious figure of Margerie.

> She is a gay young Oxfordian, regarding herself etc. and wanting to be regarded by others as a real misfit in the funny little town she has chosen by a pin in the TES [*Times Educational Supplement*], but slowly by an emergence of personal dullness and Conservatism fitting into her job more and more . . . (p. 312)

The portrait is less than flattering, but the subject is undoubtedly Monica Jones. Larkin had met Monica in September 1946. They were the same age, and she was a lecturer in English at University College, Leicester. They first had sex in the late summer of 1950 around the time that Larkin's relationship with Ruth was stumbling towards its conclusion. She was his second lover, and she became the centrepiece for what would turn out to be his final attempt at fiction. *A New World Symphony* was begun almost immediately following his abandonment of Sam Wagstaff's story, at the same time that Amis was reporting to him on the progress of the *Dixon and Christine* project. Although Larkin was happy to act as an adviser on Amis's rough drafts – tidying up the style, expelling redundant characters, etc. – there is no evidence that he expected it to be successful. It seemed to him to be Amis's version of the *Willow Gables* exercises – writing as an escape valve for personal discontent – with rebarbative satire and farce substituted for sexual fantasy. What it did do, however, was to provide Larkin with a new idea for a novel about Britain *circa* 1950. It would be set in a university, certainly, but a provincial university where the contrast between high-minded bohemianism and post-war ordinariness was almost absurdly pronounced. Larkin once claimed to Maeve Brennan that Amis had 'stolen' the idea for *Lucky Jim* from him. In truth it was the other way around. Augusta Bax, the heroine of *A New World Symphony*, was Larkin's Jim Dixon. As characters they had absolutely nothing in common, nor did their real-life counterparts Monica Jones and Kingsley Amis, but in Larkin's view Augusta would prove far more effective than Jim as the focus for a ground-breaking tale of provincial academia.

Monica was an attractive woman, a natural blonde with piercing blue eyes. There is a photograph of her by Larkin from 1947 in which she appears about to either seduce or wreck the camera or possibly both. She wore the kind of hand-made, brightly coloured clothes that might feature in contemporaneous films about Americans in the Mediterranean. Her taste in jewellery was self-consciously eccentric, ranging from ropes of imitation pearls to bejewelled rings that looked as though they put severe strain on her arm muscles. There was certainly a fair degree of sexual chemistry between them during their early, tentative meetings, owing partly to the fact that they were continually discovering similarities between their respective temperaments, backgrounds and behavioural peculiarities. She had grown up in Worcestershire, the child of a lower-middle-class family – her father was an engineer – and went to high school in Kidderminster. There in her mid to late teens she won the approval of her teachers for her abilities in English literature. She went up to Oxford, St Hugh's, on a scholarship to study English in October 1940 and graduated with a starred first in 1943 – an identical profile to Larkin's, although they never met at university. She taught briefly at a private school near her home, but she had been advised that her future lay in academia. She narrowly missed getting a job in King's College, London, but within two months, in late 1943, was appointed Lecturer in English at Leicester. Her Oxford references – one from the esteemed Helen Gardner – opened doors.

Soon Larkin began to find that their resemblances masked as many differences. Both projected a colourful unorthodox image to shield various states of inadequacy and uncertainty, but while Larkin combined his with an almost manic creative output Monica's inner character was of the inescapably defensive, watchful type. She knew that she had intellectual strength – Oxford had assured her of that – but she did not know what to do with it. Like Larkin and Amis she produced parodies of celebrated mainstream poets. An ability to imitate the stylistic idiosyncrasies of a writer indicates a critical intelligence, but even more is revealed by the nature of the caricature. Monica's spoof on Blake's 'Songs of Experience', for example, begins:

> Dryden, Dryden, hidden quite
> In the uncut leaves from sight
> What unpleasant ear or eye
> Could bare thy fearful symmetry?
> In what distant shelf or nook
> Rots thy dull and mouldering book?
> On what grounds dids't thou aspire?
> What made thee think we should admire?

The passage almost begs for explication, particularly by someone who shares the author's scholarly aplomb. You see, it seems to say, if Blake *had* written about Dryden, acknowledged founder of Augustanism, he might have rejoiced in his fall from popularity ('uncut leaves' – an image from nature combined with one from dusty old bookshelves). And Blake's resounding image, 'fearful symmetry', could also refer to Dryden's dutiful obsession with the symmetrical order of couplet poetry. The piece trembles with erudition. Compare it with Larkin's sensitive reinterpretation of Keats.

> And this is why I shag alone
> Ere half my creeping days are done
> The wind coughs sharply in the stone
> . . . there is no sun.

Or Amis's rendering of Hardy's 'Afterwards':

> When the Gents' has received my last consignment of turds,
> And they piss in the bogs where an odour of vomit clings,
> Will they say, as they scan the wall for dirty words
> 'He was a man who used to notice such things?'

The caricatures offer intriguing reflections of the personalities of the three of them. Larkin and Amis show a confident disrespect for their targets; they take over and deface the images of their esteemed predecessors. Monica, while demonstrating a mastery of technique, seems jittery, apprehensive about imitating figures she has been taught to respect as members of the literary elite. Her caricature is a polite, learned but deferential dialogue with Blake and Dryden, and in certain respects it was an accurate predication of her extended relationship with another writer who would in their lifetime join the elite.

Part 3

The Death of the Novelist

6

Single to Belfast

Larkin's first impressions of Belfast are recorded in a postcard to his mother sent on the day of his interview in June 1950: 'Belfast is an unattractive city. Oh dear, oh dear.' The words seem unambiguous enough, but with knowledge of Larkin's maturing temperament one detects a hint of masochistic glee.

After boarding the Liverpool–Belfast ferry in September he sat on deck and composed a poem called 'Single to Belfast', a title which refers of course both to the nature of his ticket and his love life. The poem was never completed, but what remains is a series of rather pompous reflections on this moment of departure, such as:

> The present is really stiffening to past
> Right under my eyes,
>
> And my life committing itself to the long bend
> That swings me, this Saturday night, away from my midland
> Emollient valley, away from the lack of questions,
> Away from endearments.
>
> Through doors left swinging, stairs and spaces and faces

And so on, with undeclared thanks to Auden and an echo of the workbook of *No for an Answer* which has Sam Wagstaff departing for a transformative new existence. But the *Ulster Duke* ferry was not quite the *Queen Mary* and Belfast was certainly not New York.

Larkin's prior knowledge of his new home was slight, but within the first few months Belfast and environs began to impress upon him a condition and a state of mind which suited his sometimes depressive sense of irony and farce. Physically Belfast bore a close resemblance to the cities of northern England that were effectively products of the industrial revolution. At its centre was City Hall, a flamboyant, assertive piece of late Victorian neo-baroque, just to the west were the giant cranes of the Harland and Wolff shipyard and round about were distributed terraces of working-class back-to-backs. The south of the city was made up predominantly of Victorian–Edwardian middle-class dwellings spaciously deposited along tree-lined avenues. Queen's University sat with comfortable solemnity in this area.

Larkin's first rooms, a bedsit in a Victorian hall of residence, overlooked the old quadrangle of Queen's, which unlike many of its Oxford counterparts did not attempt to disguise its medievalism as anything other than nineteenth century. As an institution, however, Queen's dutifully imitated Oxbridge traditions and not simply as an aspiration to status. Northern Ireland was part of the UK but was also a uniquely devolved pseudo-state, with its own parliament, legislative structure, education system and unusual police force. Also it was obsessively concerned – or at least 60 per cent of its population was concerned – that its neighbour the Republic was continually plotting to swallow it up. Queen's was its only university and quite accurately saw itself as serving a vital role as a production line for the local Establishment. A fair number of the doctors, lawyers, politicians, senior civil servants and police-men of Ulster were the products of Queen's. So quite soon Larkin found that he was living within what appeared to be aspects of his student life in minia-ture, with touches of the surreal thrown in for good measure. Queen's was a middle-class version of Oxford, while Belfast and the rest of the province resembled a kind of neurotic, torpid parody of Britain at war.

Appropriately he began to revert to the kind of lifestyle he had enjoyed as an undergraduate. The bright shirts, bow ties and patterned sports jackets replaced the relatively sober attire of his Leicester years, and Larkin soon began to realize that he could operate much as he had in Oxford, comfort-ably displaying his mildly exotic artistic persona among a group of tolerant peers – now made up of junior academics rather than undergraduates. Within weeks he had met Alan Grahame (history), Arthur Terry (Spanish), Evan John (music) and James Bradley (classics), all lodging in the same hall of residence. Soon he bumped into Colin Strang, a near contemporary of his at St John's who had recently been appointed to the philosophy depart-ment at Queen's. In the intervening years Strang had met and married Patsy Avis, another Oxford graduate. The Strangs had a house in Kincotter Avenue, South Belfast, and Larkin became a regular guest.

More and more Larkin began to find that Belfast was not simply a rerun but a considerable improvement on Oxford. Now he had independence. He no longer dwelt in the intimidating, expectant shadow of his late father; he had his own money, and the responsibilities for his widowed mother were devolved to his sister and her family. Despite the dour influence of Presbyterianism Belfast could be a lively town. The city centre pubs were busy meeting places – particularly the famous Crown; there were regular jazz concerts in the University Union and the city hospitals; and the Queen's senior common room parties would often be riotously drink-fuelled. Larkin entertained his new network of friends with well-matured versions of his Oxford retinue of anecdotes and imitations and gradually acquired the reputation in Queen's-based society as an agreeable, multi-faceted personality – a comic extrovert and boozer but also learned and cultured; after all, he had published two novels and a volume of poems and was busily producing more of both.

Larkin's five years in Belfast were transitional in a number of ways and for several reasons. To state that he sorted out his love life would be further to exploit an already ageing cliché. More accurately, he faced up to – and indeed made the best of – tastes and predispositions that had previously troubled him. His collection of pornography was expanding as rapidly as his library of mainstream literature. Caton of the infamously versatile Fortune Press, publisher of *Jill* and *The North Ship*, had inadvertently made Larkin aware of the best London-based outlets for illegal and decadent material (Caton's interest in new radical authors was a means of providing his pornographic publications list with a distracting shroud of respectability). Vicarious acts of stimulation were for Larkin an immensely honest and far less troublesome substitute for the real thing.

In a typically candid letter to Amis in 1947 he had offered an analysis of the practicalities of attempting to seduce Jane Exall without ruining his already unsettled relationship with Ruth Bowman. One can see why, even then, librarianship suited key aspects of his temperament because the letter reads like an exercise in cataloguing.

> It seems to me that while pocking Miss Jane Exall is infinitely desirable, preparing Miss Jane Exall to be pocked and dealing with Jane Exall after pocking is not at all desirable – and that pocks do not exist in the void . . . a pock is a pock, and . . . pocking Miss Jane Exall wouldn't be nearly so nice in reality as it is in my imagination WHEN I'M TOSSING MYSELF . . .

Tossing himself accompanied by his ample supply of pornography was the equivalent of much-desired promiscuity but without the tiresome obligations of seduction, deception or even, God forbid, continuity. In Belfast, however, he also found the opportunity to make life imitate glossy representation.

The Strangs' marriage was not quite deserving of the term 'open' – this was still Britain in the early 1950s – but 'ajar' would not be an overstatement. She, Patsy, came from an immensely wealthy South African family – owners of diamond mines – and had spent a relaxed, culturally rich childhood in London. After Roedean she had at Oxford made the best of her natural brilliance, temperamental flirtatiousness and taste for the idiosyncratic. Colin Strang, lecturer in philosophy and son of a distinguished diplomat, was her *alter ego*, her stabilizing presence, an arrangement which is often successful but which by 1951 was becoming strained.

Larkin's improved reinvention of his Oxford style certainly worked with Patsy. She found him entertaining, enigmatic and, in Belfast, agreeably incongruous. For Larkin she was a version of Diana Gollancz, but because she was married and he had become a friend of the family – he also got on well with Colin – the prospect of sex was far more realistic. She could, as it were, be borrowed and, like the glossy magazines, she required no long-term attention.

Most of the private diaries that Larkin himself had not destroyed were shredded by Monica and his secretary Betty Mackereth after his death, and the only surviving account of what they might have mentioned came from Patsy via her second husband, the poet Richard Murphy. One day she had arrived early at Larkin's rooms and while waiting for him read his recent entries. When later in the day she disclosed this to him she generated a once-only encounter with Larkin in state of anger verging upon rage. The most prominent entries involved detailed accounts of his masturbatory activities. Patsy, being a broad-minded, indulgent sort, was mildly amused and not at all unsettled by the disclosure that Larkin was indeed like most other people, but for him it was worse than being caught, literally, in the act. He was not infuriated so much by the nature of what Patsy had found out as by the fact that she had caught him writing about it. She had known him for little more than eighteen months, and despite the fact that they had become lovers he was still cautious about showing her what really went on behind the presence with whom she shared secret liaisons. It was already evident to her that he was capable of disingenuousness – how else could he maintain an unflustered social life with her and Colin while conducting their affair? The diary had shown her briefly, and to his distress, another level of secrecy where the different segments of his public and private worlds would become part of the same experience – writing. For Larkin, aged thirty, his notebooks and diaries had become the point at which the sometimes divergent, irreconcilable dimensions of his life intersected. The writing of them did not provide a solution to his problems but it offered an adequate compensation – confidential omniscience. He could contemplate the entirety of what he had, for others, distributed only as perspectives.

The only person with whom he voluntarily shared this experience was Amis. Their letters often read as if produced by men subjected to a radical truth drug which allowed them to maintain deft stylistic control while emptying their minds of everything from their most recently purchased jazz record – via their immediate need for a piss – to thoughts on the state of contemporary verse. The letters to Amis were a version of his note-books: 'I masturbated and thus fell asleep, waking only at 2.45 and 7.14'

(21 July 1942); 'flogging chart . . . down to 2.3' (23 July 1942). Larkin's commendably precise account of his masturbatory regime was not offered to his friend as a prurient thrill. It was offered as a testament to the comprehensive, honest fabric of the letter – nothing would be left out. That he felt able to make the various dimensions of his life available to his closest male friend while maintaining an anxious selectivity for his lover reflects the anomalous, costive nature of their friendship. To an extent each treated the other as a kind of confessor, except that their respective outpourings were certainly not founded upon a desire for conscience cleansing or the expurgation of guilt. The attraction, at least on Larkin's part, was the sense of having a special kind of diary in which he could give verbal shape – albeit chaotic – to the whole spectrum of his life, from literary ambition, through matters trivial and peripheral, to sexual frustrations and relationships; this diary would reply to him with equal and equally amusing candour. Within three years of his arrival in Belfast, however, Larkin would discover that their exchanges had provided Amis with another species of attraction, or more accurately a potential that involved turning their confidentiality into a means of amusing the reading public; *Lucky Jim* would be born out of these letters.

The success of Amis's book would cause Larkin to give up on his own ambitions to become a successful novelist. Instead he would turn his attention to his poetry and begin to produce the work that made and sustained his reputation. But with caustic Larkinesque irony parallels would emerge between Amis's source of inspiration and his own. The dynamic between secrecy and quiet disclosure that fed his addiction to the diaries and notebooks – and in an adjusted way his exchanges with Amis – would become an equally important feature of his best verse. In 'Best Society', completed shortly after Patsy's discovery of his notebooks, he contemplates the pleasure of being alone: 'I lock the door' and 'uncontradicting solitude / supports me on its giant palm.' (And one cannot but wonder if the nature of what Patsy found might have played some part in the formation of the final image: he had once remarked to Amis that 'I don't want to take a girl out and spend circa £5 on her when I can toss myself off in five minutes, free, and have the rest of the evening to myself.') He did not crave detachment from other people; rather, he was becoming aware that solitude meant something more than being alone. It was the point at which the various strata of his life were available only to him and from which he could cautiously select, perhaps edit, and reassemble material for writing poems. The anger provoked by Patsy's inquisitiveness would eventually be transposed into something cautiously planned. We, like Patsy, would be fascinated, amused, even shocked, but in the poems Larkin would maintain control. Almost thirty years later he might well have recalled the incident with Patsy when planning the opening line of what would be his last significant poem, 'Love again: wanking at ten past three'. It reads like a diary entry; and by 1979 he was beginning to lose interest in what his poems said of him and running out of things to say.

Along with his affair with Patsy Strang Larkin became closely attached to two other women while at Queen's. Judy and Ansell Egerton's marriage was, relative to the Strangs', stable and would endure until 1974. Ansell lectured in economics and after leaving Queen's employed his expertise more profitably first by becoming City Editor of *The Times*, later as a merchant banker and eventually as a director of Rothmans International. Judy was born in Australia, did a degree in history and in London in the 1970s made use of her interest in art, working first on Paul Mellon's collections and then as curator at the Tate Gallery. Larkin found in Judy reflections of the more agreeable aspects of his own character. She often gave the impression of being shy and unsettled by the presence of loquacious and intelligent companions, but in truth she was keeping in check a shrewd, thoughtful perspective upon matters in which she and genuine friends shared interests. She and Larkin found that they had similar tastes in twentieth-century fiction and poetry – predominantly English and conservative – and he enjoyed encouraging her interest in jazz with his encyclopaedic knowledge of it. After Belfast he, sometimes with Monica, would stay with the Egertons in London, usually at the time of the Lords Test Match – Ansell, seconded by Harold Pinter, would in 1973 successfully propose Larkin for membership of the Marylebone Cricket Club.

Larkin's relationship with Judy was not exactly asexual – she was strikingly pretty and he was certainly attracted to her – but it came more and more to resemble that of brother and sister. Their letters read like the correspondence of two people intimately acquainted in an agreeable but diplomatically restrained way. Larkin would address the same topics to her as those in his letters to Amis and eventually Robert Conquest, be just as amusing and, apparently, candid regarding his ongoing concerns and irritations, yet with Judy some polite editing would have occurred.

Winifred Arnott was born in London in 1929 but during the Blitz joined her father's family in Belfast and stayed on to read English at Queen's. In 1950 when Larkin arrived she had recently graduated and had taken a part-time job in the library. Quite soon she would become Ruth Bowman the second. She was seven years younger than Larkin and, although intelligent and well read, in awe both of his presence – a mixture of the esoteric and the early middle-aged – and his reputation as a writer. They attended parties together, went to concerts and the cinema and on Sundays would cycle along the Lagan and into the countryside south of Belfast. She already had a boyfriend in London and although they were not formally engaged theirs seemed to be the kind of conventional relationship that would eventually result in marriage. This was an attractive prospect for Larkin. He could play the role of learned suitor, comfortable in the knowledge that things would never reach the stage that they had with Ruth where he would continually equivocate between commitment and fear of the same: a boyfriend across the water could enable him to surrender to circumstances. In the meantime, however, he might savour the prospect of a developing relationship with someone whose company he enjoyed and whom he found attractive, in the full knowledge that its conclusion was predetermined.

Winifred spent the spring and early summer of 1952 in London, largely in the company of her boyfriend C.G. Bradshaw. She returned to Belfast in early August and was asked by Larkin's senior, Jack Graneek, if she would take up a more permanent post in the library. Larkin had encouraged Graneek in this as part of his own cat-and-mouse game of continuance without permanence, but Winifred returned with the news that she had become engaged to Bradshaw and within a year would go back to London for good. Their marriage took place in 1954 with Larkin politely declining his invitation.

Things had not gone quite as he had expected. It was not that he was stricken with her choice of Bradshaw before him – he had seen this as inevitable, on his part as a kind of goods-returned-with-thanks – but he was mildly irritated by the timing. They had not had sex, and he had hoped that her continued presence in Belfast would enable him to consummate the relationship before the unavoidable closure of operations. She now insisted that the suggestive, flirtatious element of their earlier attachment would not continue.

'Lines on a Young Lady's Photograph Album' was begun soon after Winifred's announcement of her engagement and completed in September. The poem strikes a brilliant balance between a mood of intimate informality, as if addressed to the young lady of the album, and a series of more introspective reflections on emotions prompted by the photographs themselves. The quality of the piece is without doubt, and critical accounts of it abound, but what is never mentioned is the curious image of the speaker which stays in the mind long after one's appreciation of its artistry. It invites comparison with Browning's 'My Last Duchess' except that Browning's speaker is deranged and self-evidently an invention of the poet. With 'Lines' Larkin is evasively present, and he gives away just enough to suggest that the deeply moving nostalgia of the apparent theme – the past recorded beautifully and timelessly – is intercut with something else, a kind of lewd masochism. There is a subdued sensuality in the opening stanza, in which she 'yields up' the photographs 'Matt and glossy on the thick black pages'.

> too rich:
> I choke on such nutritious images.

And later:

> the theft
> Of this one of you bathing . . .

Read by a sensitive and incorrupt person these images could remain just on the decent side of ambiguous, but the more inquisitive might be prompted to speculate on what lies behind them.

Photographs, for Larkin, played a special role in his sex life and not merely as a substitute for what could not be had in the flesh. His affair with Patsy Strang was the most satisfyingly erotic of his life, and it is significant that he suggested, eventually successfully, that they supplement their love-making with pornographic pictures, taken of and by themselves on previous occasions. This might be subjected to all manner of psychosexual divinations, but common sense leads to the conclusion that for Larkin the photograph operated across a whole spectrum of sexual, emotional, even aesthetic registers. In pragmatic terms photographs of naked women provided him with masturbation material, but his activities with Patsy indicate that he was also attracted to the prospect of incorporating the best aspects of visual record with the real thing. Larkin bought his first camera in October 1947 as a relief from boredom, but within a year photography had become and would remain his favourite hobby. He never quite accorded photography *per se* the status of a serious art form, but his own work shows that he was alert to its stylistic range, and this is particularly evident in his pictures of his women friends. There is one of Monica Jones, for example, at her desk in Leicester, which involves a stunning combination of intellectual presence and pure sexuality – and one suspects that Amis saw it, because Margaret Peel in *Lucky Jim* is a cruel parody of the very same effect.

Amis tells a story of when Larkin, after learning of Winifred's engagement, went out, got drunk and on returning to his rooms 'noticed how, more than usual', his photograph of her brought out resemblances to Stan Laurel. Consequently he deliberately spilled beer over it, leaving a permanent vertical stain, which makes one think again about why he chose such a curiously archaic title for his poem about photographs of her: 'Lines on . . .'

Photographs capture and indeed offer back a moment of intimacy without requiring anything in return, and in 'Latest Face', written before Winifred's engagement, there is a curious sense of being shown a prelude to what would be made more explicit in 'Lines'. The poem is not one of his best, with the particulars of the text almost suffocated by cloudy metaphors ('move / Into real untidy air', 'Lies grow dark around us', etc.), but what is striking is the way in which the anchoring image, Winifred's face, seems so inanimate and inoperative. Indeed it is the prompter to Larkin's circling ruminations on the nature of love and commitment. The poem is certainly about his responses to Winifred, but it begs the question of what state he perceives her in: a presence with her own perhaps unpredictable inclinations or a muted record of this presence?

Such ambiguities are both covert and autobiographical. In 'Lines' there is a double-edged moment when he almost celebrates the photograph as something which simultaneously records the past while cleansing it of what were once attendant emotions:

> We know *what was*
> Won't call on us to justify
> Our grief, however here we yowl across
> The gap from eye to page.

Not only does photography of the pornographic type provide unemotive stimulation; at the other end of the spectrum its more respectable counterpart preserves matters such as 'grief' without obliging participation.

There is no doubt that Larkin's relationship with Winifred involved for him a complex network of emotions, that his attraction to and affection for her were genuine, but it is equally certain that her perception of it was incomplete. There were things he could never tell her, such as the fact that he was as much fearful of, even repulsed by, permanence as he was enamoured of her. In his notebook he recorded, at the same time as 'Lines', a couplet of easy and pitiless symmetry:

> Not love you? Dear I'd pay ten quid for you:
> Five down and five when I got rid of you.

The struggle between 'love' and disposable pleasure is ineluctably tied into the verse. The two states become inseparable, and one is reminded of the time during his previous relationship when he wrote to Amis complaining of how his commitment to Ruth was proving too expensive.

Larkin was beginning to discover that the competing, irreconcilable dimensions of his personality – which would only appear together for the likes of Amis – could if properly managed offer a framework for his verse. Obviously the above couplet was too blatant for publication, but if he could indicate without fully disclosing the least agreeable half of his divided presence, while distributing the other more generously, he would have a poem which at once implied transparency and something more intriguing.

'Lines' certainly succeeded in this, as would 'Maiden Name', again inspired by Winifred and written shortly after her wedding in 1954.

It would be one of the poems which made *The Less Deceived* so popular and successful, and its closest formal relative would probably be the early seventeenth-century lyric practised by the likes of Donne and Herbert. The syntax and diction sit somewhere between the elegant and the languid, and both carry their stanzaic framework like a well-made suit of clothes. The title introduces the conceit with which Larkin plays games, turning it this way and that and opening it out into figurative excursions. Mostly he switches between reflective tenderness and tongue-in-cheek stoicism:

> you cannot be
> Semantically the same as that young beauty:
> It was of her that these two words were used.

Occasionally, however, there is a hint of something less agreeable. Her marriage is described as her being 'so thankfully confused / By law with someone else', with the phrase 'thankfully confused' carrying a smirking ambiguity. Is Larkin thankful for her departure or does the term involve its older usage of fortuitousness and to her benefit? Similarly, 'confused' could involve both its archaic meaning of combined (including physically combined) and its more familiar usage.

Such effects are of course part of the standard retinue of poetic stratagems, in this case brilliantly executed, but what makes the poem more intriguing is that it obsesses with a name: the 'five light sounds [that] no longer mean your face' become the hub for meditations on the nature of a relationship, but the name is not disclosed. The quality of the poem is not diminished by this, certainly, but when we read it accompanied by the knowledge that the maiden name is Winifred Arnott the strange tension between cordiality and part-restrained bitterness tells us something more about its writer. Appended to the manuscript draft of the original poem is the phrase 'you are not she', which raises the question of whether Larkin was wondering about incorporating it into a rewritten text or leaving it simply as a private comment. Either way it opens a new perspective upon the furtive verbal gymnastics of the piece: 'you are not she' = 'you Arnott she'. The girl has gone from the almost intimate familiarity of 'you' to the absence of 'she', the transformative phrase involving the aurally identical and equally effective 'Arnott' (maiden name) and 'are not'. Rarely can one claim to have access to the conditions and thought processes which brought a poem to completion, but it must be the case that the above piece of verbal quiddity was in his mind as he put together 'you cannot be / Semantically the same as that young beauty'.

More than twenty years later, when Winifred's marriage to Bradshaw broke up, they resumed correspondence, and in one letter he tries to disperse her anxieties that the best aspects of their past were an illusion. 'Anyway your memory is Balls if you think you weren't beautiful. Belfast was full of small groups of men saying how beautiful you were.' Writing this it must have seemed to Larkin as though a poem written two decades before was coming home. They never actually met again, so apart from their letters a significant aspect of her, for Larkin, was still aged twenty-four, recorded in photographs and embalmed in verse. He continues in the letter, 'I *think* you knew "Maiden Name" was about you, because I remember you said in a slightly chilly voice that you didn't care for the phrase "thankfully confused"' (16 November 1976).

This memory must have given Larkin much pleasure because Winifred, bright and certain of her future, had noticed that he had sewn into the poem a mild critique of her decision, and he would have recalled, too, the closing lines:

> your old name shelters our faithfulness,
> Instead of losing shape and meaning less
> With your depreciating luggage laden.

Of course, he is referring here to how a name resists the dispersals of memory. Isn't he? Surely the terms 'losing shape', 'meaning less', 'depreciating' and 'laden' cannot refer to the physical effects of age? His next sentence in the letter informs her that 'As for myself, I am tall, fat and bald.' He does not ask, 'What about you?', but perhaps if, as one suspects, he had the poem before him, such a question was unnecessary. He had frozen her youth in the verbal equivalent of a photograph, and whatever thereafter was lost was her concern.

During his time in Belfast Larkin evolved a balance between technical control and expressive idiosyncrasy which would be the cornerstone for much of his best verse, but it would be wrong to assume that 1950 was the year in which he became affiliated exclusively to poetry. He took with him to Belfast the early plans for *New World Symphony* which for the next three and a half years he refused fully to abandon. His failure to complete the book extinguished finally his long ambition to become an accomplished novelist, and the cause of this is a miniature chronicle in its own right.

7

The Making of Jim

In 1950, shortly before Larkin was to depart for Belfast, Amis had written him a curious letter of thanks; curious because the cause of Amis's gratitude is not immediately evident. The letter is crammed with nostalgic recollections of stages in their friendship – odd for 28-year-olds who had known each other for less than a decade.

> Do you remember, old trencherman, reading my sheaf of poems in Johns (that room I had in the North Quad) sometime in late '45 or early '46 and sang you liked them on the whole and thought they were quite good? (27 August)

Amis goes on in this manner for a few hundred words, recalling events more or less at random but returning continually to moments when Larkin had helped him out with his writerly ambitions – most of which he omits to add, diplomatically, have been failures – and one wonders, as indeed would Larkin, where all this is leading. Weirdly, Amis does not say, but he provides a clue.

> During the week I turned out all my drawers, and re-read some of your letters . . . they are much *funnier* than mine ever were . . . Today you are my 'inner audience', my watcher in Spanish, the reader over my shoulder, my often mentioned Jack and a good deal more!

Larkin would have understood most of these private code words, but the full implications of the letter would only become clear to him later. Amis was announcing, albeit obliquely, that he had decided to take his writing in a new direction. He had found the formula that would eventually become *Lucky Jim*.

Lucky Jim worked so well because there were effectively two Jims: one inside the narrative, struggling with his various feelings of impatience, frustration and rage; and the other controlling and orchestrating the story, ensuring that the reader will share Jim's private thoughts on the idiocies and pretensions of his colleagues and acquaintances. This arrangement, as indicated in Amis's letter, was inspired by his correspondence with Larkin. Each was the other's confidant, and they would discuss and disclose to each other things that no one else would ever hear. For example, in July 1946 Larkin included in a letter a shameless imitation of Ruth Bowman's self-consciously upper-class habits of pronunciation, such as 'the same (sam) time'. Ruth was never aware of this but she would, via Larkin, become ultimately responsible for one of the most widely quoted comic episodes of Amis's novel. Amis transplants the same vocal idiosyncrasy to Bertrand the pretentious 'artist' son of the Welches, and it eventually leads to the fight with Jim in Chapter 20.

> 'If you think I'm going to sit back and take this from you, you're mistaken; I don't happen to be that type, you sam.'
> 'I'm not Sam, you fool,' Dixon shrieked; this was the worst taunt of all . . .

The most blatant borrowing from their language game occurs when Jim, signing himself as Joe Higgins, sends a letter to the nasty, obsequious Johns accusing him of the attempted seduction of a university secretary. It begins, 'this is just to let you no that I no what you are up to with yuong Marleen Richards, yuong Marleen is a desent girl and has got no tim for your sort, I no your sort . . .' It closely resembles Amis to Larkin on the latter's sexual relationship with Ruth ' . . . All right. I know why you don't. All the sam, I bet you wish you could, eh (ha ha)!, you old bugar, I no yor sort', and bears some similarity to a piece from Larkin to Amis where he thanks him 'for Yuor letar, yuo can certainly Spinn a yarn, I was fare peng myself at the Finnish: rekun you ave the nack of writting . . .'

The letters themselves provided Amis with inspiration for a large number of the comic set pieces for the novel – as early as 1946 he had recognized the uniqueness of their private, shared discourse by starting to keep copies of his own to Larkin – and also they were a token of something unique in their friendship. Amis believed that they knew each other better than anyone else knew either of them – hence the untidy metaphor of the 'watcher in Spanish' indicating that their exchanges were, at least for others, a mixture of the silent and the inaccessible. In naming Larkin as his 'inner audience' Amis borrows a phrase he had invented in his Oxford B.Litt. thesis to describe a private interior dialogue that occurs during the writing of poetry. For him Larkin was a real, embodied version of one half of this exchange, and as well as drawing upon moments from their friendship and sewing them into the early drafts of the novel he began to send these pieces to Larkin for comment. There is no evidence at that point that Larkin regarded the project as potentially successful. Amis had already had a completed novel turned down by three publishers. His new excursions into what appeared to be working-class-Wodehouse-in-academe were not the kind of thing which, in Larkin's experience, mainstream fiction publishers were likely to welcome. Nevertheless he worked as Amis's adviser and copy-editor. Between 1950 and 1953 he received something like 150,000 words of sprawling, uncertain, sometimes directionless drafts from Amis. He worked hard, particularly on cutting out characters which seemed superfluous to the most interesting parts of the story, the latter principally involving Jim's tenuous status as an academic and his relationships with the irritating Margaret and the alluring Christine. In the letter of 8 September 1952, for example, Amis responds to a list of his detailed suggestions on various stages of the narrative including what would turn out to be the most famous passage of the novel:

> The lecture: I see what you mean about this, though it would be awfully difficult to do. I could have a shot at it, anyway, and you could decide whether it could go in . . .

We will never know exactly the extent to which Larkin was responsible for the brilliant timing of this scene, but later in the letter we encounter something which suggests that at this stage at least the novel was operating as the site for private jokes:

> I think the best thing about Veronica's name would be to change it to Margaret Jones; then I could enjoy cutting at Margaret Ashbury as well as at Monica. You tell Monica I'm cutting at some frightful Welch girl, and I'll tell Margaret that I'm cutting at some frightful Leicester girl. How would that do? It's a common enough sort of name, God knows. (8 September 1952)

It is beyond dispute that Monica Jones was the model for the odious Margaret Peel of *Lucky Jim*, but the story which attends this particular borrowing by Amis shows her to be a pivotal figure in post-war literary history; that she played this role unwittingly adds a note of drollery to the tale.

Despite Amis's argument that Larkin could claim that Margaret was based on a woman social worker friend of the Amises in Swansea, the rhyming association of Monica's full name of Monica Margaret Beale Jones with Margaret Peel's would have been clear enough. Also the effect of Margaret upon the texture of the novel is both striking to the general reader and, for Amis, Larkin and Monica, privately reverberant.

Every time Jim meets her, or even thinks about her, the passage involves a precise description of what she is wearing, often supplemented by a comment on her posture or physiognomy. She wore 'a sort of arty get-up of multicoloured shirt, skirt with fringed hem and pocket, low-heeled shoes, and wooden beads', and in the next chapter 'She was wearing her arty get-up, but had discarded the wooden beads in favour of a brooch consisting of the letter "M".' No one else in the book receives anything like the attention to physical detail given to Margaret.

> As if searching for a text he examined her face, noting the tufts of brown hair that overhung the earpieces of her glasses, the crease running up the near cheek and approaching closer than before to this eye socket (or was he imagining that?) and the faint but at this angle unmistakably downward curve of the mouth.

Jim's apparent obsession with her appearance might be his way of empha-sizing his dissatisfaction at being attached to a woman he finds unattractive. But at the same time one suspects that Amis is suggesting a causal rela-tionship between women who look and dress like Margaret and a propensity for pretentiousness and faked psychological intricacy.

Margaret's face, hair, spectacles, her taste in clothes and jewellery, would have shown anyone who knew Monica, and knew of Larkin's friendship with Amis, that Margaret was based on her. And there were parallels, too, between their cultural predispositions and their verbal habits, so much so that Larkin was later prompted to ask Amis if 'you weren't actually there taking notes [of our conversations] were you?' (Jacobs, p. 146).

Over three years Larkin not only witnessed the fictional recreation of Monica, he assisted in it and in the construction of the world she would inhabit. Indeed Larkin read the novel as a better-organized version of the private chronicle of complaints, confidences and daydreams that accom-panied it. For example, Amis's father-in-law, Leonard Bardwell, was the model for Jim's boss Professor Neddy Welch, and Amis kept Larkin simul-taneously informed of the construction of Neddy and the ever-irritating activities of his real-life counterpart. Neddy's surname is an undisguised reference to Bardwell's interest in Welsh language and culture, and Amis also christened the latter 'ape-man' – his obsessive concern with folk culture and medieval England being as relevant in the 1950s as a case for the return to the lifestyle of our simian ancestors. This private joke with Larkin inspired in the novel the famous scene where Jim does an ape imitation as a comment on the lecture he was obliged to write celebrating medieval England. While Amis was amusing his friend with his accounts of week-ends with the in-laws Larkin was also reading equally hilarious versions of these involving Jim, assisted by his narrator. Larkin felt himself becoming part of a peculiar circle of literary incest in which private confidences and droll reports on Amis's personal life were being interwoven with their fictionalized counterparts. It felt like a game in which he played the role of straight-faced copy-editor, much as Amis had done with their collaborations on *Willow Gables*, and it was this sense of farcical unreality that prompted him to borrow some of Amis's ideas for a publishable version of the provincial academic novel.

Jim Dixon would change sex to become Augusta Bax, based upon the woman whom Amis was so mercilessly caricaturing in his drafts, Monica Jones. Bizarre and improbable as all of this might seem, there was from Larkin's perspective a purposive logic behind it. A number of temperamental features shared by Amis and Larkin were very similar to those that attracted Larkin to Monica. She, too, was irritated by the tendency for provincial universities to concern themselves obsessively with bureaucratic ritual. English litera-ture as a university discipline was in Britain attaining a reasonable level of acknowledgement and respect; in the inter-war years it had been widely mocked as an upstart, amateurish affair, a second-rate alternative to Classics. After the war English gradually, systematically, set about creating a scholarly and disciplinary framework for itself that would rival established arts subjects. The so-called New Critics – including in Britain the likes of William Empson, I.A. Richards and F.R. Leavis – were producing books of and about literary criticism which involved the sharp intellectual rigour more usually associated with history and philosophy. Monica, while showing an impres-sive ability to engage critically with literary texts – her first in Oxford was acknowledged as one of the best of that year – found herself at Leicester becoming more and more irritated by the systemization of criticism. She was a curious combination of a Johnsonian and an anarchist. Like the good Doctor she was opinionated and judgemental – some writers were good, others were not – but she balked at grounding evaluation in consensual or abstract formu-lae. Instead she favoured such quixotic measures as instinct and inclination and as a consequence developed a reputation in Leicester as an eccentric rebel. She never published a word of criticism in her life, but in lectures and tutorials and in the marking of student papers she was the model of idiosyn-cratic arbitrariness. This, along with wearing tartan to lecture on *Macbeth* and a waist-length rope of pearls for *Antony and Cleopatra*, made her a small legend in her equally compact provincial domain.

Larkin in *A New World Symphony* offers a complex and unnervingly honest picture of Monica. When the novel was eventually published after Larkin's death Monica read it for the first time and drew the editor's attention to a passage describing Augusta Bax's youthful, creative enthusiasm for clothes both fashionable and unusual. 'Yes. That's me,' she said, but she did not, however, comment upon how this unremarkable trait was but a slight element of Larkin's depiction of a more puzzling, almost baroque persona: the printing of a hundred cards 'reading *Miss Augusta Bax*' and kept in 'an ivory and silver case with concertina pockets inside'; the attendance of Evensong on Sundays (despite her indifferent agnosticism); the placing of a three-branched candle on her writing desk; her singing of nineteenth-century love songs in French while being punted on the Cherwell. During the early years of their relationship, before Larkin finally broke up with Ruth, each of them had cultivated an image of affected, perverse bohemianism. His stationery, for example, included pink, searing lemon and, most strikingly, the black-bordered mourning paper left over from his father's funeral – 'This paper must be used up and by who better than myself,' he commented. He sent Monica elaborately designed cards like those that Augusta has printed for herself. Larkin, sensing Monica's taste for arch formality, advised her to use them 'for cancelling tutorials, refusing dinner parties, postponing lectures and declining invitations to rambles, discussion groups, coffee circles . . .' In the novel:

> By setting up as an eccentric – vague, wispy, slightly distracted but exquisitely-bred – she gained a reputation in College many envied . . .
>
> What prompted this attitude? . . . Partly it was a daydream of the kind of person she most admired. Partly it was a reaction against the kind of person she most disliked . . . But partly – perhaps mostly – it was a guard, a mask, hiding an enormous vacancy. (p. 399)

By 'vacancy' Larkin most certainly does not mean shallowness. As the novel and its central figure evolve it becomes evident that he is creating what would have been his most intricate fictional presence, based principally upon Monica and, more obliquely, himself – a character for whom vacancy was synonymous with absence of realization, anticipation of failure. Augusta/Monica compensated for this by becoming the person Larkin had met, and to a degree recognized, during his first year in Leicester.

> Augusta admired the amateur tradition, the dislike of plodding, the careless production of masterpieces. She saw herself reading widely, pointlessly, fantastically, trailing through eighteenth-century libraries, lounging in embrasures with folios, one hand turning a globe. Then a subject would spring up in her mind: a single strand electrifying several centuries . . . one followed one's nose, perhaps now and again a book might result.

It is fascinating to compare Larkin's version of Monica with Amis's. Provided that one accepts that perception is partly a function of the predis-positions of the perceiver, then both are accurate and realistic.

Amis was introduced to Monica by Larkin during a 1947 visit to Leicester, and although she was willing to tolerate some of the more strident social habits of Larkin's closest friend Amis decided almost immediately that she was not the right kind of partner for Larkin. Monica and Amis would meet five or six times thereafter up to 1950, but following his move to Belfast Larkin made sure that their encounters were as infrequent as possible. She never once accompanied Larkin on his regular visits to the Amis house in Swansea. It was not that Larkin felt unable to deal with the simmering antagonism that soon became a standard feature of their meetings; more that he found their incompatibility reflected a division within his own personality, which he was content to maintain. Monica's only public statement on Amis was terse but perceptive: 'Kingsley wasn't just making faces, he was actually trying them on. He didn't know who he was' (Motion, p. 169). This comment was retrospective, made after Larkin's death, and as such it goes beyond her remembrance of the three of them in the late 1940s and 1950s. She knew from Larkin that Amis's renowned talent for mimicry was the public manifestation of a private world in which his taste for dissimulation served also his addiction to promiscuity. Monica had no particular moral objections to whatever Amis got up to, but she was aware that Larkin would when appropriate be drawn into an alliance of shared confidences in which Amis was the senior partner. It was not quite that he 'didn't know who he was'; to be more accurate he could choose to be someone else and take Larkin with him.

Amis said of Monica, again after Larkin's death, that 'There was a sort of adhesive thing about her . . . Not quite predatory, but still' (Motion, p. 169), which is an almost perfect description of Margaret Peel. At the time that Larkin and Monica first started to see one another he was less diplomatic:

> It doesn't surprise me in the *least* that Monica is studding Crab; he's *exactly* the sort of *priggish, boring, featureless* (especially *that*; there isn't *anything* about him, is there?) *long-winded, inessential* man she'd go for. (8 September 1948)

This could be Jim Dixon speaking at the end of the novel when he, and indeed the reader, have become fully aware of the nasty manipulative tendencies of the real Margaret. Crabbe, one should note, is described not as the poet but the 'man' Monica would 'go for'. The implied message is that while Larkin is the complete antithesis of this Monica would try to mould him suitably to meet her expectations – exactly the way that Margaret had behaved with Jim.

In truth Monica provided Larkin with a counterbalancing alternative to Amis. The latter had from their Oxford days onwards virtually forbidden from their exchanges anything that resembled the, as Amis saw it, false earnestness of tutorials. Literature could be discussed, certainly, but in a manner that had more in common with Byron than Leavis. Larkin and Monica shared a genuine, thoughtful enthusiasm for the profundities of

Hardy, Yeats and Lawrence and would exchange ideas and reflections on them without a hint of self-consciousness.

The other main character of *A New World Symphony* is Dr Butterfield, Augusta's head of department. Butterfield, thirty years her senior, embodies the amateur tradition of scholarship to which she aspires, and the plot focuses upon the conflict between Butterfield's ethos and the commerce-based pragmatism of post-war England. The university wishes to expand and its administrators are attempting to supplement government funding with local business sponsorship. Chairs for all departments are being advertised and the successful candidates will be expected to show as much entrepreneurial flair as scholarly dedication to their subjects. Clearly Butterfield will not get the job.

In Amis's version Jim exposes academia as a nest of neurotic bohemians, egotists and audacious time-wasters; he gets the pretty, unpretentious girl and after dumping Margaret/Monica exchanges scholarship for a well-paid job in the real world of industry and high finance. Larkin would have been entertained by this. It was an amusing, fantastic rewrite of the retinue of complaints about colleagues and working life with which Amis's letters from Swansea had been strewn for the previous five or six years. It was not, however, a presentation that he imagined would be taken seriously by a publisher. *A New World Symphony* would; it involved themes and narrative foci that Larkin had cautiously selected from Amis's material and inverted, so that civilized, almost languid intellectualism became a bulwark against the invasions of corporate anti-culture.

He never discussed *A New World Symphony* with anyone. There are vague references between 1950 and 1954 in letters to Amis and Sutton to his having restarted a novel, but nothing more. He was convinced that Amis's work would not get into print, and while he was preparing his own he understandably did not want to admit that he was using his friend's writing as inspirational counterpoint. Proof that he was can be found in the draft itself.

The likeliest candidate for the Chair is an egotistical bully and his name is Welch. Amis had bombarded Larkin with material in letters on his loathing for his father-in-law Bardwell and in drafts on his vengeful caricature of him as Professor Neddy Welch. Throughout *A New World Symphony* there are randomly distributed references to matters 'Welsh', involving the nationality of minor characters, places sometimes visited, locutionary habits and so on. These seem to be completely arbitrary, at least regarding the novel itself, but they gather significance with the knowledge that Amis was continually sewing into his letters and drafts jokes about Welch the character, and the Welsh, in whose country Amis lived and with whose culture Bardwell was obsessed. It was often Larkin's habit in early drafts of fiction to name characters in a talismanic, idiosyncratic manner, with the intention of changing these to something more unpremeditated when the text was offered to the public. We can assume that had *A New World Symphony* been completed and published he would have done so here, too. (And we should here recall 'Sam' Wagstaff, boyfriend of a fictionalized version of Ruth, whose pronunciation of 'same' as 'sam' became a running joke with Larkin and Amis.)

Amis stalks the pages at this early draft stage like the ghost of Larkin's conscience. There is even a reference to a minor character called 'Mumbles the Librarian'. Mumbles was the suburb in which the Amises had lived during their first three years in Swansea and which of course appeared atop Kingsley's regular letters – letters to a librarian with a slight speech defect.

The exact date at which Larkin finally abandoned *A New World Symphony* is uncertain, but the cause is clear enough. He became aware, during 1953, that *Lucky Jim* was turning into something more than a shared joke. John Wain had known Larkin and Amis from their Oxford days and had thereafter done well as a writer and academic. He had spent the war years as a Junior Fellow at St John's and then acquired a Lectureship at Reading University where he established himself as a kind of amateur patron of the arts. He launched a series of short poetry volumes, sponsored by the university, which can be seen as the first recognition of a new wave of contra-Modernism, and in 1953 he secured a contract with the BBC to edit a radio series called *First Readings* which would introduce Third Programme listeners to the work of new writers. Larkin's poem 'If, My Darling' would appear on this in July, but the opening broadcast on 26 April featured an extract that had far more significant reverberations. It was a short piece from Amis's as yet unpublished novel. The typescript was with Gollancz, and as soon as Amis's eventual editor Hilary Rubinstein, following the broadcast, found most of his office colleagues discussing it and in states of uncontrollable laughter he immediately telegrammed Amis with the offer of a contract. Amis informed Larkin of this on 5 May, adding 'It will be dedicated to you.' He concludes that he is 'Glad about your novel . . .' but confesses that he can't remember what '"The Leicester one" was going to be'. The 'Leicester' novel was up to that point a private reference to Larkin's admiration for William Cooper's *Scenes from Provincial Life* (1950), which he had christened, with well-meant irony, 'the great Leicester novel'. It appears that Larkin had recently informed Amis that his own contribution to this sub-genre was under way. He did not tell him that it was to be an alternative to *Lucky Jim*, and Amis would also never learn that his letter of 5 May would effectively put an end to it.

Later that summer Larkin wrote to Patsy Strang, who had since moved to England: 'You know, I *can't* write this book: if it is to be written at all it should largely be an attack on Monica and I *can't* do that, not while we are still on friendly terms, and I'm not even sure it interests me sufficiently to go on' (5 July 1953). This is fascinating in its disclosure that Patsy was the only person with whom he had discussed anything regarding the nature of the book and also because he seems to be addressing the problem as much to himself as he is explaining it to her. The emphatic, repeated *'can't'* relates not to his inability to write the book but to his realization that he needs comprehensively to alter it, shift the perspective so that Monica's/Augusta's flaws and idiosyncrasies are no longer treated sympathetically. As he states, this would be difficult while he and Monica are still on 'friendly terms', but he does not explain why such a major change has to be made in the first place. A week later he offers, involuntarily, a clue, writing to Patsy that 'I still feel a good deal worried by art (writing) and life (MMBJ) [Monica Margaret Beale Jones] . . . Now I've begun writing I find I've nearly nothing to say' (12 July 1953). The rest of the letter is mostly a chronicle of general complaints regarding the replacement of gloom and depression with a 'restless and bored' condition, and for no apparent reason the observation that 'I expect getting his novel accepted has made Kingsley a bit cocky.'

The workbook for the new draft, all done during 1953, reads like the jottings of someone lost in a maze, constantly choosing another potential route while knowing that he will never reach the exit. Larkin plays with alternatives: Perhaps he could give more attention to Butterfield (now called Praed) as the central figure? How can Augusta be changed? Focus upon her background – her parents' marital problems – as the cause of her serrated temperament; make her more forceful, even irreverent? Transform the story itself, with Augusta leaving the English provinces for the USA? All the time the options are driven by an unstated imperative: Try not to prompt comparisons with *Lucky Jim*. Larkin knew this was impossible, and at the end of November 1953 he gave up for good, little more than a month before review copies of Amis's novel went out. In February 1954 it was again to Patsy that he offered his genuine feelings about the attention being generated by its publication: 'the reviews it has been getting are the kind of thing *I don't like to see* – Anthony Powell for instance in today's *Punch*. Well, well. Success, success.' He concedes that 'The Kingsley humour I think quite unrivalled, quite wonderful.' But of course he always had; Amis had been one half of a private double act. Now, however, their world was public property, and Larkin's unease is evident. 'Apart from being funny I think it is somewhat over simple.' 'It's in the general thinness of the imagination that he falls down', and he compares *Lucky Jim* with a story from Angus Wilson's *The Wrong Set*, which 'to my mind makes the Welch family hardly satire at all' (3 February 1954). He did not add that the reason none of this occurred to him while he was spending so much time helping Kingsley rewrite first drafts was that he had misjudged the literary world that would in a month turn his friend from a nonentity into a star. In a letter to Monica in February 1955 Larkin offers an account of his friendship with Amis which is partly an apology for the latter's creation of Margaret Peel and, more strikingly, a moment of recognition that Amis had exploited their friendship. He states, with regard to *Lucky Jim*, that 'I refuse to believe he can write a book on his own – or at least a good book', a clear disclosure that for Larkin his role as unwitting collaborator in Amis's ascent to first-novel fame had now become part of his menu of dejection.

Lucky Jim has been held responsible for many things – progenitor of an unprofound, witty, rational, sardonic mood in post-war fiction and so on – but it should also be recognized as a pivotal moment in the creation of a poetic repertoire that few would dispute is one of the finest of the twentieth century. The novel and its author played this role unwittingly but none the less effectively; Larkin gave up fiction.

Amis and *Lucky Jim* are acknowledged in the typescript of *A New World Symphony* as the presences who brought about its stagnation. No direct reference is made to them in the 1953–4 verse, but if we bring them with us into a reading it becomes evident that they were present when Larkin wrote the poems. 'Poetry of Departures' and 'Toads' are meditations upon the same condition felt, it is inferred, by everyone at one time or another: ennui, *Weltschmerz*, the irksomeness of having to work and live in a way that is a dispiriting obligation. It is a familiar theme, but in both poems there is something opalescent in Larkin's treatment of it. In 'Poetry of Departures' he first harnesses his frustration to familiar escapist clichés:

> So to hear it said
>
> *He walked out on the whole crowd*
> Leaves me flushed and stirred,
> Like *Then he undid her dress*
> Or *Take that you bastard*;
> Surely I can, if he did?

One is prompted to ask; if you can, then why don't you? He goes on to add that he would go today,

> Yes, swagger the nut-strewn roads,
> Crouch in the fo'c'sle
> Stubbly with goodness, if
> It weren't so artificial,
> Such a deliberate step backwards
> To create an object:
> Books; china; a life
> Reprehensibly perfect.

The first set of images seem drawn from the world of B-movie fantasy, but the second, the ones potentially open to him, are equally unreal, although this time with a tinge of adolescent adventurism: 'swagger the nut-strewn roads', 'crouch in the fo'c'sle', 'stubbly with goodness'. Humphrey Bogart has been replaced by the Famous Five. He posits two types of release from an apparent sense of dissatisfaction, one self-evidently unattainable, the other perversely irrelevant; so why bother with either? The answer involves tracing a thread of meaning only half disclosed in the fabric of the poem itself. Both types of release, while apparently incompatible, share certain characteristics: they are disagreeably 'artificial' and involve 'a deliberate step backwards / To create an object: / Books . . . a life / Reprehensibly perfect'.

The one person to have made them compatible and to have revelled in the outcome was Amis. *Lucky Jim* was a fairy-tale which had, overnight, earned its author immense literary esteem. It was, and only Larkin knew this, fantasy made real and vice versa; a blending of Amis's actual life with Jim Dixon's, who 'walks out on the whole crowd', taking with him the kind of girl who will, we know, allow him to undo her dress, after of course he had belted her unworthy boyfriend. Jim had not said, 'Take that, you bastard', but '"You bloody old towser-faced boot-faced totem-pole on a crap reservation," he said', just before thumping Bertrand, would do.

The imperatives of the first part derive in truth from Amis's letters, which read like the promptings of an amiable, almost kind-hearted Mephistopheles. He responds, for instance, to Larkin's convoluted account of his pursuit of Winifred with 'I fucking give you up as far as sex is concerned. Don't you e pe *want* a poke? More impressive too, to stop believing in sex *after* pocking AWA rather than before' (16 April 1953).

Barely a month before *Lucky Jim* was published and little more than two before Larkin composed the poem, Amis wrote to him that 'I wish that something would happen to me, like having a fuck or selling the film rights to *Jim*. That'd be funny wouldn't it? Dixon, Alex Guinness; Christine, Gina Lollobrigida; Margaret, Dulcie Grey; Bertrand, Orson Welles; Welch, Boris Karloff . . . Directed by Alfred Hitchcock. Just pipe dreaming dear' (26 November 1953). By the end of January 1954 the pipe dream was becoming real. John Betjeman wrote Amis a private letter, at the same time as his fulsome review in the *Daily Telegraph*, complimenting him on a beguiling mixture of fairy -tale and realism. Amis had informed his friend of this, adding that 'they can't stop me now!' Larkin had witnessed and been kept regularly informed of this unlikely incidence of adolescent escapism made real from its very adult initiator. Five days after he completed 'Poetry of Departures' he included in a letter to Patsy an aside on his writing. 'I sometimes read a poem over with a tiny Kingsley crying *How d'you mean* at every unclear image, and it's a wonderful aid to improvement' (3 February 1954).

One suspects that alongside this imagined helpmate is the recollection of how he, Larkin, had played a similar role in the making of Kingsley's fantasy. In 'Toads' he returns to the same field of complaint. He asks,

> Why should I let the toad *work*
> Squat on my life?
> Can't I use my wit as a pitchfork
> And drive the brute off?

As rhetorical questions go it is one of the best, sullenly pre-empting its answer, but the alternative seems to involve unfocused absurdism.

> Lots of folk live on their wits:
> Lecturers, lispers,
> Losels, loblolly men, louts –
> They don't end as paupers;

'Lecturers' probably found their way into this alliterative cascade by an accident of 'l's and 's's – probably. Later he concedes that he is not 'courageous enough' to shout *'stuff your pension!'* because not only does 'the toad *work*' squat *on* his life 'something sufficiently toad-like / Squats in me, too;'

> And will never allow me to blarney
> My way to getting
> The fame and the girl and the money
> All at one sitting.

It is not that he cannot do this; rather, that his innate toad-like characteristics cause him not to. All of a sudden the digressive whimsy has become precise in the fame, the girl and the money. The lecturer who is now anything but a pauper has indeed got them all: Amis again.

The final stanza,

> I don't say, one bodies the other
> One's spiritual truth;
> But I do say it's hard to lose either,
> When you have both.

seems at first puzzling, but the first 'one' is the toad that sits on him, the second the 'toad-like' condition that configures his temperament. The subtext for 'Toads' becomes bitterly evident in a letter that Larkin wrote to Monica ten months after completing the poem. 'I sought his [Amis's] company because it gave me a wonderful sense of relief – I've always needed this "fourth form friend", with whom I can pretend things are not as I know they are – and pretended I was like him. Now I don't feel like pretending any longer . . . He doesn't like books. He doesn't like reading. And I wouldn't take his opinion on anything, books, people, places . . .' The most striking, puzzling feature of the letter is Larkin's apparent sense of surprise. He writes as though he has only just discovered that this friend's intellectual hooliganism was not a pretence, while he, Larkin, had treated their 'fourth form' antics as a release, an escape from 'things . . . as I know they are'. In truth, he had known this all along. The shock was due to the fact that Amis had turned their private, adolescent fantasy world into a recipe for literary success. The letter was written in February 1955 six weeks after W. Somerset Maugham had in the *Sunday Times* 'Books of the Year' supplement cited *Lucky Jim* as presaging the decline of Western civilization. Its author, a provincial academic with an Oxford degree no less, had written a distressingly autobiographical novel which recommended, justified, a blend of hedonism and philistinism. 'They [that is, Amis *and* Dixon] do not go to university to acquire culture', wrote Maugham, 'but to get a job, and when they have got one scamp it. They have no manners, and are woefully unable to deal with any social predicament.' Larkin had read the piece, and Maugham's litany of negatives is echoed in his letter to Monica. He knew that their private fantasy had become Amis's route to fame and also that what faced him was the 'toad', work, a career as a librarian. How else would he earn a living, at least enough to allow himself the time and opportunity to abandon 'pretending' and turn his attention to the unprofitable realm of 'things . . . as I know they are' in his poems.

'Toads' leaves us with an impression of curmudgeonly contentment, signals of the misanthropic presence of his later work, but there is something else. Three years earlier Larkin, in response to Sutton's praise for the self-published pamphlet *XX Poems*, had offered perhaps his most coherent account of how and why he writes verse. 'For me, a poem is the crossroads of my thoughts, my feelings, my imaginings, my wishes and my verbal sense: normally these run parallel.' He then stops typing and provides a diagrammatic representation of these five elements following parallel lines adding in longhand that 'Often two or more cross . . . but only when all cross at one point do you get a poem' (10 July 1951). All this is leavened with a hint of self-mockery – he also provides a diagram of the lines conjoining, adding, 'Poem!! Yippee!!', and a sketch of a glass of bubbling champagne – but such was his habit with Sutton when he was saying something about himself where significance was not quite matched by confidence.

Larkin does not claim that such interweavings come about by accidental promptings or unsolicited moments of inspiration. They are, on the contrary, the result of planning, calculation, stylistic design and, most significantly, selective appropriation. He sews together the elements so that each is variously reshaped, obscured, transformed or delineated by its convergence with the others. In 'Poetry of Departures' and 'Toads' the predominant mood is that of stoic resignation, an acceptance that some aspects of his world cannot be altered but are by their intransigence recognizable to him as appropriate, albeit distorting mirrors of his temperament. When we examine the circumstances of their composition, best evidenced in his letters, we can almost watch how the diagram he had offered to Sutton is brought into operation. The abandonment of *A New World Symphony*, the success of *Lucky Jim*, the recollected and still present voice of Amis as at once his *alter ego* and enviable opposite, are never in the poems explicitly referred to, of course, but they become hidden talismans and provide the 'crossroads of my thoughts, my feelings, my imaginings, my wishes and my verbal sense'. Evidence of Larkin's developing expertise in negotiating such interchanges emerges when we compare these poems with those inspired by and addressed to Winifred, in which the mysterious subject engages our attention almost as determinedly as the poem itself. Now Larkin leads us into the texture of the poem, and the question of why he is doing so becomes a dimension of the experience, not its pretext.

8

The Making of Larkin

During his period in Belfast Larkin's relationship with Monica acquired a degree of continuity, or so it appeared to her. On his visits to Britain he would divide his time between periods with his mother and sister, trips to the Amises in Swansea, occasional meetings with Bruce Montgomery and regular encounters with Monica. They might stay at her flat in Leicester or after 1951, particularly during the Easter and summer vacations, take holidays in various parts of southern England, North Wales or Scotland. She first visited Belfast in March 1951, and after a few days in the city they took the train to Portrush and then on to the Glens of Antrim, staying in the pretty, well-preserved village of Glenarm. In later summers they would explore Donegal, and on one occasion they briefly visited Dublin; generally they preferred the countryside.

The remarkable thing about their relationship during these years was the way in which Larkin organized and oversaw it. Monica met Patsy several times but at the time did not suspect that anything other than close friendship existed between them – indeed she knew little of the affair until after Larkin's death. Similarly, she knew of Winifred but trusted Larkin's account of her as a junior colleague with whom he shared interests and often socialized. Again, until the 1960s she assumed that the subjects of 'Lines on a Young Lady's Photograph Album' and 'Maiden Name' were inventions, conceits.

Patsy was the living realization of the fantasies for which pornography provided him with more reliable deliverance. On several occasions she suggested that since they enjoyed each other so much, sexually and temperamentally, they should go public and have a proper relationship. She offered to leave Colin, marry him and, as she put it, 'do all the earning so that he could write'. Larkin was honest enough in his responses. Theirs was an affair in the deliciously improper sense, and he enjoyed particularly its furtive aspect. They would leave letters for one another in post offices under the false names of Mr and Mrs Crane and book into hotels in Larne or other Belfast satellite towns, again as the Cranes. Belfast with its dour Victorian countenance and abiding distaste for anything indulgent or exciting – bar the marching season and 12th of July bonfires – provided the ideal counterpoint for their secret adventures. The choice of Crane was their amusing commentary upon all of this, given that the most omnipresent public couple in Belfast were the two giant Harland and Wolff cranes. In March 1953 he wrote to her with a further explanation of how they were unsuited to a long-term relationship. She was, he contended, far more exuberant and impassioned than him. 'Please don't think of me as frightfully sophisticated . . . I'm not. You're only my second young lady, and look like being my last.' The first, as far as Patsy knew, was Monica. He said nothing of Ruth.

In mid-summer 1953 Larkin spent a week in Mallaig in the Highlands of Scotland, with Monica, and following that they went south for ten days in Weymouth. Larkin never disclosed a particular taste for the epistolary novel, but during this period it might occasionally have occurred to him that he was in one. On 20 July he wrote to Winifred from Mallaig, informing her of the view from his hotel window of a church 'with a cross on top (and a gull on the cross)', a cottage and 'beyond, the grey sea and the dim shape of Skye. I can hear gulls calling and hotel guests padding about.' Later he shifts to the anecdotal – an account of a notoriously drunken fisherman of the village – and finally to the intimate, recalling their cycle rides around the Ulster countryside, particularly the one just before his departure 'ending with your soft *shy* goodbye (lock this up) on Thursday in the darkness' (20 July 1953). Before he left he had set her a task. In his absence she was to read a number of seventeenth-century amatory poems, chosen by him. (The exercise would in due course inspire his own borrowing from the Metaphysical sub-genre in his poem on and to Winifred, 'Maiden Name'.) All involved the commanding yet gentle and learned presence of the seducer addressing his generally innocent and always subdued addressee. 'How are you getting on with *your* holiday task? When you know it thoroughly, you might go on to Herrick's *To virgins, to make the most of time*.' This must have seemed, at least to him, mordantly appropriate. He had clearly not give up in his pursuit of her despite the presence of her London-based fiancé, and he was writing her provocatively amusing letters. He ends, 'I rage, I pant, I burn for a letter from you . . .', knowing of course that, like Herrick's virgins, she would remain the secret recipient of his beguiling sophistry.

And where was Monica when he was writing this? 'The only time I can write to you [Winifred] is before getting up, which is what I'm doing now . . .' Larkin and Monica were sexual partners, but this was 1953 and offering false names to hotel receptionists and other guests was simply too much trouble, given that their relationship had already taken on aspects of the reliably mundane. They took separate bedrooms.

Two days later on 22 July he begins, 'Hotel paper, hotel pen, but I can still write you the beginnings of a letter before breakfast, as M [Monica] hasn't finished dressing yet.' On this occasion the letter is to Patsy, and one cannot help finding parallels with Fielding's *Clarissa* or Smollett's *Humphrey Clinker* as Mr Larkin, hidden in his study, hurries a message across the paper before the return of 'M'. A week later he is in Weymouth, snatching a few spare moments while Monica is elsewhere, this time 'sitting in the sun lounge looking across the front' and informing Winifred of how, when no one was looking, he had 'plucked your letter from the rack like a cormorant snapping up a bit of bread'. He commends her for reading the next on his list of lyrics, this time Marvell's 'To His Coy Mistress', adding that 'I'm not really playing my *own* game in all this. By the time I've convinced you that virginity is just an underdeveloped talent you'll be setting yourself off alone and defenceless, with young Sparks' (Graham Bradshaw, her fiancé).

His ability to switch personae for three different women, let alone overcome the practical difficulties of secretly writing to two while holidaying with the third, is formidable, and on 28 July he delivered an urbane finale in a letter from Weymouth to Colin and Patsy, simply two close friends you understand, on what he and his girlfriend Monica had got up to in the Highlands and on the English south coast.

Larkin's attempt at duplicitous promiscuity carried with it the atmosphere of an Ealing Comedy, that characteristically English sense of something naughty going on beneath the calm surface of nothing terribly untoward. He could share a bed with his clandestine, adulterous partner while he and her unconcealed long-term counterpart were obliged to have separate rooms. And then there was Winifred, the Coy Lady he would like to share with Marvell, if only she were not so determined to begin a proper relationship with someone a little more conventional. Larkin was enjoying himself and he knew that before too long matters would reach a conclusion, all the more painlessly because he would not be a participant.

Soon after his return to Belfast in August Patsy wrote informing him that Colin had applied successfully for a lectureship in Newcastle and that, apart from clearing their house, they would not be returning to Ulster. Their relationship was not over, not quite, but the move would cause practical difficulties. It was at this point that she suggested that she leave Colin for him, and he with disingenuous concern for her advised against such a precipitous act. She left Colin anyway, went to Paris to study at the Sorbonne and there met the poet Richard Murphy. At the end of November 1954 she informed Larkin that she and Murphy were to be married. He answered tactfully that 'I think I'd better retire into the background of your life for a bit' (7 December 1954), and both of them knew that he meant for good. Later in the letter he informs her, offhandedly, that 'I got this blasted Hull post, and am going there in March'. He had first mentioned the Hull post to Patsy in October. It was one among many that his boss Jack Graneek had advised him to apply for, 'but', he informs Patsy, 'it is true that I shall not' (9 October 1954). He adds enigmatically that he does not 'think that's the answer'. Three weeks later, however, he had almost changed his mind, telling Patsy that, yes, he wants the job but only 'in a way;

knowing that it will mean harder work and more responsibility' (28 October). He repeated for his mother the same display of ambivalence shot through with indecision when called for interview, writing to her that 'it's a bit chilly here – and smells of fish' and describing his approach to the interview as more an act of endurance than the pursuit of an objective. However, one member of the panel, Roy Brett, recalls him as by far the most impressive and self-assured candidate, displaying a comprehensive command of the business of running a library, which he made 'intensely interesting, with a wealth of detail which never approached the tedious. Above all I remember the exact and lucid sentences formed without hesitation and the incisive mind' (Brett, p. 101).

Larkin had at some point made a final decision to leave Belfast. He had been happy there, but the move was an acknowledgement that he had become, more than ever before, unflinchingly, almost dispassionately aware of who he was and what his life amounted to. The five years in Belfast had contributed to this, not by virtue of the place itself, but the place would, if he remained there, provide memories of mutation when what he required was a sense of completion. For those who knew him the move was simply that; a change of place, to a new, more senior post. It neither indicated nor reflected a significant change in him, at least not in terms of the personae he shared with friends and colleagues. It was, however, connected with something that had begun to happen at a more private level in his poems.

The poems he composed during his last two years in Belfast contain the quintessence of what would become Larkin the acclaimed poet. They would form the core of *The Less Deceived*, the collection that effectively altered his status from obscure, occasional novelist and versifier to one of the outstanding voices in the motley chorus of post-war English writing.

'Success Story' is an intriguing piece of work partly because it has been ignored completely by virtually every commentator upon Larkin. It is an uncomplicated reflection upon failure, inferring that his – and the speaker is certainly Larkin – lack of success involves an unrealized literary ambition. The closing two stanzas are fascinating:

> The explanation goes like this, in daylight:
> To be ambitious is to fall in love
> With a particular life you haven't got
> And (since love picks your opposite) won't achieve.
> That's clear as day. But come back late at night,
> You'll hear a curious counter-whispering:
> Success, it says, you've scored a great success.
> Your wish has flowered, you've dodged the dirty feeding,
> Clean past it now at hardly any price –
> Just some pretence about the other thing.

What, he prompts us to ask, has he failed at in 'daylight', yet compensated for with the private counter-whisper of the night? It seems that he has become aware that his governing, overarching ambition was a falsehood, weirdly described as 'dirty feeding' or, more mundanely, the 'pretence about the other thing'.

The poem was written on 11 March 1954. A week earlier he had written to Patsy, caught between admiration for a novel that he had helped to construct and pure envy that it had piloted Amis to a position he had so long craved: 'Success, Success', he had written of Amis in the letter, with teeth clenched in indignation, but in the poem this becomes endurable irony. The alternative to what has been denied to him is not specified, but it does not need to be: the speaking presence of the poem is perversely aroused by failure because of his self-evident mastery of something else, the poem that he is writing.

The letters to Patsy during this period are like a sketchbook of his literary progressions and an index to their promptings. On 6 March he writes that having 'hurled himself' at the novel again he has now, finally, 'packed it up . . . and I am still suffering from injury to self esteem'. Six weeks after that he tells her of his Easter break in Britain, including a weekend in Swansea with the Amises 'which rather put me out of humour . . . I was rather jealous of his success'; that word again, and the newly acclaimed novelist and old friend who has attained it. Ten months later he remains unable, perhaps unwilling, to rid himself of the envious feelings that had become stubbornly attached to a single word. 'I came up from London this morning, feeling pretty tired and fed up after another glimpse of the rich life of the Amis household,' he wrote to Monica in January 1955 and added, 'It's not his success I mind so much as immunity from worry and hard work, though I mind his success as well.' Which brings to mind the passage from 'Toads': 'Why should I let the toad *work* / Squat on my life' when 'Lots of folk live on their wits: / Lecturers . . .' In the poem the question is fecklessly hypothetical, while for Monica he provides the bitter particulars that prompted it.

In his letter of 6 March 1954 to Patsy he reports on his week in the Midlands spent mainly with his mother. On Easter Tuesday they had paid their annual visit to the 'family graves' in Lichfield, and the Easter weekend had involved 'a queer mixture of hell and a rest cure, with a bit of gardening and church-going along with the big meals'. The term 'church-going' rests among his weary report on family obligations like a diamond in the mud. We will never know if Larkin recollected his use of it in that passage, but three weeks later he wrote to Patsy that 'I have been writing a long poem about churches recently that I hope will be finished tonight.' It would be his most celebrated early piece.

'Church Going', like all other poems, is not perfect, yet it shares with a select few the condition of being unimprovable. One is aware of that token of excellence, the contrast between the easy, elegant passage of the words and the immense difficulty of making this effect possible. The register with which Larkin informs the poem involves a mixture of incongruity, discordancy and acceptance. He feels comfortable in this vast, ancient building and persuades us that his presence, alone, as a dry commentator upon its span of false mythologies and centuries of unremembered ritual is somehow fitting. The church both as a physical setting and an accumulation of significances is treated neither dismissively nor with customary respect, but with sympathy; which, via the words of the poem, it seems to return.

The idiomatic coupling of the title is reinterpreted by the poem. This is a particular, personal encounter – not the kind that one would share with members of a congregation. Nowhere, however, does Larkin treat those who might still be churchgoers as pitiable or credulous. The final stanza is a masterpiece of consolidated meditation. There appears to be a covenant formed between his own scepticism and a building resonant with faith, yet he does not force the issue. And one here recollects the sentence in the letter to Patsy containing the phrase 'church-going' where he describes his period with his mother as 'a queer mixture of hell and a rest cure'. It was not quite that he resented having to accompany his mother to church services, nothing so unambiguous as that. His relationship with her was always at once a wearying necessity and a gathering of intimate, emotional registers. It seems appropriate then that this same sense of states incongruous but not dispersible should re-emerge three weeks later in a poem where again he is 'Church Going' except this time he is alone, better able to choreograph the conflicting states of mind that attend his presence in the church. He is able to because he can rebuild them as something else, a poem which like the church building contains and prompts but does not coerce him.

It was not that before the Belfast years Larkin had lacked the mental conditioning or stylistic competence to produce excellent poems. Both were certainly present, but with a few exceptions they failed to cooperate. There is no single reason for their relatively sudden coming together in the verse of 1953–5, but the poems themselves indicate how via a panorama of moods and conditions Larkin began to feel that poetry was his *métier*; not necessarily his choice, as 'Success Story' infers, but at least his accepted destiny.

'I Remember, I Remember' was written in January 1954, soon after his arrival back in Belfast following a Christmas and New Year shared with his mother, Monica, and for a couple of days the Amises. It has him on the train from Swansea via Bristol to Liverpool. As he states in the first line he is 'Coming up England by a different line / For once'. Usually the train went through Birmingham, but this time it stops in Coventry. Perhaps the line was being repaired; we will never know, but of course he recognizes the station.

'Why, Coventry!' I exclaimed. 'I was born here.'

This is true, of course; the untruth involves the person to whom he addresses this exclamation. He was alone on the journey to Liverpool, Monica having, customarily, not accompanied him to Swansea. The other person in the carriage is a fiction, a conceit, and as such a version of Larkin himself. He has this presence ask 'Was that . . . where you "have your roots"?' and in response Larkin offers a retinue of sardonic negatives, each extinguishing standard expectations of a remembered childhood – the garden where 'I did not invent / Blinding theologies of flowers and fruits', 'the splendid family / I never ran to when I got depressed' – and offers nothing of substance in recompense. The absence of anything to report on his past is decanted into the final line.

'Nothing, like something, happens anywhere.'

In 1959, after *The Less Deceived* had earned him prestige as one of the first team of the Movement, he wrote a short essay which took its title from the penultimate line of the poem, 'Not the Place's Fault', and ostensibly gave an honest account of his childhood. His admission that before leaving home he had known no girls and his dry comment that 'How I reconciled this with my total acceptance of Lawrence I have no idea' seem embarrassingly candid enough. It is the kind of statement which could satisfy the curiosity of his now considerable number of fans who after reading 'I Remember, I Remember' might wonder why the poem is a web of obfuscation and what really happened. Of his father's views and disposition, his mother's supine indifference and his own developing sense of entrapment between affection and revulsion he says, of course, nothing.

This prompts the related question of why exactly he chose a self-evidently autobiographical theme for a poem when he knew that in doing so he would have to systematically avoid an honest recollection of his past. In 1956 he offered an account of his personal intuitions on writing poetry to accompany his pieces in D.J. Enright's *Poems of the 1950s*.

I write poems to preserve things I have seen/thought/felt (if I may so indicate a composite and complex experience), both for myself and for others, though I feel that my prime responsibility is to the experience itself, which I am trying to keep from oblivion for its own sake.

This affirmation of a 'prime responsibility . . . to the experience itself' seems at first to be rebutted by 'I Remember, I Remember', but the 'experience' which the poem does indeed capture in an impressively vivid and enigmatic manner is a moment of being prompted to remember and the systematic extinction, at least for public scrutiny, of the particulars of memory. Larkin offers us a picture of his mind busily exchanging painful facts for their risibly fantastic counterparts. Of course we are now faced with the question of whether our knowledge of the actuality of Larkin's childhood contaminates or enriches our reading of the poem. I would argue that it does the latter, because it provides us with a picture of the artist at work and this cannot diminish the quality of the artefact. Our fuller knowledge of the poem's context and background brings to mind both his crossroads theory of composition and the energetic maelstrom of letters that attended his holidays in Scotland and England during the previous summer. His statement to Sutton that in normal circumstances the sub-elements of his character and state of mind 'run parallel' is premised upon himself as the only person with a comprehensive, commanding knowledge of these otherwise separate compartments of his life. He obviously took some pleasure in this during his various reinventions of himself for his correspondents. With poems, however, the lines would intersect, become a crossroads. What was disclosed would be immaterial. More important was the release of energy as these states of consciousness were brought into contact. At the station in Coventry Larkin found his present and past held before him for scrutiny. He invented an interrogator, and the words on the page show us how in his mind he is dealing with the crossroads between what he remembers and what he might have said if asked.

During his Belfast years Larkin became conscious of his individuality as a poet, and he perfected a technique which fed upon his temperament. He was a man who selected and redistributed aspects of himself for different people and different circumstances; he had become a poet who had found a means of controlling and harvesting moments of contact between these otherwise separate dimensions.

Evidence of this is provided by Larkin himself in his unpublished and unfinished piece 'At thirty-one, when some are rich'. The provisional title is its first line, and the topics of the poem involve a fascinating, introspectively candid account of who and what he was.

> At thirty-one, when some are rich
> And others dead,
> I, being neither, have a job instead . . .

When he wrote this, *Lucky Jim* was four months short of going into print, but Larkin knew it would succeed. And what does he do with the time not given over to his 'job'?

> instead of planning how
> I can best thrive,
> How best win fame and money while alive,
> I sit down, supper over, and begin
> One of the letters of a kind I now
> Feel most of my spare time is going in . . .

He was aware, of course, that their private correspondence was the foundation for his friend's forthcoming novel. With this recognition came another, that his destiny lay not with the genre that might 'win fame and money while alive'. He does not refer to poetry specifically; more revealing is his focus upon the kind of letters that he now feels have become at once an addiction and a reflection of his personality: 'letters to women . . . love letters only in a sense: they owe / Too much elsewhere to come under that head'. The poem was begun and left unfinished during the three weeks following his return to Belfast in late summer 1953 after the period spent variously in the company of two women – Monica and his mother – while two others – Patsy and Winifred – received accounts by letter; his curious epistolary odyssey from Mallaig to Weymouth. Now he comes, 'each evening back to a high room', and writes letters to all four. They are, as he states, love letters 'only in a sense'. He is not telling lies exactly ('I'm kind, but not kinetic'), but rather

> Just compromise,
> Amiable residue when each denies
> The other's want . . .

He is selecting appropriate dimensions of himself for each correspondent, and the question posed is whether this technique of splicing and redistributing Philip Larkin will amount to anything more than an emotionally bankrupt, private world of letter writing. The answer is at once implied but blindingly obvious. The poem he is writing is about the poet he recognizes himself becoming.

A coda to Larkin's Belfast years was provided by Patsy Strang who in 1957 began work on a novel which would be published posthumously as *Playing the Harlot*. It is autobiographical, involving several of the people she knew in Belfast and later in Paris, including her husband Colin. Larkin appears as Rollo Jute. Her portrait of him is revealing in that it reflects her sense of loss at the ending of their relationship and something that can only be treated as painful intuition. For much of the novel he is presented as a dry, intelligent, misanthropic figure. Often she seems to be disclosing aspects of Larkin that were confidential to her and which, if the novel were published, she knew that only he would be likely to recognize. Few are flattering. Jute is almost self-mockingly parsimonious. He lives by 'private means', supplemented by 'afternoon classes in Musical Appreciation of the Girl's Public Day School Trust'; Larkin had confessed to her his fantasies regarding school-girls. A thinly disguised version of Winifred is offered briefly as the anxious late-adolescent Arabella, who is introduced to Jute by friends aware of his predilections. In Chapter 15 Jute and the composer Anderson Cully – based upon Bruce Montgomery – visit Paris. Montgomery and Larkin had done so in April 1952, and Patsy's fictional account is drawn partly from a letter he had written to her and Colin.

> On Friday night we drank till late, on Saturday we saw the Monet, drank what can only have been a bottle of champagne each in the Ritz Bar and saw Benjamin Britten. (16 May 1952)

In the novel we find:

> Two months later Anderson and Rollo were drinking champagne in the Ritz bar . . . 'Did you see that?' Anderson pointed his cigarette at a group standing at the bar. 'Benjamin Britten,' he beamed triumphantly. (p. 118)

Larkin, in the letter, states, without a hint of self-parody, 'Today we had better spend in the Louvre, which I am told does not charge on Sundays,' and Patsy's narrator informs us that 'Since their arrival the previous evening they had, between them, spent fifty pounds. And Rollo was regretting every handful of his share.'

> 'What about the bookshop?' Rollo said.
> 'Now, now. Don't fret.' Anderson patted his shoulder manfully.
> 'We'll find it, all right. There can't be more than one shop round there specialising in sweets got up to look like fruit . . .' (p. 121)

The kind of 'bookshop' they're looking for becomes evident as Rollo imagines being handed over 'to a gang of fuzzy wuzzies in the back yard . . . Monsieur want preety pictures of my sister. Rightoh.'

Rollo features specifically in only about an eighth of the novel, but such is the attention given to his presence – perverse, irritating but quietly engaging – we finish the book with the impression that it involves two principal characters – Mary, its subject, a version of Patsy herself, and Rollo. The two of them are alone in the closing chapter, at Mary's house in Somerset. The events and their attendant spoken exchanges seem inconsequential, even discontinuous, a threadbare attempt at symbolism; or rather they would if one were not aware of the recollections that underpin them. Rollo is there to take photographs of the landscape, and like Larkin he shows a dedication to photography as an art through which its practitioner can possess a subject without endangering its separateness. Patsy was also, of course, intimately aware of the fabric of predilections that went with Larkin's hobby, from his musings on the photographs of Winifred to the pictures of themselves together. The closing two pages have him attempting to photograph a deer enmeshed in wire. Mary runs away and is found by him later in the woods, distressed, and concerned about the fate of a fawn, which neither of them has seen but which both tacitly acknowledge as missing. The closest that Patsy and Larkin had come to something permanent had been in 1952 when she became pregnant. She had suffered a miscarriage.

The novel is not an act of vengeance or a dispirited character assassination. Rather it is a perceptive account by one of the few people who had known the different compartments of Larkin's life, the intersections of which impelled his verse. At one point an exasperated Cully tells Rollo that 'I sometimes wonder . . . why you bother to live at all,' but it is Patsy speaking here. She has, in full knowledge of the answer, posed Larkin's fictional counterpart a question and, quite brilliantly, anticipated the reply he, the poet, would offer four years hence, in 'Dockery and Son'.

> Life is first boredom, then fear.
> Whether or not we use it, it goes,
> And leaves what something hidden from us chose,
> And age, and then the only end of age.

Part 4

Movements

9

Conquest

Much has been written about the Movement, and as far as the undisputed facts are concerned little more needs to be said. The term was given its capital letter by J.D. Scott in an anonymous *Spectator* leader on 1 October 1954, but it had for several years been attached by reviewers, albeit tentatively, to a definite article. 'The' Movement referred to a group of writers – mostly but not exclusively poets – who had started to publish in the late 1940s. By the early 1950s reviewers were beginning to notice common features in their work. Most frequently they counterpointed informal, sometimes even demotic, contemporary locutions against traditional verse forms and throughout the poem maintained a prose-like coherence.

Donald Davie, himself deemed a Movement poet, argued that they had revived a Popian blend of accessibility, correctness and journalistic relevance; he called them 'the New Augustans'. The critic Anthony Hartley (1954) thought they had as much in common with the sardonic, conversational ironies of the School of Donne.

The 1953 PEN anthology contained verse by Larkin, Amis, Elizabeth Jennings and Robert Conquest, who edited the collection. The archetypal Movement collection, *New Lines* (1956), was also edited by Conquest and contained verse by himself, D.J. Enright, John Holloway, John Wain, Elizabeth Jennings, Donald Davie, Amis and Larkin. In the Introduction Conquest propounded a manifesto. Poetry, he wrote, should be 'empirical in its attitude to all that comes', should 'resist the agglomeration of unconscious commands' and 'maintain a rational structure and comprehensible language'.

Like practically all other literary groups the Movement has suffered from a general wish to dissociate expressed in varying degrees by its supposed members, which is of course understandable given that few if any literary artists are content to have their individuality compromised by collective association. At the same time, however, the Movement can make a minor claim to uniqueness as probably the only cultural enterprise which is disliked by virtually everyone who writes about it. It has earned little more than grudging tolerance from academics and routine helpings of opprobrium from assemblies of poets, novelists and dramatists who regard affiliation to conservative or traditional habits of composition as the equivalent of betrayal. Blake Morrison's book *The Movement* is acclaimed justifiably as the best scholarly account of the people involved and their work, yet throughout it Morrison's prose puts one in mind of a court pathologist's report upon a tragic accident. Due consideration is given to all involved, commendable acts are noted, but it would of course be unthinkable actually to celebrate the events.

The question of why attitudes to the Movement rarely shift outside a spectrum between stoic acceptance and distaste has not been fully addressed, but the answer is self-evident. Never before in literary history has there been a collection of writers who appear to deserve, indeed welcome, the epithet reactionary. Even the Augustans, with whom Davie concedes tenuous association, can claim to be innovators. True, they venerated principles of order, symmetry and transparency in poetic writing, but they saw these as radical alternatives to the unlicensed indulgences of the Renaissance: something new was happening, the poetic equivalent of the sharp symmetries of Bauhaus. After Modernism, however, nothing unprecedented could ever be done again. Certainly reworkings of Modernist precedent offered, and still offer, virtually limitless possibilities to writers so disposed, but reworkings are all they can be – variations, improvements, sidelong glances upon or self-referring acknowledgements of the work of Pound, Eliot, Joyce, Woolf et al. In short, after Modernism literary history came if not to an end then to an endless network of recirculations. Was the only alternative a return to the past?

Conquest in his Introduction to *New Lines* does not bother even to mention Modernism. Instead he begins by examining how the poets of the previous three decades had failed to unshackle themselves from its influence. While not actually referring to the Auden group he accuses them of giving the 'Id . . . too much of a say' and with similarly polite discretion he laments the more recent 'debilitating' obsession with metaphor, 'diffuse and sentimental verbiage, or hollow technical pirouettes' without naming Dylan Thomas as principal offender. Having pressed the point that the poets of the volume have successfully detached themselves from Modernism and its aftermath, he raises the inevitable question of whether they are engaged in some kind of nostalgic atavism. 'Restorations are not repetitions. The atmosphere, the attack of these poets is as concentratedly contemporary as could be imagined.' Poetry informed by contemporaneity is, he argues, by its very nature new. Just as significantly these poets are the first literary grouping whose unity is guaranteed by the fact that they neither share nor individually pay allegiance to 'great systems of theoretical constructs'; their work stands determinedly separate from anything resembling an aesthetic or intellectual formula.

In 1958 William Van O'Connor, an American academic, wrote to Larkin asking him if he had felt as though he was part of something that could be treated as a Movement, an assembly of writers with recognizably shared characteristics. Larkin replied that he had never even met Elizabeth Jennings, Thom Gunn, John Holloway or Iris Murdoch. He conceded a 'recent and intermittent acquaintance' with Donald Davie and a slightly closer one with John Wain. Amis, he stated, was the only alleged member of this nebulous formation whom he knew well. Larkin's impression of indifference might seem to imply that he thought the Movement a chimera, but at the same time one suspects that he is not so much denying its existence as reflecting his puzzlement at how such an enterprise could have been brought about without any kind of collaboration. In a slightly obtuse manner he is underlining Conquest's point that the Movement was born out of a reaction to recent literary history. Its members were escaping the net of Modernism, and their similarities bore witness to the fact that this exodus could only lead them in one direction; as Conquest put it, 'to be empirical in [their] attitude to all that comes' and to 'maintain a rational structure and comprehensible language'.

The prevailing opinion is that by about 1957–8 most members of the Movement had already begun to disown it, which is not so much an untruth as a misinterpretation of the facts. Certainly during the couple of years following the appearance of Conquest's volume (1956), Enright's *Poets of the 1950s* (1955) and G.S. Fraser's *Poetry Now* (1956), those included in each were taking the opportunity to reflect upon what, if anything, had happened, and Larkin's letter to O'Connor typifies their response, with puzzlement rather than outright denial as the keynote. The factor which caused virtually all of the poets involved so much confusion was the Movement's unforeseen and unplanned advent. Apart from the disclosure by the likes of Conquest that they had participated in this broad, discernible transition and crystallization of literary mores, none appeared to be aware that it was happening. The result was often ambivalence prompted by a conflict between opportunism and disbelief.

In a letter to Patsy in 1954 Larkin writes:

> People like Anthony Hartley and G.S. Fraser are very stupidly crying us all up these days: take my word for it, people will get very sick of us (or *them*; that is, Wain, Gunn, Davie, Amis) and then, UNLESS they produce some unassailably good work, I think the tide will turn rapidly and they will rapidly be discredited. I'm sure I don't care. (9 October 1954)

The last sentence is disingenuous to say the least. He certainly did care, and although he refers to reviews by Fraser and Hartley which contributed to a sense that something was indeed happening he would also have recalled a letter from Amis earlier that year which reads like a celebration of fantasy made real. Along with reports on sales of the film rights for *Lucky Jim* and his daily baskets of fan mail he tells of a recent trip to Oxford and London where of course he was celebrated as the most outstanding new arrival, a poet who could also write hilarious fiction. Along the way he had met Hartley, J.D. Scott, C.P. Snow, G.S. Fraser, Harry Hoff, Ken Tynan, all keen to offer him unstinting praise. 'I feel in a sense that "they can't stop me now" ... There's no doubt, you know, but we are getting to be a movement, even if the only people in it we like apart from ourselves are each other.' In 1960 Amis would dismiss the Movement as a 'phantom', but in truth what he meant was that it was real enough to have served a purpose in 1954–5, when Amis rode its tide of publicity, but that by 1960, when he had published three more novels, it could conveniently disappear.

Larkin in 1954 was beginning to feel left out, hence his only partially successful attempt in the letter to Patsy to disguise envy as indifference and scepticism, but within six months he, too, was moving closer towards the centre of things and his mood changed accordingly. To Enright he wrote with enthusiasm regarding his selections for the forthcoming volume – in which not only his own verse but his 'Statement' on contemporaneous poetry would be included. He comments on Enright's choices as 'well balanced' and, significantly, 'representative' – from which one might infer that there was something which the volume would represent. A month later he asked Conquest if he could look at a pre-proof copy of the introduction to *New Lines*, indicating that he was aware that it would be treated as a kind of manifesto. Larkin offered sceptical comments on some points – particularly Conquest's contention that the new writers had completely detached themselves from self-conscious literariness; not all of them, averred Larkin – but his most telling sentence is:

> For my part I feel that we have got the method right – plain language, absence of posturings, sense of proportion, humour, abandonment of the dithyrambic ideal – and are waiting for the matter: a fuller and more sensitive response to life as it appears from day to day, and not only on Mediterranean holidays financed by the British Council.
> (28 May 1955)

A year before this he had no concept of a 'we' with whose 'method' he might concede affinity, and his description of them as 'waiting for the matter' subscribes exactly to Conquest's 'empirical in our attitude to all that comes'.

Two weeks later he wrote again stating that he was 'glad' Conquest had found his comments 'useful' – he had made some slight alterations following Larkin's letter – and offered further reflections on the nature of this curious community of writers having suddenly discovered themselves. 'I certainly don't think attacks on other people help a "movement": the way to attack bad work is to produce good yourself: that's about all you can do.' Larkin is referring here to Conquest's distancing of the new writing from any given aesthetic or theoretical confederation and surmising that in abjuring the support of association they are guaranteeing themselves a form of courageous unity; they will each be judged purely by the quality of their work.

Larkin felt that he was participating in a moment of recognition, that the features which in his view made poetry important were gradually regaining a just and natural ascendancy after approximately four decades of marginalization. The poets who appeared in *New Lines*, and indeed in the Enright and Fraser volumes, were joined by a thread of affinity made all the more evident by their differences. They had without planning or consultation all been drawn to those mainstays of traditional verse, regular metre and the stanza. These had not of course been abandoned in previous decades, but what made the Movement poets recognizably new was that each was prepared to test his or her own temperamental presence, voice, idiom against an abstract structure to see if the former could be at once sustained, sharpened and certainly not obscured by the latter. As a consequence the Movement reminds one of a room of people painted by an exemplary representational artist – a sense of separateness and individualism within and almost in spite of a shared fabric is palpable.

Conquest had begun to discover the existence of the Movement approximately three years earlier. Donald Davie's *Purity of Diction in English Poetry*, published in 1952, proposes a model of literary history involving regular, periodic tensions between radicalism and established convention. He argues that the latter will always eventually restore poetry to an affinity with the reading public, that 'pure' rather than arbitrarily distorted or obscure diction will ultimately triumph. Most significantly Davie claims that the poetry of the mid-twentieth century has faced a greater threat than ever before from the forces of impurity and that there is evidence of an accordingly decisive return to transparency.

In June 1952 Kingsley Amis was invited to a party in Chelsea at which the first PEN anthology of verse would be launched (PEN being an organization founded in the 1920s to promote international freedom of expression). He was a contributor, along with Conquest, with whom he had previously only communicated briefly by letter. Their first meeting in person began formally enough with the discovery that they had each read Davie's book and found it to be both prescient and encouraging. Quite soon and after a few more drinks their focus shifted to other fields of shared interest – particularly caricature, parody and women – involving appropriately enough a recitation by Conquest of 'Mexican Pete', his own sequel to 'Eskimo Nell'. Conquest suggested that they go on for a late dinner, but Amis, already drunk, had to be back in Swansea the following day and regretfully declined the offer. It was the beginning of a friendship that lasted until Amis's death, and when the latter learned about a year later of Conquest's plans for a collection that would embody Davie's diagnosis he made sure that Conquest was aware of Larkin. *The North Ship* had faded into obscurity by then, but during 1954–5 the *Spectator* had begun to publish several new poems a week which in various ways gave witness to Scott's polemical leader article, including four by Larkin, fruits of his discovery of a more confident lyric voice during the last years in Belfast. Amis had encouraged Larkin to approach the *Spectator*, with whose editors and regular contributors he had become well acquainted since the success of *Lucky Jim*. Amis and Wain, already friends of Conquest, were by the end of 1954 involved with plans for *New Lines* and prompted by Amis Conquest wrote to Larkin in January 1955 asking him if he would be willing to participate. It was the beginning of their correspondence, and by mid-summer they had arranged to meet. Larkin and Monica were to take their summer holiday late that year, in September. They were going to Sark, the smallest and most unusual of the Channel Islands, owned and governed by an aristocrat and having no motor vehicles. It would be another in their by now regular excursions to parts of the UK which satisfied their mutual taste for places remote, mildly idiosyncratic and unfashionable. First, though, they would stay over in London at the Strand Palace Hotel where, Larkin wrote to Conquest, 'I look forward to meeting you . . . I don't know the place at all, but I expect we shall be where drinking takes place. I am tall, bespectacled, balding (sounds like Time), probably wearing a sea-water coloured suit' (7 September 1955).

In their letters each had gradually discovered reciprocal opinions on poetry and during the same period learned, vicariously through Amis, something of their respective temperaments and dispositions. In the hotel bar drinks were bought, jovial informality replaced polite curiosity and both soon became aware of why Amis had encouraged them to meet. The Amis–Larkin partnership had found a new member, which meant that subsequently confidentiality would play some part in their exchanges. Monica was present at the Strand Palace, but in October Larkin spent a weekend unaccompanied at the Conquests' house in Hampstead. Larkin had previously informed Conquest of how six of his nine pieces for *New Lines* were due to appear around the same time in a collection of his own, *The Less Deceived*, but that the publisher was a somewhat obscure, provincial organization, based, coincidentally, in Hull, run by, owned and indeed comprised entirely of a married couple, Jean and George Hartley. Conquest was intrigued and promised to include some reference to 'the Marvell Press' in the Introduction to *New Lines*, partly to illustrate his point that the new writers were as yet unrecognized, even snubbed, by the major houses and partly as a promotional boost for Larkin's forthcoming volume.

Following the visit Larkin wrote to him with details of the Marvell Press, congratulated him also on an essay of his recently accepted by *Essays in Criticism*, suggested a meeting with Amis in London in early January and concluded, 'Glad about the Bizarre – pabulum is very thin these days. "Modèles academiques" – crikey' (9 November). *Bizarre* was a pornographic magazine whose most recent special feature involved what it claimed were French female undergraduates engaged in demonstrably unacademic pursuits. Throughout the next two decades Conquest regularly supplied his friend with magazines and other material that were well before their time with regard to the complexity and sophistication of acts depicted. Nothing particularly perverted would be involved, and it was almost entirely aimed at a composite heterosexual readership, but Larkin remained impressed by its vivid, imaginative spirit. His letters to Conquest are littered with expressions of sincere admiration, such as 'I got the pictures – whacko. I admired the painstaking realism of it – I mean, the teacher did really look like a teacher, and I greatly appreciated the school-like electric bell on the wall. The action and standard of definition left something to be desired – I'll leave you to guess what.' The rest of the letter concerns a Donald Davie piece in the *Listener* on the Movement, specifically its most pronounced antagonist, Charles Tomlinson, plus a modest tribute to Conquest for spotting an autobiographical essay by Larkin in the Coventry arts magazine *Umbrella*. It ends, '*Silky* is not v. good: try *The Fabulous Rosina* 216. Most extraordinary tits, like saucers – Areolae, that is, as opposed to breasts' (4 July 1959). The detailed scrutiny which Larkin brings to erotica betrays the temperamental stamp mark of a New Critic, but what is most remarkable about the letters to Conquest is their likeness to the Amis correspondence. Both resemble surrealist paintings of the mildly farcical Magritte type, where each image is familiar but not quite where it ought to be. The most noticeable difference involves the function and status of women, with the likes of Patsy, Winifred and Ruth featuring in the Amis letters while for Conquest he is mostly preoccupied by their unnamed, glossy counterparts.

It was not that Conquest replaced Amis, but from *Lucky Jim* onwards there was a subtle but discernible change in Larkin's relationship with the latter. Before that the Larkin–Amis interchanges had been for each of them unique. For everyone else in their respective lives, from closest family through friends to colleagues, a judicious process of editing and selection would come into play, but with each other they shared everything. Once Conquest had joined this exclusive club Larkin gradually began to redistribute his confidences, including in letters remarks which though certainly not vindictive carry a hint of envy and resentment. 'I haven't had a letter from Kingsley for ages, despite letters of condolences [on the death of Amis's mother], cheerings up etc. is he cross or just lazy? Of course, now term's started he's got 6 hours work to do every week, mustn't forget that's pretty tough going' (7 May 1957). 'Yes, Swansea's secret weapon screeded me at last, with *some* information regarding his year's experiences [as Writer in Residence at Princeton] but not much. He seems to have spent his time drinking and fucking, as if this should surprise me' (13 August 1959).

Conquest himself has been given due credit as one of the most effective polemicists for the sub-genre of tough, unpretentious writing associated with the Movement, but his role in the lives and work of Amis and Larkin is both intriguing and largely unrecognized. He functioned for both as a strange combination of provocateur and wise uncle.

Born in Great Malvern in 1917, he retained dual US–UK citizenship and after education at Winchester and Magdalen College, Oxford, and war service in the infantry and intelligence corps he joined the diplomatic service. He was working in Whitehall and environs when he met Larkin and Amis, but for both, at least in the early years of their acquaintance, he remained coyly evasive about what exactly he did there. Larkin was caused to enquire about why for instance he had 'chucked up [his] job' which he did in 1956 to become a Research Fellow in the London School of Economics. 'I can't imagine what you are doing,' pondered Larkin; 'is it *research*?' (5 October 1956). Yes, but not quite the kind that Larkin envisaged. Along with his literary involvements Conquest's principal claim to fame is as a political historian, specifically a Sovietologist. During the 1950s and 1960s he regularly produced articles which chipped away at the established middle ground and leftist consensus that the Soviet Union was flawed but profoundly well intentioned, and in 1968 he published *The Great Terror*, a book which showed that the Soviet State had evolved a machinery just as efficient and relentlessly evil as that of its Nazi counterpart. His knowledge of Soviet affairs went beyond that of a standard home-based Foreign Office officer and academic.

Also he provided Amis with alibis and sometimes the use of his flat in Buckingham Gate for adulterous liaisons with women in London, one of which was memorably alluded to in the poem 'Nothing to Fear'. This relates to an incident when Conquest had rigged the door of the flat to cause tape-recorded messages such as 'Lucky sod' to echo reprovingly around the rooms. Their relationship had a subtle effect on the development of Amis's novels after *Lucky Jim*. Conquest never became a fictional presence in the books, but his actual presence provided Amis with a supplement to the interchange with Larkin that had fed *Lucky Jim*. Virtually all of the novels up to the early 1960s engage with the themes of domestic contentment, monogamy, mature and loving commitment and the factors which make each of these variously absurd or impossible. Conquest joined Larkin as Amis's confessor and supplemented this as a magician of promiscuity.

For Larkin he played a slightly different role. If he had needed alibis Conquest would no doubt have provided them, but it soon became evident that Larkin's requirements were of a slightly more introversive, voyeuristic character. 'I greatly enjoyed our tour of the dens', he wrote in June 1957 'and reckon that place in Greek Street is as good as any.' This one apparently allowed customers to take photographs: 'my 2 sets were very mixed – one bloody awful and I enclose it, you can have it (hope the letter doesn't go astray!)'. Approximately three months after this Conquest played a practical joke upon Larkin which, although in the same vein as his tape-recordings for Amis, proved to be far more unnerving for its victim. One morning in October 1957 Larkin opened a Scotland Yard-embossed envelope to find a letter from the Vice Squad detailing proceedings already being undertaken under the Obscene Publications Act of 1921 and informing him that as yet no decision had been made regarding the prosecution of Philip Arthur Larkin. He should, however, make himself ready to attend court proceedings if summoned. Larkin telephoned the library apologizing for an unforeseen bout of illness and spent the rest of the day with his solicitor who eventually advised him that they were unable to offer him proper assistance unless or until a prosecution or warrant for his arrest was actually issued (without noticing that the 1921 Act was an invention of Conquest's). Eventually, Conquest confessed to the ruse and took care of the solicitor's expenses; after he had informed Amis, the latter wrote to commiserate. 'What a day for you . . . The bloody fool [Conquest]. And in his letter to me he seems to think it a bit farcical on your part not to have smelt a rat straightaway. God if it had happened to me I should have been suicidal' (15 March 1958). There is a hint, just a hint, of disingenuous sympathy here, combined with the type-script equivalent of a straight face.

Suspicion that Amis and Conquest would always in some way be the wags and himself the stooge in such manoeuvres is likely to have prompted his letter to Conquest stating that it all 'left a frightful scar on my sensibility, which will probably mean that nude pics will act as a detumescent in future, not that I shall ever have the courage to buy any. You've probably turned me homo, come to think of it. Perhaps you'll be the first to suffer the fearful consequences of this. What?' (9 September 1958). His readiness to take the joke is as convincing as Amis's commiserations.

Larkin's role in the threesome with Amis and Conquest involved a blend of stoical acquiescence and masochistic enthusiasm. During 1955–6 he acquired a presence on the literary landscape that would prove to be far more enduring than the brief flickers of potential prompted mainly by his two novels. *The Less Deceived* went into print in November 1955 with an initial subscription-only run of 300 copies, and for the first month it seemed to have taken the same direction as *XX Poems* and *The North Ship*, disappearing without trace. But just before Christmas *The Times* included it, with generous words of praise, in its books-of-the-year list. This was intriguing, given that no one else had even acknowledged its existence, and this sense of a significant new figure arriving unannounced prompted and often informed a sudden rush to review the collection following the new year. Anthony Hartley, who had recently invented the Movement, wrote in the *Spectator* that he saw it as 'in the running for the best [poetry collection] published in this country since the war'; G.S. Fraser, ally of Hartley and editor of one of the founding Movement volumes, contended that Larkin could now be seen 'to exemplify everything that is good in this "new movement" and none of its faults' (*New Statesman*, 21 January 1956); and the anonymous reviewer in the *Times Literary Supplement* found him to be now established as 'a poet of quite exceptional importance'. F.W. Bateson in the new academic journal *Essays in Criticism* contended that *The Less Deceived* could spearhead a return of serious poetry from the sequestered impenetrability of Modernism to the approval and appreciation of the broader reading public – 'Come buy!' he urged them. And they did. By August 1956 the paperback edition had sold more than 1,300 copies, and by the end of the year the volume had reached its third 1,500-copy impression. Impressions four and five followed in 1957.

Some reviews were less celebratory, such as David Wright's in *Encounter* which denounced the volume as attempting to replace the avant-garde element of Modernism-and-after with the 'palsy of playing safe'. Most famously there was Charles Tomlinson's 1957 *Essays in Criticism* piece, 'The Middlebrow Muse', in which he accused the Movement writers in general and Larkin in particular of 'middle-cum-lowbrowism', 'the suburban mental ratio' and 'parochialism'. Larkin responded, privately to Conquest, by asking 'why can't these chaps emulate Yeats and say simply "It may be a way but it is not my way?"' (7 May 1957). In short, write and let write without invoking some higher authority from which it would be ruinous of poetry to diverge. In Tomlinson's case the authority was T.S. Eliot, particularly his 'Tradition and the Individual Talent' which treated continuous innovation as the necessary lifeblood of verse. 'And why does he think I haven't read Tradition and the etc?' asked Larkin. 'I have and I think it piss.' Larkin's principal point was that the notion of poetry as fulfilling some kind of duty to an abstract notion of formal radicalism meant that its focus would be shifted disastrously from its carefully shaped message to its shape. He had elaborated on this, publicly, in April 1956. 'I am always very puzzled when I hear a poem condemned as "mere personal emotion".' How, he asks, can emotion be abstract and impersonal? Surely, he contends, an emotion that is 'merely' personal is a contradiction in terms. To even recognize it as an emotion testifies to its universality. The phrase is misleading and he implies ill-applied. 'I think it enormously important for us to recognise that what has failed is not the poet's emotion but his technique. What we should be saying, in other words, is "mere incompetent writing"' (*Further Requirements*, p.65).

This piece deserves to be treated as a significant contribution to the Movement's shared, sometimes precariously shared, sense of identity: technique is important, but only as a test of a poet's skill and as a means of appropriately delineating his message. Just as significantly it reflected Larkin's transformation in less than a year from relative obscurity to some kind of public status. Richard Murphy, now married to Patsy Strang, had become the editor of the BBC Third Programme series *New Poetry*, and he had commissioned Larkin to do a talk on anything he liked. It was broadcast live on 13 April 1956. Larkin was speaking to the entire United Kingdom, or at least those who elected to listen to the sophisticated Third Programme, and with merely the slightest ghost of the stammer which would have been recognized only by those who had known him in his teens and early twenties. To Conquest he wrote, 'Is that plum voiced pansy, gobblingly unsure of his baying mongrel vowels, really me?' The statement, despite its protective self-deprecation, is full of self-satisfaction. He might have added, 'Yes it is. I've made it.' He had. In June the *Times Education Supplement*, at the time the professional magazine for both schools and universities, celebrated him as contributing to 'the triumph of clarity over the formless mystifications of the last twenty years'. Apparently prompted by his Third Programme broadcast the *Guardian* approached him in May 1956 to become a regular reviewer, a task he maintained with a sedulous and exhausting balance between opinion and evaluation.

Yet throughout this period Larkin continued to regard himself as if not an impostor then at least an anomaly. He had, he knew, ceased to be an ambitious novelist and become exclusively a poet more as a consequence of circumstance than choice. Now, within two years of this change in his literary persona, he had succeeded, but it was a slightly bizarre sense of success, one that would always invite comparisons with what had happened to his closest friend.

His arrangement with the Marvell Press could have provided material for the kind of dry, satiric realism that the fiction branch of Movement writing was establishing as its signature. Jean and George Hartley blended enthusiasm, energy and naïvety in a manner that commanded admiration while generating, particularly for persons of a methodical disposition such as Larkin, frustration. The press was based in the living room of their early-nineteenth-century labourer's terraced house in Hessle near Hull. The 'contract' for *The Less Deceived* was actually signed three months after the collection went to press, mainly because George had forgotten to draft it. In the end he drew up the kind of agreement more familiar to players of *Monopoly* than book-trade professionals, undertaking to pay Larkin 'an equal share of the profit'. This amounted to brown envelopes stuffed with bank notes, a means by which Hartley could secure his company from the attentions of the Inland Revenue. Larkin routinely began to refer to Hartley, mainly in letters to friends, as 'the ponce of Hessle', partly because his enterprise had an air of the eighteenth-century Grub Street sub-culture about it, when publishing coexisted with other profitably amoral practices. Also, Hartley needed a regular salary to keep his publishing house on its feet and he worked for the popular gents' outfitter Austin Reed, one step up from Burtons and suppliers of his own rather louche attire. Larkin, always radically debonair as a dresser, thought Hartley resembled a late 1950' version of Graham Greene's Pinkie. When he reported, mainly to Judy Egerton and Conquest, on Hartley's apparent addiction to catastrophe he must have seen himself as having stepped into a parallel universe in which the atmosphere of the new literary culture – with John Osborne's *Look Back in Anger* the Movement had been joined by the Angries – was attended by its mildly farcical counterpart.

There was, for example, Hartley's launching of Listen Records in 1958 which would provide the rock-and-roll generation with 33 r.p.m. performances by new arrivals on the poetry scene. The first attempt to record *The Less Deceived* with HMV in London was interrupted from one side by building works and from the other by an ambitious rock-and-roll group. Collaborative realism perhaps, but as Larkin reported to Conquest, 'God I'm so angry I could kick sodding little G from here to Hessle Market Cross and then stick him on top of it' (28 October 1958). He probably was angry, but his account in the letter of the incidents at the studio by far outdo a Michael Balcon film for dry timing and were clearly designed to make Conquest laugh. Larkin, too, would at least have been smiling resolutely as he typed up the piece. Within about a week of *The Less Deceived* going to press Larkin received a letter from Charles Monteith of Faber and Faber, publishers of *A Girl in Winter* and probably the most prestigious poetry imprint in Britain. Monteith wondered whether Larkin had enough poems finished to merit a collection because Faber would publish it. This apparently rash offer had been prompted by the appearance a week earlier of 'Church Going' in the *Spectator*. Monteith thought the poem so astounding that he was willing to offer a contract on the strength of it. Sorry, replied Larkin, he was already committed elsewhere. 'Church Going' had been sent to the *Spectator* in July 1954, but being an organization of High Tory eccentricity they had mislaid it for sixteen months. It would have seemed to Larkin as though God, fate or whatever agency determined the nature of events and their consequences was imbued with a particularly dark sense of humour.

Alongside all this he was witnessing Amis's rapid ascent to literary superstardom. *That Uncertain Feeling* had won him the prestigious Somerset Maugham Award which in turn provided Amis and family with funding for a four-month sabbatical in Portugal. *I Like It Here* was the result, a novel that prompted widespread debate on whether or not the Movement was intrinsically xenophobic and generated welcome controversy and sales for Amis. The *Daily Mail* bought Hilly's ghosted reports on life with a famous novelist, which gave particular attention to how this handsome charmer was, unlike his creations, a loving, family-orientated monogamist. Larkin was fascinated. 'The Amises seem on the way to being the World's Sweethearts: did you see Hilly's article in the *D. Mail* on why she married Kingsley? Didn't equate with my recollection of the facts. God the auto-biography I'm gonna leave' (letter to Patsy Murphy, 1 March 1958).

Larkin's autobiography would in the end be his *Collected Poems*, which make up for their lack of chronicle with the author's veracious presence. The poems written during his Belfast years which formed the core of *The Less Deceived* established a precedent for much of what would follow. At their centre would be a uniquely Larkinesque paradox: he evinces a sympathetic interest in other states and lives because of the fact that they are not his.

10

Detachments

When he arrived in Hull Larkin went through a well-rehearsed ritual of finding the most convenient and consequently disagreeable place to live and then repeating the act. In March 1955 he moved into Holtby House, a student residence, in Cottingham, once a village but now part of the northern suburbs of Hull. To Ansell and Judy Egerton he wrote of his '*not* suitable' lodgings, 'small, bare floored and noisy', and comparable with 'some penurious doss house at night, with hobos snoring and quarrelling all around me' (24 March 1955). How very similar this is to his report five years earlier to Jim Sutton on the 'bleak "Hall of Residence"' opposite Queen's, Belfast, with its noisy trams outside, minimum furniture within and '42 blundering students, who are always coming in pissed or waking me up in some way or another (an outburst of hammering from the next room)' (5 November 1950). After a month he moved out of Holtby Hall to a private boarding house through an arrangement with the university. This, too, turned out to be 'a nightmare' with the constant irritation of a 'blasted RADIO which seems to feature in everyone's life these days' (letter to D.J. Enright, 26 April 1955). Similarly, his move to an apparently superior set of rooms in Belfast had brought with it only a variation in grievances: 'so many flies . . . smelly and untidy . . . dirty marks on my living room walls. Who's going to get them off?' (to Patsy Strang, 25 August 1952).

In June 1955 he moved once more to another boarding-house a few streets away in Hallgate, owned this time by an elderly lady, Mrs Squire, with quieter habits, but again the rooms were cramped, poorly heated and uncomfortably furnished. Within a week Mrs Squire fell ill and announced that her lodgers would all have to find alternative accommodation, which Larkin did with the Drinkwaters in the same street. This time the top-floor rooms were a little more spacious, but one reason for the Drinkwaters' acceptance of a lodger was to provide extra cash for their new and reliably noisy child.

'Mr Bleaney' was of course the result of all this. It was his first full excursion into mordantly dark comedy, and it also began to indicate, while maintaining a cautious film of indifference, his sense of distaste for many people with whom he was obliged to share time and space.

The landlady's dreary account of the previous occupant of the room is supplemented by its appearance:

> Flowered curtains, thin and frayed,
> Fall to within five inches of the sill,
>
> Whose window shows a strip of building land,
> Tussocky, littered.

The bed inspires no comment, the 'upright' chair is one assumes uncomfortable, the 'sixty-watt bulb' – not forty or one hundred, you understand – seems unshaded, the door has no hook and there is no room for 'books'. He adds a dash at the completion of this itinerary, indicating the brief moment between impression and decision. 'I'll take it,' he states. Thereafter he settles down to enjoy the ambient misery and reflect upon his occupation of what is not just Mr Bleaney's room but the summation of his drab existence. 'I knew his habits,' he states, particularly regarding the choice between sauce and gravy, summer holidays in Frinton and Christmas with his sister in Stoke,

> But if he stood and watched the frigid wind
> Tousling the clouds, lay on the fusty bed
> Telling himself that this was home, and grinned,
> And shivered, without shaking off the dread
>
> That how we live measures our own nature,
> And at his age having no more to show
> Than one hired box should make him pretty sure
> He warranted no better, I don't know.

Mr Bleaney himself is pure invention, but the poem is a record of Larkin's imaginings. In a letter to D.J. Enright written in the midst of his farcical odyssey from one dreadful room to another he states that 'Every day I sink a little further' and gives an account of 'this indefinite interim period' (26 April 1955) involving all of the grim objects and conditions that make up the likes of Mr Bleaney's world. It is not, he points out, the fault of 'the town or the university', but, he implies, he cannot be held responsible for the experience either.

In the poem this is transformed, with 'I'll take it,' into a deliberate act of slumming, the poetic equivalent of Orwell's *Down and Out in Paris and London*. Also, the impression of him calculatedly borrowing someone else's circumstances adds an edge to the questions which make up the two final stanzas. Of course he cannot be sure of whether Bleaney was prone to asking himself how he had ended up in a dump like this, which lends the closing 'I don't know' a degree of credence. He is, however, fully aware that someone like Bleaney would not have been further moved to reflect upon whether our lifestyle 'measures our existence', let alone 'grin' at the Socratic complexity of all this. These elegantly crafted musings are Larkin's, prompted by his almost masochistic contemplation of the joyless pit that was once Bleaney's.

Ever since Wordsworth graciously invited the likes of 'The Idiot Boy' and 'The Mad Mother' into his balladic sphere there had always been an air of aesthetic altruism attendant upon making the apparently unpoetic worthy of treatment by versification, particularly when this involved people, but Larkin, notably with Mr Bleaney, began to change things. Never before had the dreadfulness of conditions, objects and individuals been augmented by their presence in poems, nor had the quality of the poems themselves been so improved by this process of mediation.

The mood of sardonic melancholia that informs 'Mr Bleaney' would soon find more to fuel it in the real world. As usual he arranged to spend Christmas 1955 and New Year with his mother in Loughborough. On arrival he found friends and neighbours in a state of concern regarding a curious affliction besetting Eva and of which he had not been forewarned. No specific record of what this amounted to survives, but enough can be inferred from the fact that her GP found he could do little and referred her to the nearby Carlton Hayes Hospital. Carlton Hayes dealt with various forms of mental illness and instability, and in a letter to Judy Egerton (10 February 1956) he implies that Eva was suffering from depression. A treatment was prescribed which allowed her to return home in early January. What remained most vividly in Larkin's mind was his experience of the hospital itself.

> Large and dingy as a London terminus, it was filled with the apathetic or moping inmates and their stolid families and in the very centre stood a tea trolley, at which a small queue endlessly waited. If it was like anything on earth it was like a German expressionist film. Around the walls and corridors lingered the hospital servants (all harmless certifieds) grinning as you passed. (10 February 1956)

This vision of a living purgatory was made no less dreadful by the fact that he had for at least a month been suffering from a persistent stomach disorder and was booked to undergo a barium meal and X-ray in Hull in late January, these being the tests generally employed to identify cancers.

Between his mother's return from Carlton Hayes and his own return to Hull he met up with Monica, and they decided upon an impromptu visit to somewhere which might relieve the preponderant sense of gloom. They went south to the Sussex coast and stayed in Chichester; pretty, quintessentially

English and at that time almost empty. It was here in the cathedral that they encountered the tomb of the Fitzalans, Earl and Countess of Arundel. Larkin scribbled some notes, including details provided by the cathedral authorities on the history of the monument, but he was not sure at present what he would do with them. The resulting poem, 'An Arundel Tomb', would become one of his best known and most frequently cited and reprinted. He wrote it during the two weeks following his tests in mid-February 1956, before he knew the results.

Below the finished poem on the manuscript draft he wrote that 'Love isn't stronger than death just because statues hold hands for 600 years', which is generally taken to reflect the poem's mood of cynical detachment, but something more than this appears in 'An Arundel Tomb'. It was prompted and written during a brief period when Larkin had witnessed and experienced a catalogue of horrible images and terminal potentialities worthy of Brueghel. In the middle of all this he encountered an iconic representation of love as both mortal and transcendent. He would have found this by equal degrees affecting and absurd. The poetry that engages most with the brutal contrariness of life as brief, nasty and pointless while pretending to be something else is that of the seventeenth-century lyricists, the Metaphysicals, and 'An Arundel Tomb' nods sardonically towards that tradition.

Among its diction and syntax is found a light distribution of registers which are, if not quite anachronistic, self-consciously unusual. 'Proper habits vaguely shown' carries a hint of the naughty ambiguity of the Renaissance lyricist, and the words 'lie in stone' would if found in a poem three centuries older than this prompt a suspicion that the verb 'lie' is playing beyond its apparent reference to a recumbent final posture. This suspicion is further encouraged in the final stanza, in which we learn that

> Time has transfigured them into
> Untruth.

Many commentators upon the poem have failed to recognize that its speaker is robustly unpersuaded by everything that he apprehends, that the poem is in truth an affirmation of cynical disbelief both in the significance of love as anything beyond the emblematic and in the possibility of there being something after death. Such misreadings testify to the brilliance of Larkin's counterpointing of the respectful, deferential manner of the poem against what it actually says. I would aver that one poet was patrolling Larkin's consciousness as he wrote it: Andrew Marvell. Larkin would later write of him as 'the poet of enigma, of concealed meaning, of alternative explanation, of ambiguous attitude' (*Required Writing*, p. 252). He is not referring here to wilful stylistic indulgence but to Marvell's ability to lull the reader into a state of expectation so compelling that when the real sense of what he is saying becomes apparent the effect is all the more disturbing. This same interface between predominant mood and underpinning message is the most striking feature of 'An Arundel Tomb', and it perfectly mirrors the circumstances in which the poem was conceived and completed. It was when he was preparing the final draft that he constructed in the letter to Judy Egerton the vivid image of the interior of Carlton Hayes Hospital, and one cannot help but wonder whether his use of the sinister image of the tea trolley around which the drugged and dispirited patients seemed to float was transposed with his recollection of another space, this time empty but similarly centred upon a lifeless object, an effigy to which 'the endless altered people come'. In Chichester Cathedral the tomb and its resonances would have offered themselves to Larkin as an essay on life and death which, compared with his ongoing thoughts regarding his mother and his own imminent date with X-rays and a barium meal, would have seemed impressively, almost hilariously irrelevant in its grandeur. He responded appropriately, and the closing stanza could make a claim to being the most calculated, brutally misleading use of syntax in English verse:

> The stone fidelity
> They hardly meant has come to be
> Their final blazon, and to prove
> Our almost-instinct almost true:
> What will survive of us is love.

Read with emphasis upon the euphoric cascade of verbs and nouns – 'stone fidelity', 'has come to be', 'their final blazon', 'instinct', 'true' – the last line appears to be a triumphant celebration of what it says. But the deceptively innocuous modifiers 'hardly', and, twice, 'almost' assassinate this optimistic motif; an 'almost true' will always be a lie. He sent Monica an early draft and offered his own comments on what prompts our desire to be entombed near our loved ones: 'love being stronger than death' is, he concludes, a 'sentiment . . . only justifiable if love can stop people dying', which, of course, it cannot.

The barium meal and the X-ray disclosed no signs of a cancer, indeed offered no indication of a medical condition at all beyond, as his GP advised, the need to improve and vary his diet.

In October 1956 Larkin finally escaped the merry-go-round of dismal bedsitting rooms and boarding-houses crystallized in 'Mr Bleaney' and moved into an unfurnished self-contained flat. Despite the fact that he would live on the top floor of 32 Pearson Park for the subsequent eighteen years it would be wrong to treat his new home as the mark of settled domesticity. Shortly before moving he wrote to Monica that the thought of becoming 'Practically a *householder*' – including rates, the obligation to buy and own furniture, insuring the contents and so on – 'gives me a sort of sinking feeling' (18 September 1956). He does not explain why, nor does he offer any reason for the faintly apologetic manner of his account, but Monica by now knew him well enough to appreciate the subtext. He wrote also that 'I'm being woven into the fabric of society so fast my head is spinning'. Anything that carried even a remote indication of permanence, including such apparently innocuous activities as choosing and purchasing objects to live with, felt ominous to Larkin; as though he were undergoing some kind of transformation which might lead to that conclusive surrender of selfhood to belonging, marriage.

Pearson Park was a mid-Victorian terrace of characteristically eclectic architectural inference, with tinges of Gothic, Tudor and Baroque all politely suburbanized. Larkin's flat was comprised of a moderately spacious living-room, one bedroom and a small kitchen and bathroom. The living-room window offered him a view of the park itself. Quite soon he had placed a pair of binoculars permanently on the sill and would eventually invest in a telescope. The image of him as unaccompanied observer, monitoring the activities of those passing through the park, became part of the mythology of Larkin. On the first anniversary of his death Amis listened to a Radio 4 programme in which friends and colleagues in Hull had reminisced on his habit of unobtrusively watching the world, assembling, they implied, material for his poems. Amis offered his own interpretation to Conquest: 'The only point of interest was that P had a telescope on his windowsill to get a better view of passing tits' (6 December 1986).

It is curious that while Monica visited him regularly in Hull it was not until late 1958 that she began to stay overnight in Pearson Park. For two years she used a nearby hotel. David Rex, the ground-floor tenant of No. 32 until 1962, commented that 'he kept very quiet about [Monica]', and even though Rex and his wife knew of her 'we noticed that whenever we and other tenants were away Monica would come to stay'. This arrangement was instituted by Larkin, arguing that at least until he had become established in his new post he did not want to present himself as a debauchee. This was nonsense, of course, but Monica accepted it while being aware that in truth his reluctance to share his flat's bedroom was based on his fear of this being one more stage on the route towards permanence.

He wrote 'Self's the Man' shortly after Monica had begun to become an occasional cohabitee. The Arnold of the poem was based upon Larkin's colleague and junior in the library, Arthur Wood. Wood for no obvious reason became the persistent target of Larkin's virulence – never to his face and usually in letters to friends. Douglas Dunn in *Larkin at Sixty* presents him as an eccentric, an acquisitions specialist with a taste for the arcane and curious yet with a tendency to treat books in the same way as the worst kind of collector treats butterflies or stamps, his obsessive acquisitiveness matched by an indifference to their content or intrinsic worth. In other circumstances such idiosyncrasies would have prompted in Larkin a degree of affinity, but by 1958, when the poem was written, his running of the cramped, existing library and supervising the construction of its replacement had become if not as important as his writing then at least as demanding upon his sense of commitment. Larkin was, despite himself, coming to respect the benefits of collective efficiency and teamwork, and Wood was a throwback to the time when academia, including its libraries, was a refuge for aberrance. In Larkin's letters to his mother, to Monica and Judy Egerton, Wood features variously as a 'grinning subnormal gnome', the 'Glasgow bookie' and 'the sawn off little rocking horse of stupidity' over whom he wishes he could 'drive a horse and cart', which might, given Wood's irritating yet harmless propensities, seem a little excessive. But Wood also showed Larkin a version of his recent self, the Sub-Librarian in Queen's, Belfast, who had taken his job seriously only so far as it allowed him to indulge his personal predispositions. Wood's obtuse refusal to conform became for Larkin a reminder that he had now taken the opposite route. This irritated him, and in 'Self's the Man' he found a merciless and perversely apposite means for revenge: irrespective of his behaviour at work Wood was always obliged to return to the demanding conventions of wife and family.

During the first five stanzas of the poem Larkin takes pleasure in observing the grim consequences of Arnold's decision to get married – with 'the kiddies' clobber and the drier / And the electric fire', emptying his pay-packet, the mother-in-law's dreaded presence for the summer, the wife's insistence that he puts 'a screw in the wall', and paints the hall – but what makes the poem most fascinating is its tendency to blur the distinction between Arnold/Wood and Larkin's reflective contemplation of himself. He begins,

> Oh, no one can deny
> That Arnold is less selfish than I.
> He married a woman to stop her getting away
> Now she's there all day,

which contains a contradiction: surely the fact that he married to 'stop her getting away' invalidates the declaration of his selflessness. Eventually Larkin seems to recognize this:

> But wait, not so fast:
> Is there such a contrast?
> He was out for his own ends
> Not just pleasing his friends;
> And if it was such a mistake

> He still did it for his own sake,
> Playing his own game.
> So he and I are the same . . .

Indeed they are, because Larkin, too, had proposed marriage to a woman 'to stop her getting away', Ruth Bowman. Eight years earlier he had written to Sutton shortly after his untidy disengagement from his fiancée, and despite the intervening years it sounds like a prose commentary upon the poem.

> I have . . . learned how *bad* living can be, and am sure that no man should ever run the risk of being married to a complaining, nagging or otherwise unserviceable wife. There is no hell like marriage. And all for what, eh, you just tell me that? Christ fuck! To put forward all one's self control and resilience *just to go on living with someone* – by God!

The poem was begun at the beginning of November 1958, shortly after Monica had spent her first weekend, inclusive of overnight occupancy, at Pearson Park, and Larkin's letter to her of 3 November includes a fascinating picture of how circumstances contributed to the words on the page. He regrets that their recent 'encounter' had had such 'unhappy results for you'; unhappy because Monica's experience of being admitted to her partner's inner sanctum, his bedroom, after they had been having sex for more than a decade had struck her as a sour parody of Victorian courtship rites, and she had said so.

They parted on good terms and as was their custom chose a forthcoming radio programme – usually a play or concert which would hold interest for each – and agreed that they would listen to it while imagining the other's response. Larkin in the letter offered his. 'I hope you liked the music tonight, but it distracted me from you and wasn't really a good idea. I felt as if there was a distance (as there is) between us, only a physical one, but a distance.' Here he borrows from his poetry the entangling of the literal with the figurative and applies it to his relationship with Monica, and the next sentence is added without any indication of causality or irony. 'Funnily enough, I settled to write a short "comic" poem . . . not very good, wanting a last line. It's based to some extent on Wood, horrible cadging little varmint.' It is evident that while 'Self's the Man' was 'based to some extent on Wood' it was driven just as much by Larkin's reflections on his own love life, past and present. The closing stanza has him comparing his state of mind with Wood's on the issue of a permanent relationship:

> Only I'm a better hand
> At knowing what I can stand
> Without them sending a van –

But as he disclosed to Monica he could not think of a final line. After reflecting upon his experiences with Ruth and more recently with a partner whom he had obliged to accept a relationship which was habitual yet informal, unfixed and to his benefit, the final line became embarrassingly insistent:

Or I suppose I can.

He knew that he could, of course, but it was a troubled knowledge.

Larkin's poetic output between 1956 and 1960 was relatively infrequent – on average two and a half poems a year – and in letters to friends he usually claimed that he lacked inspiration. The true cause was at once more mundane and intriguing. He was giving more and more of his time and attention to his job, and when he did have the opportunity to draft poems he found that a single preoccupation took precedence. The circumstances and the perspectives of the poems might be different, but they turned upon a persistent subtext: his sense of separateness.

The best known is 'The Whitsun Weddings', inspired by a train journey from Hull to London on 28 May 1955, the Saturday of the Whitsun weekend. This first experience became a mild addiction. Two years later, in May 1957, he wrote to Monica, 'I went home on Saturday, 1.30 to Grantham – a lovely run, the scorched land misty with heat, like a kind of bloom of heat – and at every station, Goole, Doncaster, Retford, Newark, importunate wedding parties, gawky and vociferous, seeing off couples to London.' By this time the poem was at draft stage, and between 1955 and 1958 he would make the Whitsun journey three times, a silent witness to this curious social ritual. In the finished poem he would, as in 1955, accompany the new couples the full distance to London.

The poem has been submitted to dozens of exegeses, but by far the most telling comments come from Larkin himself both in an interview with Melvyn Bragg and privately, implicitly, in letters to friends. In the interview he speaks of how the newly married couples boarded at subsequent stations 'all looked different but they were all doing the same things and sort of feeling the same things!' and recalls that with each stop it was as though 'fresh emotion climbed aboard'. The previously slow train seemed to have acquired an inexplicable momentum; 'you hurtle on, you felt the whole thing was being aimed like a bullet – at the heart of things you know. All this fresh, open life. Incredible experience. I've never forgotten it' (*South Bank Show*, 16 April 1981).

His description catches perfectly the beautifully executed change of pace and perspective in the poem itself, and it also replicates an even more significant feature of the verse – studied puzzlement. For much of the piece Larkin adopts the persona of the genial anthropologist, a poetic Sir David Attenborough maintaining a balance between sympathetic affinity and objectivity. He records the rituals of this curious other species, to whom he knows he is related yet, for reasons he does not bother to explain, from whom he will remain always detached. The train provides him with a perfect means of activating this sense of ambivalence, because by frequently switching as he does between 'we' and 'they' he leaves us uncertain of whether he is simply sharing the journey with them or if this 'frail/travelling coincidence' in which each couple unwittingly participates involves him, too, and as something more than an observer.

Larkin did not record his immediate impressions of the journey, but it is evident that over the subsequent three years the poem evolved from a mixture of recollection and reflection. The voice that we eventually hear is a polite, circumspect version of its private counterpart. For example, the opening passage in which

> We ran
> Behind the backs of houses, crossed a street
> Of blinding windscreens, smelt the fish-dock; thence
> The river's level drifting breadth began,
> Where sky and Lincolnshire and water meet.

is hardly an idyllic description of Hull but it improves upon his account to Patsy Murphy in July 1955, 'The town smells of fish. And everywhere creep the new cars with L on the front, Auntie Cis and co. learning to drive' (28 July), and his more succinct verdict for Conquest a week earlier, 'Hull. It's a frightful dump' (24 July).

The figures he observes in the poem, the 'girls' 'grinning and pomaded' 'In parodies of fashion', the fathers 'with broad belts under their suits / And seamy foreheads', the mothers 'loud and fat' and the uncle 'shouting smut' all seem possessed of a beguiling transparency. They are not exactly dignified but their honest vulgarity is something that Larkin uncritically accepts. Could these be the same type of people who, two days after his return from London on Whit Monday, he encountered during an outing to Haworth?

> a traumatic experience . . . being jammed among 999 other trippers ('Old ain't it' – 'Here, Luke here' – 'Mam, I want the lav') . . . I really felt it was England at last. What an impossible place it is, really . . . (Letter to Egertons, 31 May 1955)

Or, to Conquest again, 'England at present – God what a hole, what witless crapulous people' (24 July).

In stanzas 4 and 5 he reflects upon the marriages themselves and fixes upon the way in which at each station the train enacts a more consequential state of departure, the sense of every couple having detached themselves from their previous lives, 'Free at last, / And loaded with the sum of all they saw . . . A dozen marriages got under way.' The question never addressed but attendant upon this is of what exactly Larkin feels. In a letter to Judy Egerton in May 1958 he pondered the same notion of transformation, a beginning and a conclusion overlapping, that he had witnessed on the train, but on this occasion conviction displaces observation:

> Life is a funny business. The only way of getting shot of your family is to put your neck in the noose of another one. Such is nature's abhorrence of a vacuum. (25 May)

The closing lines of the poem are a masterpiece of evasion; the coincidence,

> and what it held
> Stood ready to be loosed with all the power
> That being changed can give. We slowed again,
> And as the tightened brakes took hold, there swelled
> A sense of falling, like an arrow-shower
> Sent out of sight, somewhere becoming rain.

The poems ends, but its concluding juggling act between inference and bold imagery will go on for ever. The 'arrow-shower' might well, as he disclosed to Jean Hartley, have been inspired by Olivier's *Henry V*, but this does not account for it 'becoming rain', unless one simply accepts that both images involved things quintessentially English – outdated patriotism, dismal weather and a sense of resignation. Whatever all of this signifies, Larkin gathers himself into it with the collective 'We', and if one suspects that this act of sharing is tinged on his part with a sense of relief that on leaving the train his future will be very different from theirs one should consult his account of a very similar experience which occurred two months later during that same summer of 1955. He had spent the weekend in London with Richard and Patsy Murphy and in his letter of thanks two days later he digresses.

> I had a hellish journey back, on a *filthy* train, next to a young couple with a slobbering chocolatey baby – apart from a few splashes of milk, nothing happened to me, but the strain of feeling it might was a great one – and I wasn't sorry to get back . . . (17 August 1955)

There is something more here than irritation at having to travel alongside a child, and the phrase 'the strain of feeling it might' carries an unnerving echo of the last lines of the poem, with a brief inference in both that such encounters might involve a kind of fate-by-association.

In a 1980 interview John Haffenden asked Larkin if the poem did give 'unqualified assent to hopefulness' and Larkin answered, 'There's nothing to suggest that their lives won't be happy, surely? I defy you to find it', sounding curiously like a conscience-stricken defendant. Certainly there is nothing in the poem itself, but sufficient evidence can certainly be found in 'Afternoons' which might reasonably be subtitled, 'Whitsun Weddings, Part 2'. It was written less than a year later and the newlyweds whose 'lives would all contain this hour' are now 'Young mothers' with 'husbands in skilled trades', the numinous 'sense of falling' as the train slowed become a state of inertia. We know without Larkin having to tell us that the 'new recreation ground' – not unlike the park viewed from his flat – where the mothers assemble with their kids is a dispiriting place, a routine alternative to the 'estateful of washing', where living-rooms contain 'albums, lettered / Our Wedding, lying / Near the television'. As with paintings so with poems, the true artist can make the most melancholic condition the subject of a superb artefact without causing it to be any the less depressing. With Larkin, however, one cannot help but intuit a degree of ghoulish satisfaction in his manner, as if he knew all along what awaited the couples as they left the train and was simply postponing the opportunity to observe that now

> Something is pushing them
> To the side of their own lives.

A considerable number of the poems that make up The Whitsun Weddings collection give attention to the kind of people who inspired the title poem. To categorize them as working class is too vague and perhaps anachronistic. This was the period in which Harold Macmillan declared that everyone had 'never had it so good', a sentiment mordantly endorsed in the Boulting Brothers' I'm All Right Jack where the iniquities of capitalism appear to have been exchanged for a farcical desuetude of traditional structures in which no one is particularly poor and the better off are almost apologetic for being so. Larkin had always remained unaffiliated to a particular political or ideological thesis, probably as a result of having witnessed his father's self-destructive extremism. He would lean by instinct towards conservatism in general, but the gradual transformations in British society set in train mostly by the post-war Labour government hardly registered for him, at least not in a conventional manner. In 'The Importance of Elsewhere', written during the month following his move from Belfast to Hull, he muses on the paradox of how in Northern Ireland being 'not home' had been accommodating, how 'difference made me welcome'. But now:

On holiday with Eva and Sydney, 1939

Larkin outside Bruce Montgomery's Oxford lodgings, 1943

J.S. (Jim)
Sutton, 1946

Amis in Oxford, *c.* 1946

Monica Jones,
1947

Ruth Bowman, 1947

Judy Egerton, 1954

Larkin and Patsy Strang, Belfast, 1952

John Wain, mid-1950s

The Amises in Swansea, late 1950s

Winifred Arnott, early 1950s

Monica in Leicester, late 1950s

Larkin and Monica on holiday in Devon, late 1950s

Robert Conquest,
c. 1960

Anthony Powell, Kingsley Amis, Larkin and Hilly Amis, London, 1958

Bruce Montgomery with Bentley, late 1950s

Larkin with Maeve Brennan, 1961

Larkin on the
Scottish border,
Coldstream, 1962

Larkin conversing with John Betjeman in Pearson Park flat for BBC *Monitor* film, 1964; 'Bun', in the absence of namesake Monica, looks on from desk

Larkin and Brynmor Jones Library staff, photographed from his first-floor office, 1967

Larkin outside Brynmor Jones Library, mid-1970s

Larkin and Monica outside Buckingham Palace following receipt of his CBE, 1976

Larkin and Eva, late 1960s

Luncheon party to mark the twenty-fifth anniversary of Larkin's appointment at Hull, 1980. Maeve Brennan is rear left and Betty Mackereth middle front

Larkin at work, c. 1981

> Living in England has no such excuse:
> These are my customs and establishments
> It would be much more serious to refuse.
> Here no elsewhere underwrites my existence.

This seems a trifle gnomic, at least until one considers how frequently he refers in letters to friends to the mixture of shock and distaste that attended his return to England.

> I'm passing through an anti-English phase at present – they are miles uglier and noisier and vulgarer than the Irish: the pubs here are nightmares of neo-Falstaffianism, coughing laughter well soused with phlegm . . . And the young folk all indulging in healthy mixed activities. And the university staff OOYA BUGGAR . . . (To Patsy Murphy, 28 July 1955)

> I'm feeling a bit out of sympathy with England at present . . . [its] people, delivered over gagged and bound to TV, motoring and Mackeson's stout. (To Robert Conquest, 24 July 1955)

> What an impossible place it is, really: everyone eating rubbishy ice-creams and drinking coca-cola, disregarding the beer and ham sandwiches. Home along the still sweating tarmac . . .
> (To the Egertons, 31 May 1955)

It was not that the Ulster proletariat was entirely immune from vulgarity and hedonistic abandon – although the constitutional system embodied in Stormont and institutionalized inhibition ensured the six counties would always be several years behind collateral social shifts in the rest of the UK – rather that finding himself among a people to whom he felt he belonged made their habits seem all the more abhorrent.

During the late 1950s and early 1960s Larkin wrote a number of review articles on John Betjeman. Each reflects a genuine admiration for the man and his poetry, but it is possible to detect another quietly understated agenda: an implicit positioning of himself as comparable with, separate from and most certainly not beholden to Betjeman. In the longest, 'Betjeman En Bloc' (1959), he offers a critique of Betjeman as satirist and social commentator, particularly his pictures of post-war England, such as

> Civics, eurythmics, economics, Marx
> How-to-respect-wild-life-in-National-Parks;
> Plastics, gymnastics – thus they learn to scorn

> The old thatch'd cottages where they were born.
> The girls, ambitious to begin their lives
> Serving in Woolworths rather than as wives.

In Larkin's view, 'Satire in Betjeman . . . dissolves in laughter and affection before it reaches its target.' Betjeman's is a 'Peter-simplified view of England'; he is 'too much of his age . . . to attack it convincingly' (*Further Requirements*, p. 210). Larkin implies that Betjeman's treatment of contemporary England is condescending, sympathetic and in turn reassuringly inaccurate.

Betjeman's cheerful brand of irony causes Woolworths to seem as picturesque as the 'old thatch'd cottages' and if anyone is tempted to ally Larkin with, let alone treat him as beholden to, Betjeman they should compare this image with Larkin's in 'The Large Cool Store', prompted apparently by his visit to the recently opened Hull branch of Marks and Spencer.

The poem's two closest relatives in the Larkin *oeuvre* are its obvious parent, 'The Whitsun Weddings', and its less legitimate forebear, 'An Arundel Tomb'. The sculpted 'proper habits' of the late earl and countess have been replaced by 'Knitwear, Summer Casuals, Hose / In brown and greys, maroon and navy . . .' This, implies Larkin, is the cathedral of the present day, its well-stocked shelves 'Conjur[ing] the weekday world of those / Who leave at dawn low terraced houses / Timed for factory, yard and site'. Whatever once was worn beneath the 'jointed armour stiffened pleat' of the two fully clothed aristocrats during their 'supine stationary voyage' through eternal repose is now more incautiously represented in the 'Modes for Night' department, including 'Bri-Nylon Baby-Dolls and Shorties'.

> To suppose
> They share that world, to think their sort is
> Matched by something in it, shows
>
> How separate and unearthly love is,
> Or women are, or what they do,
> Or in our young unreal wishes
> Seem to be: synthetic, new
> And natureless in ecstasies.

Larkin is here reacquainting himself with the train passengers and their platformed relatives. This is where 'they' shop, and it also provides the opportunity for Larkin to experience with them a sense of sharing. Monica was quite happy to satiate his tastes for sexy underwear and night garments, and in 'The Large Cool Store' he encounters a commonality of impulse. The closing sentence winds through a stanza and a half and leaves in its wake a sequence of hybrid registers: complaint and resignation, condescension and affiliation, and finally a mock battle between the esoteric philosophy of love and its erotic counterpart, with the former never standing a chance.

Bri-Nylon nighties might serve as appropriately brief tokens of equitability, but three months later, in 'Here', the 'residents from raw estates', the 'cut-price crowd, urban yet simple', are removed again to a comfortable distance, Larkin preferring the 'unfenced existence' beyond the suburbs where 'Loneliness clarifies' and 'silence stands / Like heat'.

Larkin's dealings with the common people, particularly those of Hull and environs, are far too cunningly equivocal to be condemned as snobbish – Betjeman's patronizing affability is more deserving of that title. Morbid fascination with a hint of relief would be a more accurate description. Their lives are a blend of conformity and material ambition with marriage as the common constituent, but not the type of marriage that Larkin feared so horribly. Theirs was the habitual, plebeian kind; something to be put up with, a routine. Consequently Larkin could contemplate lives that carried the emblem of unadorned simplicity without feeling he had missed out.

Part 5

Women

11

Letters Between Friends

Jean Hartley states that while Larkin's friendship with Amis remained 'strong and intimate' it was just as consistently 'tinged with a perhaps inevitable rivalry'. Philip would call regularly at Hull Road during the eighteen months following the publication of *The Less Deceived* and, with Jean and George, pore delightedly over that week's accumulation of reviews and related articles and note with equal satisfaction the increasing number of subscription slips. With a mixture of admiration and stoical despondency Larkin would also give accounts of how his friend's second novel, *That Uncertain Feeling*, published within two months of *The Less Deceived*, was astounding the reading public: most were amazed by how rapidly the author of *Lucky Jim* could produce yet another book which, while impressively different, could so brilliantly paint a picture of contemporary life and mores. 'Philip told us, good humouredly,' says Jean, 'how after reading . . . *That Uncertain Feeling* he complained that Kingsley had cannibalised his letters for some of the material. "Life transmuted into art" Kingsley had retorted. Philip replied, "But God damn it, Kingsley, my letters ARE art."' In truth, Larkin's good-humoured complaint provided only a selective account of the complex web created by the two men and used by one of them with such ruthless versatility.

That Uncertain Feeling is a first-person account by John Lewis of a couple of months of his life in a South Wales town remarkably similar to Swansea. Lewis spends much of his time weighing up the attractions of adultery with the posh and sexy Elizabeth Gruffydd-Williams against the potential damage this might cause to his marriage to the pretty Jean. They have two lovable children, and so far the story is based almost entirely on fact. Amis was a serial adulterer who could never properly distinguish between genuine feelings of guilt and the more pragmatic instinct to ensure that Hilly did not discover what was going on. The novel makes effective use of this dilemma by allowing the reader an exclusive perspective upon the various layers of Lewis's life, beginning with the practical difficulties of telling lies and keeping secrets and graduating to the emotional kaleidoscope of commitment, infidelity, remorse and excitement.

The dynamic of the fiction evolved out of Amis's friendship with Larkin.

While Conquest played a straightforward role in the provision of accommodation in London and plausible alibis, Larkin was Amis's emotional release mechanism, his confessor. Amis's letters to him would mix anxious reports on how he was concealing his latest liaison from the increasingly suspicious Hilly with reflective passages on life as a successful seducer and a family man and its inherent paradoxes. In this respect the letters were a rehearsal for the fabric of effects spun by John Lewis. Throughout the novel the reader's potentially empathetic relationship with him is tested by the growing suspicion that if he were not such a brilliant raconteur we could easily come to despise him. We wonder what we would have felt, indeed what we would have done, had we known real versions of John and Jean, rather than listened to an exclusive account of events by the former. Larkin had to deal with the fictional and non-fictional experiences simultaneously. Amis provided him with a private commentary on his extra-marital activities plus a philanderer's disquisition on life in general, while on visits to the Amises' house Larkin was obliged to behave with Hilly, whom he considered as much a friend as the wife of one, as though nothing was happening. When he read the novel he would have undergone the disquieting experience of having to share all of this with tens of thousands of amused readers, knowing privately that it was based on fact and that he had played the role of reader-surrogate in its construction.

It was *Lucky Jim* revisited, except on this occasion it was the adulterous subterfuge and reflective contrition played out in Amis's letters that had been transformed into the successful novel. For Larkin it would have seemed as though his friend had discovered the key to fashioning all aspects of life, however licentious and paradoxical, into a profitable vehicle for literary fame. A subdued, even tolerant level of envy might have attended this were it not for the fact that Amis seemed intent on continually reminding Larkin of his role as contributor and spectator.

As early as 1953 Amis had written to Larkin confessing that he could not think of a setting for his next piece, specifically a profession for his main character. He had done 'carledge life' in *Lucky Jim*, and his only other significant personal experience had been in the army, which offered too limited a menu of plots. But he did have access, albeit secondary, to a lifestyle that was so mundane that it yearned to be made more interesting. John Lewis becomes a provincial librarian, and the contrast between the grinding monotony of his working life and his droll, expertly timed account of it is one of the best features of the book. Larkin would when reading it have recognized his letters to Amis, particularly those offering caustic accounts of his time in Wellington Public Library. Jean Hartley had either misunderstood Larkin or he had offered her a diplomatic account of things. Amis had not cannibalized the letters verbatim. He had, from Larkin's perspective, done much worse than that by stealing part of his friend's life and reconstructing it in a way that could cause Larkin to feel a combination of bitterness and amazement. John Lewis is a hybrid of Larkin and Amis in the sense that he draws all of his disgracefully hedonistic and undeniably attractive features from the latter and presses the former into service for everything else. Larkin was watching his friendship with Amis re-enacted in a single fictional presence, an embodied double act in which he was an involuntary participant.

Amis had kept Larkin up to date with the progress of *That Uncertain Feeling* throughout 1954, and when they met in Cheltenham in late November he showed him the substance of the final draft. Larkin laughed, dutifully but saved his actual feelings for Monica to whom he wrote in February 1955, shortly after Amis had informed him of having sent the finished text to Gollancz, 'Oh please God, make them return it, with a suggestion that he "rewrites certain passages". Nothing would delight me more.' He was particularly aggrieved by Amis's presentation of Lewis the librarian. At no point in the novel does he confess to literary ambitions, which is puzzling given his dextrous command of so many stylistic registers. To this extent he is an unnerving and pitilessly accurate version of Larkin as he presented himself in his letters to Amis: a man with no enthusiasm for his job but at the same time not blind to the irony of having to spend his working life with the material of literature and cater for the ridiculous range of obscure and philistine tastes of his daily customers. The subtext in both instances – self-evident in the novel and a continuous feature of their correspondence – is that we find a writer with enormous potential and ambition in circumstances that resemble a living parody of each.

Larkin's commitment to librarianship was born out of immutable realities. By the middle of what would be his last year in Belfast he had come to accept that even if he could find a publisher for one of his ongoing attempts at fiction this would be no more profitable than his two previous novels. He knew he could never support himself as a writer, and his decision to apply for such a senior post at Hull was prompted by this recognition. Within months he was obliged to undergo a transformation of his professional life. On arrival he found himself in charge of eleven members of staff, a library stock of approximately 125,000 volumes and library premises that involved a random collection of buildings, including Nissen huts, adapted from other functions. The positive aspect of this had been indicated during his interview and substantiated by his seniors shortly after his appointment. Student numbers would be increased from approximately 800 in 1955 incrementally to at least double that over the following five years. Brynmor Jones took over as Vice-Chancellor shortly after Larkin's appointment and made it clear that it was his intention to pilot Hull to a position which at least bore comparison with such established, wealthier provincial universities as Manchester, Birmingham and Leeds. He initiated what became known as Stage 1 of the library development, a completely new building (which would eventually bear his name) designed to hold a million books and accommodate at least five hundred readers. Stage 2 would expand this to include further space for books and readers and incorporate an administrative block. Provisional plans for this had existed since the university received its charter in 1954 and immediately Larkin began to find flaws, particularly in the original conception of an administrative block which physically separated the main reading area from the principal book stack.

Common sense told him that a rethink would be necessary, but he also recognized that in order to fulfil his role effectively as the chief of this new project he needed more than qualifications in librarianship. As a consequence he undertook a three-month period of self-education in the practicalities of civil engineering, surveying and architecture. By 1956 he felt confident enough to offer the University Buildings Officer, Donald Campbell, revised ideas for Stage 1 – which would be to a large extent implemented – and to use Campbell as an ally in liaisons with the architects, Forsyth and Partners. While Forsyths offered plans and design strategies Larkin contributed practical advice based partly on his experience of the day-to-day operations of libraries and partly as a result of his own innovative concepts of how modern materials, lighting and heating systems could best be made use of. Amis told of how once, around 1960, he was sitting in the senior common room in Swansea when he heard the name of his oldest friend repeated again and again in a conversation between a couple of senior administrators and a professor of social science. Larkin was, in their general opinion, 'one of the best'. Amis moved closer, fascinated that, on the strength of *The Less Deceived*, Larkin was being celebrated by persons who, in his experience, usually had no interest in poetry. They were of course addressing his growing reputation throughout the academic community as a librarian.

Alongside his new role as linchpin in this process of post-war university expansion Larkin found himself for the first time as a boss. His post at Belfast had involved some degree of seniority, but now he ran everything and everyone. He became within a year an image of the kind of benevolent dictator that bitter irony would have caused to form in his private hall of recollections. He had always known that some aspects of his father's temperament and disposition were evident in his own. Now he was faced with a very similar set of professional challenges and responsibilities, and he responded almost identically. When he moved into his large, generously appointed new office during the completion of Stage 1 in 1959 the parallels with Coventry City Hall struck him immediately; ever the dark ironist, he gave the place occupied on his father's desk by the operational statue of the Führer over to a photographic portrait of Guy the Gorilla, more a comment perhaps on the absurdity of Sydney's enthusiasm than historical revisionism. His office became his space for retreat, reflection and control. Access would only be granted via his secretary, which meant that Larkin could plan his day according to, as he saw it, the most efficient division of his time between unavoidable encounters with bodies such as the Senate Library Committee and periods during which the long-term future of his library and its staff could be planned and reconsidered without unnecessary disturbance. In 1957 he took on a new private secretary, Betty Mackereth, a woman he recognized as formidable of character and unwilling to suffer fools or insignificant visitors gladly. Their alliance would develop effectively and amicably and last until his death.

All but two of the original eleven staff members were female, a proportion that would remain roughly consistent through the first years of expansion; in 1964 there were twenty-eight women and five men. This arrangement suited Larkin for several reasons. During the mid to late 1950s most women had been taught to 'know their place', and while Larkin soon assumed the role of the avuncular autocrat, willing to share a joke and play his part in the rapidly forming sense of a collective enterprise, he also made it clear from the beginning that insubordinate or mutinous behaviour would not be tolerated. Women were easier to deal with, and in the light of this his limitless contempt for his deputy, Arthur Wood, becomes a little less puzzling. Wood was male and, like Larkin before Hull, willing to do the job but more concerned with his own agenda and set of priorities than he ought to be. Also, Larkin enjoyed the atmosphere of what soon evolved into a kind of chaste bibliophilic harem. Quite soon Betty and others became attuned to a consensually agreed code of exchange in which matters such as Larkin's eccentric footnotes of dress – bright red socks with sober grey business suit, for example – would be commented on to him by women staff as if they were discussing fashion with each other. And within a year his placing of a spyglass on his windowsill – an extension of his Pearson Park habit – to better peruse and comment upon passing female undergraduates was treated by his women colleagues as a commendable display of appreciation on his part for the best-presented members of their gender.

Even in the unreformed late 1950s one might have expected such behaviour to have been treated by some women as at least heedless and inconsiderate, a casual reinforcement of roles as predator and prey, but Larkin dispersed such reactions with his disarming blend of burlesque and candour. His reputation as a published novelist and poet preceded him, and for a short period he seemed to embody such high-cultural clichés as withdrawn, enigmatic and taciturn, at least until he made it clear to all who showed an interest that this was an involuntary impression, the result of inherent shyness and his long and still unconcluded battle with the stammer. Once all of that was established he seemed reluctant to conceal anything else. His ongoing affair with Monica – still an unusual arrangement for the time – was open to comment, as was the fact that in her absence he showed a considerable interest in other women, usually students. Larkin made no secret of all this, but he also guaranteed that a level of innocuousness would be attached to it by presenting himself as a farcically heroic failure. Maeve Brennan recalls that 'he normally overcame his own reticence by chaffing us, often about our love lives; then having secured our confidence, he would often make fun of his own predicament' (*The Philip Larkin I Knew*, p. 28).

During the spring of 1956 his comments on the attractiveness and dress sense of a particular undergraduate, reading English, had become the subject of daily exchanges comprised mostly of self-deprecating remarks on his part and responses by junior female colleagues on how she would surely be flattered by the attentions of someone of his wit and relative youth – he was still only thirty-four. One afternoon in April at least four of his colleagues assembled at a discreet distance to watch him attempt to chat her up. As Maeve Brennan reported, 'in spite of our [preliminary] exhortations, I don't think he made much progress'. Then there was a postgraduate student – whose Amazonian physique particularly excited Larkin – who did agree to accompany him on at least two occasions for drinks and a meal. Larkin kept his colleagues informed and amused with his sardonic account of the doomed progress of this affinity. She was, he reported, happy enough to tolerate him as an amusing companion but anything further would not be seriously considered. He even suggested that were she to rethink her refusal he would name part of Stage 1 after her; many sections of the library and the rest of the expanding university were each week taking on the surnames of otherwise forgotten local dignitaries, and therefore only a select few, that is the two of them, would know the true identity of this one. She remained uncertain of whether to take this seriously, but Larkin made sure that his staff could always amuse themselves with or explain to newcomers the provenance of Miss Porter's Room, briefly the imagined location for clandestine liaisons between the chief librarian and its nominee and thereafter strictly designated by order of the former as stationery store and broom cupboard.

Larkin was playing two roles. In one sense the gene which had drawn Sydney reflexively to the career and mindset of accountancy was manifesting itself in Philip in those early years of middle age when the opportune and potential give way to the unavoidable. Librarianism was in this respect dryly apposite: it was secure, and it serviced literary culture in the same indifferent, uninvolved manner as accountancy tinkered with money. The other role was tinged, if not quite equally, with parody and fantasy, involving the kind of figure he might have been had librarian John Lewis been real and not borrowed his good looks and seductive skills exclusively from his author.

That Uncertain Feeling fed Larkin's surmise that he was playing the passive, indeed anonymous half of the double act that was impelling Amis's considerable and growing literary fame, and in September 1956 he received a letter from his friend which provided confirmation. As was their mutual habit it drifted between trivialities and matters more profound – as if their shared discourse transcended such distinctions – but one issue rose continually to surface: their letters. Amis had been reading Larkin's, most of which he had kept. It was, he states, like reading an unpublished novel by, say, Isherwood or Hoff, an experience that 'made me feel happy and contented as if I was doing something significant in a significant mode of existence, just like I felt, I remember describing to you, while I was reading Scenes from p[rovincial] life'. He goes on to praise Larkin for his at once engaging and amusing accounts of his encounters with Monica, Winifred Arnott and Ruth Bowman. 'But apart from lots of causes for yelling laughter what came over was [how] you seem to observe women much more closely and sensitively and well lovingly ah ha well perhaps not that than I do' (24 September 1956). Larkin, who had only two years previously given up his ambition to become a major novelist, is informed by his closest friend that his letters are as good as fiction. The novel he could not write is according to Amis already existent in this sad chronicle of provincial lust and farcically distended pessimism. 'Anyway,' continues Amis,

> it all made me feel what a feast is awaiting chaps when we're both dead and our complete letters come out . . . Made me think we ought to try to get back into . . . our old tempo of screedswapping . . . there is a novel there, about you in Wellington-Leicester-Belfast-Hull and I shall . . . probably write it one day, if you don't.

Larkin did not respond directly to this but we can offer a confident account of what he felt. The novel suggested by Amis would involve a picking of the bones, given that the body of their friendship had already been successfully plundered by him in his fiction so far. What would, however, have struck Larkin as pertinent to their respective standing as writers, although perhaps not entirely intended as such by his friend, was Amis's fascination with their letters. Amis had used them in various ways as dialogic rehearsals for his fiction and his comment that they would constitute a 'feast' for critics when 'we're both dead' would have prompted Larkin to consider how his own work might be re-examined in terms of their 'tempo of screedswapping'. He would have recognized that the evolution of the quintessential poetic voice of Philip Larkin through the 1950s had come about not just through his acquisition of a new and better stylistic register but also because he had begun to feel more confident and comfortable with regard to his putative reader. Larkin was an addictive, almost fanatical letter-writer. When he was not producing literature, working, socializing or sleeping, much of his time was given over to composing letters for friends, literary acquaintances, family or lovers. For most he selected personae to accommodate their expectations, but with a small number – Judy Egerton and Robert Conquest to some degree and Amis extensively – he provided a more abundant, comprehensive account of himself, embarrassments, trivialities and self-contrarieties included. While the poems that built his reputation did not of course carry to their readers the same agenda of private knowledge they offered a comparable level of arch confidentiality, at once intimate, informal and cautiously entertaining.

Amis's musings, albeit self-focused, caused Larkin to begin work on the most significant poem to remain unpublished in his lifetime. The ostensible topic of 'Letter to a Friend About Girls' was sex, but its far more intriguing subtext involved Larkin's response to his friend's letter of 24 September 1956. What fascinated Larkin most was Amis's treatment of their friend-ship as at once special, secretive and something that might be worth writing about. Accordingly he made sure that the poem would register differently for Amis and the putative general reader.

> After comparing lives with you for years
> I see how I've been losing: all the while
> I've met a different gauge of girl from yours.
> Grant that, and all the rest makes sense as well:
> My mortification at your pushovers,
> Your mystification at my fecklessness –
> Everything proves we play in different leagues.
> Before, I couldn't credit your intrigues
> Because I thought all girls the same . . .

The mood of sanguine resignation carries with it the inference that his sense of recognition, almost revelation, is recent, confirmed by the first word of stanza two:

> Now I believe your staggering skirmishes
> In train, tutorial and telephone booth,
> The wife whose husband watched away matches
> While she behaved so badly in a bath,
> And all the rest who beckon from that world
> Described on Sundays only, where to want

> Is straightway to be wanted, seek to find,
> And no one gets upset or seems to mind
> At what you say to them, or what you don't:
> A world where all the nonsense is annulled,
>
> And beauty is accepted slang for yes.

Why 'Now', one might wonder? A particular reader would know the answer, given that the stanza is assembled from Amis's anecdotes of the previous decade, and one of these is particularly significant: the wife 'who behaved so badly in a bath' while her husband was watching away matches. In the letter which prompted the poem Amis had told of how he was 'getting tied up with a young woman here, not to say really tied up, just started fucking her what . . .', an arrangement scheduled by her provision of the fixture list of the Swansea Rugby Football Club and marked with matches to be attended by her husband, 'Her meaning being, then YOU CAN SLIP IN AND SLIP IT IN BACH.'

Larkin's statement that 'Now I believe' all the reports of sexual conquest on which Amis had kept him regularly updated does not imply that he ever doubted their veracity. It indicates his recognition that Amis had almost magically caused fantasy and fact to become compatible. He had witnessed first Amis's use of their friendship as the dynamic for *Lucky Jim*; next he had read *That Uncertain Feeling* where the private correspondence between the narrator and the reader is a replica – confessions, reflections and celebrations included – of Amis's with him. Finally he had seen a curious spiralling of the fact–fiction alliance, with Amis's success as a novelist and public personality causing his real-life career as a lady-killer to improve upon its made-up counterpart.

The third and fourth stanzas invite a comparison between their sex lives, at least ostensibly. When he asks, 'But equally, haven't you noticed mine?' one should remember that by now he expects Amis to pay attention to the established subtext, writing. His girls

> have their world, not much compared with yours
> But where they work, and age, and put off men
> By being unattractive, or too shy,
> Or having morals – anyhow none give in . . .
>
> . . . you mine away
> For months, both of you, till the collapse comes
> Into remorse, tears, and wondering why
> You ever start such boring barren games . . .

This is a direct response to the section of Amis's letter where he thanks Larkin for his amusingly despondent accounts of his relationships with women, such as when 'AWA [Winifred Arnott] slipped-off-from-the-expensive-dinner-I-was-giving-her-to-go-to-a-Bach-concert . . .' This raises the question of why he asks Amis, 'haven't you noticed mine?', when it is evident that he has. What Larkin would like Amis to notice, or at least consider, is the ways in which their respective literary careers have interfaced with their lives. Just as Amis had made his life and his fiction enviably interchangeable and interdependent, so Larkin's poetry had become a kind of testament to his dismal retinue of disappointments with women. The melancholic, almost masochistic presence which had come to inhabit his verse had also made it successful. It was an honest reflection of the man behind the poems, the same man who had since Oxford played his role as mordant hanger-on to Amis's witty seducer in their mutually accepted double act.

> I'm happier now I've got things clear, although
> It's strange we never meet each other's sort:
> There should be equal chances I'd've thought.
> Must finish now. One day perhaps I'll know
> What makes you be so lucky in your ratio
> – One of those 'more things', could it be? *Horatio*

The speculative circling is arch and rhetorical. Of course he knows why they never 'meet each other's sort' or what makes him so 'lucky' in his 'ratio'. That knowledge is a condition of his having 'got things clear', but he is content to play his role of dismal failure in this rich and varied pageant of male philandering.

'Horatio' was of course a figure in *Hamlet*, the old university friend of the Prince left alive to tell the story, which seems appropriate. Amis, too, had lived beyond his fictions. His principal male characters seemed always to get away with so much that credibility was threatened. But it and they survived, just like their author in his reckless pursuit of excitement beyond the ordinary. Alternatively Larkin is the failed novelist, the poet who has found his natural accomplishment in fashioning the elegant text from irredeemably depressing material.

There is an almost cruelly appropriate and risible appendix to Larkin's reflections. In October 1957 he sent Amis a rough first draft of the piece, and the latter replied that it 'sounds like an absolutely fucking marvellous idea . . . But don't get me wrong (though I suppose it needn't be "me" in the poem); what I mean is I am no Don J. at all, really, I merely work a pennyworth of fucking in with an intolerable deal of wire pulling' (9 November 1957). There is no record of Larkin's response, but one might safely assume that at this point he was slightly puzzled by Amis's inference that the 'absolutely fucking marvellous' idea was Larkin's own. Amis continues that 'it [the poem] might easily stir me to a reply, not a polemical one of course, but a further discussion of the points you raise'. It might all, he states, be 'bumper fun' and concludes, without a hint of irony, 'Or isn't that in tune with your original conception?' Well, no, Larkin would have mused, given that the poem was a thoughtful response to Amis's own enthusiastic 'original conception' in the letter of September 1956. After dismissing the off-chance that Amis might have been visited by a bout of clinical amnesia, it is possible that Larkin's taste for self-lacerating dark comedy would have prompted him to see the 'friend' of the poem as an even more accurate picture of Amis than he had first imagined. The preening false modesty of 'I am no Don J. at all' was apt. Amis had variously overlooked and forgotten screeds of past reports on his Don Juanish conquests, his cannibalization of their friendship for his own literary purposes and, apparently, his original suggestion – that they write about all this – which had prompted Larkin to compose the poem. The image of the 'friend' in the poem as so magically successful that such irritating encumbrances as memory can be sidelined is superbly accurate. Larkin did not send Amis any further drafts of the poem and the latter forgot about it completely, which is consistent with the impression Amis had left upon him during one of their meetings in London a couple of months earlier. To Judy Egerton Larkin wrote,

> Three old friends – myself, B and K [Bruce Montgomery and Kingsley] – met in London . . . last week . . . Kingsley has less and less conception of talking to you: you are simply an audience, and the more intelligent the better, since the better you can appreciate him. (4 August 1957)

On at least three occasions Larkin thought seriously about publishing the poem. In 1970, for instance, he wrote to Anthony Thwaite, then literary editor of the New Statesman, for his opinion and Thwaite replied that he thought it excellent, would be willing to publish it but asked if in doing so it might cause embarrassment to 'The Friend' who, Thwaite assumed, might be Amis or Conquest. Larkin avoided identifying the Friend as indeed Amis and instead offered an account of the poem as more inventively hypothetical than autobiographical.

> . . . in the eyes of the author, his friend got all the straightforward, easy girls and he got all the neurotic difficult ones, leaving the reader to see that in fact the girls were all the same and simply responded to the way they were treated. In other words the difference was in the friends and not in the girls. (19 March 1970)

One wonders whether this was prompted by a wish to protect his and Amis's private lives or a more complex, private inclination. Evidence would suggest the latter, because in fact the exegesis offered in the letter to Thwaite is actually lifted from Amis's letters to Larkin which pre-date the poem. For example, after advising Larkin on his relationship with Winifred Arnott (21 January 1953) Amis offers a general observation: 'it isn't that the girls [we meet] are different, it's just that we meet them differently'. A couple of months later Amis returns to this theme, contending that 'I'm *right* about girls taking colour from their squires . . . Let me tell you son; *they all do*' (3 March 1953). Larkin's letter to Thwaite was intended as the final move in the game of literary chess begun by Amis in 1956 when he first suggested that their correspondence would prove to be a kind of complex subscript to their literary output. He knew that Thwaite would keep the letter and that one day someone would puzzle over its curious promptings. It was Larkin's studied contribution to what Amis had called the 'feast awaiting chaps when we're both dead and our . . . letters come out'.

'Letter to a Friend About Girls' provides a fascinating glimpse into the nature of a distended, unequal literary partnership and less blatantly into the partnership between its author and his verse. It is unnervingly candid, and although its subject gives cause for prurient raptness there is something else far more central to a proper appreciation of Larkin's poetry which should engage our attention. Amis knew there was a feature of Larkin's letters that intrigued him but, distractedly selfish as he was, thought they reminded him of fiction. What he should have noticed was that Larkin the letter-writer, who had become to him as familiar and companionable a presence as the embodied version, bore a striking resemblance to Larkin the poet.

For those closest to him he reserves in his letters a characteristic blending of intimacy, focusing upon matters exclusive to both of them, with a bravura, entertaining display of self-flagellation. This mixture is leavened by accounts of events and occurrences with no obvious intrinsic significance – the train being late, the wind strong, the Library Committee meeting in a week's time, etc. – but which become part of the texture of the letter in the same way that the background of a good painting or photograph becomes a dimension of its subject. This same choreography of disclosure and setting operates in his best poems. The most significant difference – apart of course from Larkin's stylistic dexterity as a versifier – manifests itself in the reason for his choice of material and adjustments of persona. In the letters these would alter according to the nature of his relationship with the recipient – his letters to Monica and Amis, for example, differ in predictable and obvious ways – but in the poems, too, there are reconfigurations of tone and substance. In both cases Larkin is offering different dimensions of himself, and while the former is dependent exclusively upon the identity of the recipient the latter provides Larkin with the opportunity for eclecticism.

His life by the end of the 1950s was on the face of things assembled from a reliable schedule of routines both personal and professional, but it was when these factors began to overlap and intersect that he became more aware of the key questions that attended them. These questions had no obvious answers, nor even did they demand to be addressed. They did, however, provide the driving force for his poetry.

12

Maeve

Larkin's relationship with Monica had become unconventionally predictable in the sense that she had accepted his wish that their time together involve what amounted to recreational suspensions of other commitments. This began to change, however, in 1959. In early October her mother died unexpectedly of a heart attack, an occurrence that accelerated her father's decline. He had been ill with cancer for more than a year and effectively gave up resistance following his wife's death. He died in early December. Larkin wrote her a letter incorporating standard reflections upon 'how thin the surface of life is' and imagining that she would be 'simultaneously ravaged and numbed' by the loss of her mother (13 October 1959). He attended neither of their funerals, nor did he offer any assistance with the at once distressing and practical problems that awaited Monica in Stourport-on-Severn where she had to deal with solicitors, disposal of house and contents and all the other tasks faced by the only living relatives of the recently deceased. Monica was disappointed but not particularly surprised by this. She had gradually come to recognize in Philip a trait he shared with his mother: a tendency to observe the formalities of concern for other people's distress while reserving virtually all of one's emotional and indeed physical resources for matters much closer to home.

Larkin's concern for Monica was genuine in the sense that only the vilest hypocrite would dissemble when enquiring of their lover 'How is your father this weekend?' and empathizing with the 'awful mixture of regret and sorrow' (26 November 1959) that attended her time with a man recently widowed and terminally ill. Monica's father had, as Larkin suspected, little more than a week to live when he wrote this, and if one were to harbour any doubts regarding his sincerity then a reading of the rest of the letter would invalidate them. As is his habit he shifts focus and mood continuously, but on this occasion one can discern a desperate though unstated subtext. He piles in information regarding 'your rolls of pink toilet paper at my elbow . . . their only significance is that I've been too lazy to put them away'. He even includes the name of their manufacturer – 'only just discovered Bronco' – and adds that 'well its curious to begin a letter in this way'. Indeed it is, and even more curious to leave a sentence such as that as it stands and then launch into a manic display of randomness incorporating, breathlessly, his experience of a recent Italian film, battered pikelets with two glasses of milk, the problem of obtaining screws for his particularly heavy bedroom mirror, the SCR Kitchen Committee, Geoffrey Grigson, Richard Hoggart, Aude, and the satiating effects of Chinese food. This is the unmistakable sign of someone shy of disclosing genuine emotion. Panic has set in, verbal rambling has taken over, and the fact that Larkin exhibits this in a letter testifies to the intensity of his feelings. Normally such disordered prolixity would only affect speech, but for Larkin letters had become so closely interwoven with his emotional and mental fabric that he is typing without control, filling the page with anything that comes to mind to put off for as long as possible his engagement with Monica's ongoing state of distress. This veers between the embarrassing and the endearing – given that his pain, though differently founded, seems almost equal to hers – but hypocritical it is not.

None the less his distress was comprised partly of fear. There was no obvious reason why the loss of her parents should affect the practicalities of Monica's life in that she had not chosen to live in Leicester because of them, and until their final months neither had made particular demands upon her, but Larkin was faced with the question of how her sudden experience of isolation might cause her perhaps even subliminally to seek more from her relationship with him.

'Letter to a Friend About Girls' had existed in several drafts since 1956, but in the months following Monica's mother's and then her father's deaths Larkin returned to it again and again to finalize the two closing stanzas, which would remain unaltered after January 1960 and are present in *Collected Poems*. It is here that he gives a detailed account of the 'different gauge of girl' that makes up his and certainly not Amis's experience. She is apparently 'unattractive', 'too shy', possessed of 'morals', reluctant to 'give in' and would in any event 'go quite rigid with disgust / At anything but marriage'. This is certainly not a description of Monica or Patsy Strang, and few if any would find a convincing resemblance between the figure in the poem and Ruth Bowman or Winifred Arnott despite Larkin's persistent lack of success with the latter. So is this person an assembly of the characteristics he most dislikes but feels, masochistically, that he probably deserves? Perhaps, but one cannot help but give attention to the chronology of events that attends this poem.

During 1959 Larkin enhanced his reputation as a thoughtful, benevolent boss by starting classes for those members of his staff who wanted to take the Library Association Registration examination as the foundation for a long-term career. Seven signed up in early 1960, but by mid-summer all but one had dropped out. Maeve Brennan had spoken only occasionally to Larkin before enrolling for his classes, but as the numbers declined he began to suggest that they meet informally, and by late summer 1960 she, Larkin and the Rexes, a young couple then occupying the ground floor of 32 Pearson Park, regularly made up a 'foursome' for films, drinks, parties and on one occasion an Acker Bilk concert.

Maeve, as she herself accepted, was not a classically handsome woman, her physiognomy incorporating some of the combative, well-defined features that we more readily associate with maleness. She was not only a practising Roman Catholic but one who regarded her Church's regulations, particularly regarding sex, as more than arbitrarily imposed rules, as necessary adjuncts to a faith that underpinned any proper understanding of the world and the human condition. Larkin, when he finished stanzas 3 and 4 of 'Letter to a Friend', knew of Maeve and knew that she would be likely to enrol for his classes. Orwell and Huxley are traditionally cited as the chief twentieth-century journeymen of prophetic literature, but perhaps Larkin in 'Letter to a Friend' was staking his claim as practitioner of a very private, self-fulfilling offshoot of the genre.

Maeve states that during 1960 her 'friendship with Philip Larkin was still entirely Platonic' (*The Philip Larkin I Knew*, p. 38). In formal terms this is true, but the fact that Larkin was self-consciously honest about his ongoing relationship with Monica, and Maeve similarly candid about her steady boyfriend (only ever referred to since as 'Philip C'), suggests that a rehearsal for something potentially more than Platonic was taking place, particularly given that neither introduced the other to their respective partners. Larkin first made his intentions explicit in February 1961. Maeve had just passed her Library Association examination, and they had gone out for a celebratory meal in the Beverley Arms, in the agreeably antique town of that name some seven miles north of Hull city. Afterwards icy pavements provided the opportunity for gentlemanly supportive contact which Larkin translated to an unambiguous embrace in the taxi home. Maeve: 'from that evening our friendship entered a new and headier phase which was to have greater significance than either of us could have envisaged then' (pp. 38–9). This new and headier phase involved Larkin, while remaining respectful of her religious convictions, attempting to persuade Maeve to have sex with him, and for those with whom they worked and socialized it became evident that theirs was now more than a friendship. Foursomes became twosomes, and in the library an unspoken convention was observed that when Larkin entered Maeve's office towards the end of the working day everyone else would leave it.

Gradually he began to replicate, with appropriate adjustments, aspects of his relationship with Monica. They would read literature together – Sassoon, Owen, Betjeman, Hardy, Yeats – and as a potential bridge between their differences Larkin avowed a particular enthusiasm for Evelyn Waugh as one who combined devoutness with cynicism. While Monica was Bunny or Bun and regularly in receipt of gifts from Larkin which maintained the rabbit theme – tea cosies, wooden models and ornaments, etc. – Maeve became Miss Mouse or simply Mouse. From 1961 to 1972 they would read and read to each other ongoing novels, six in total, by Margery Sharp. These were intended for children and involved principally Miss Bianca, a rodent of almost aristocratic bearing who lived in a Porcelain Pagoda and was the favourite of the Ambassador's son. She was the Embassy mouse, Secretary and later President of the Mouse Prisoner's Aid Society and attended regularly by a rather dim mouse-slave called Bernard.

The fact that Larkin had begun to lead a double life is beyond dispute, but the fascinating question of why exactly he chose to do so still awaits a satisfactory answer. His relationship with Monica was unconventional, a curious amalgam of the clandestine and the predictable, and even though he might have feared further demands for security on her part following her parents' deaths, a tentative relationship with another woman for whom sex, marriage, fidelity and permanence were virtually synonymous would seem an unwise alternative, let alone an escape route.

Maeve herself reflected upon this more than two decades after their relationship had ended.

> Philip's fundamental ambivalence towards marriage, in spite of his occasional assertions to the contrary, prevented him from making a decisive choice between Monica Jones and me, and in effect, put a stop to any significant development in our relationship. As long as Monica was in Leicester and I in Hull the choice was not forced upon him. Furthermore, I too refused to confront my instinctive misgivings about marriage with Philip; still less did I want to contemplate the future without him. (*The Philip Larkin I Knew*, p. 50)

First of all one should note that she concedes, albeit implicitly, that he had changed her. Had she not come to accept what she charitably refers to as his 'ambivalence towards marriage' she would not have tolerated what she eventually recognized as her status as subordinate mistress. Certainly their relationship was known of in Hull, but elsewhere Larkin made sure that as few people as possible had any knowledge of Maeve. A year after Larkin's death Amis wrote to Conquest: 'I never heard a word about her except that solitary "Maeve wants to marry me" blurting; you too, I think. He didn't half keep his life in compartments.' He adds, with customary tact, 'and bollock her for trying to grab Philip for the Church'. How different this is from Jean Hartley's picture of things in her *Guardian* obituary of Maeve: 'Over the years as we met at parties, dinners, plays and poetry readings, it was clear that

Maeve and Philip were very much in love' (*Guardian*, 19 June 2003).

How exactly Monica became aware that Larkin was seeing someone else on more than friendly terms is unclear – although given that she visited Hull virtually every month and was on good terms with most of Larkin's acquaintances there some kind of deliberate or accidental disclosure was inevitable. He certainly gave nothing away, and it was during early 1961 that Monica first began asking him if it was true that he was indeed pursuing an interest in another woman. He could do no other than admit the existence of Maeve and concede that he was seeing her regularly, but he assured Monica that the arrangement was more sociable than sexual and that even if he were tempted to take things further – not that he would, of course – Maeve's religious convictions would rule out congress. She did not believe him. One is struck most of all in his letters to Monica during this period not so much by Larkin's tendency towards dissimulation as by his curious manner. He is sincere, even repentant, but all the time he gives the impression that his feelings are generated by matters beyond the control of either of them. 'I'm terribly sorry you feel so miserable these days, though not surprised – it is a most trying position to be in, and I should hate it and feel utterly down and out, hopeless, scared to death, just as you do' (1 January 1961). This resembles condolences to a recently bereaved close friend. It does not sound like a lover attempting to either excuse or disguise his potential infidelities, and the fact that it was sheds some light on the nature of his relationship with Monica. He cared for her, needed her, but his feelings were beset by, even dependent upon, what we might call perverseness but which prior to the nineteenth century had been regarded by many as the norm in human affairs.

On first reading an eighteenth-century novel such as Richardson's *Pamela* most of us are puzzled by what appear to be inconsistencies of characterization, with people apparently able to avow ideals of commitment and fidelity, behave as if these did not exist and not feel the need for explanation, let alone guilt. Richardson was, unwittingly perhaps, a commendable realist in that his society treated morality, faith, veracity and other vaunted intangibles as useful but, like the judiciary, only when necessary and practicable. Larkin, at least with regard to Monica, could have walked out of a 200-year-old novel. In 1955 he had gone so far as to broach the subject of marriage, not a proposal exactly, more a cautious reflection upon the benefits and drawbacks for both of them. He noted that, given his elevation to a better-paid, more senior post, 'this would be a good point to do so. I have a living wage, you want to pack up your job [as early as 1955 Monica had become disenchanted with academia, particularly the growing pressure to publish], we both want – or think we want – the same kind of life' (29 January 1955). He continues, listing the circumstantial conditions that urge a serious consideration of marriage ('And we are ageing!'). What follows is fascinating. 'I would sooner marry you than anyone else I know, and in any case I don't want to lose you. The sort of thing that gives me pause (paws) is wondering whether I do more than just like you very, very much and find it flattering and easy to stay with you . . . Is it right to marry without feeling "quite sure"? But am I the kind of person ever to feel "quite sure"?'

Exactly how Monica felt on being informed that Larkin would 'sooner marry you than anyone else I know' goes unrecorded, but it is possible that she would have been reminded of, say, her successful job interview at Leicester ('you proved to be the best candidate in an impressive field', etc.). Thereafter Larkin seems almost to forget that he is addressing his potential fiancée and shifts to a self-absorbed diary manner – 'Is it right . . .', 'But am I . . .' So even before he started a long-term relationship with Maeve Monica had become accustomed to her dual role as sexual partner and recipient of Larkin's disinterested musings on the nature of sex, relationships, marriage, permanence et al.

Larkin's relationship with Maeve lasted seventeen years, from 1961 to 1978, and, outstandingly, the sense of uncertainty and tension that attended its opening period became habitual. Hardly a year went by without him having to convince Monica either that she was overreacting to a relatively innocuous arrangement, that a break-up with Maeve was imminent or that whatever happened she was the one he held in highest regard and would remain as his long-term partner. Maeve experienced a collateral though far more devious strategy of retention. From the beginning Larkin was honest with her about Monica, but he convinced Maeve that he was attracted, not simply attracted but drawn, to her because he felt that there was something about her that Monica lacked. He did not indicate explicitly that he would be willing to re-examine his agnosticism in deference to her fabric of beliefs and commitments, but gradually he insinuated that these same beliefs were part of her fascination for him. In her book on her relationship with Larkin Maeve gives extraordinary emphasis to what she calls his 'moment of ecstasy' letter, which she only discovered six years after his death. It was written in 1943 to Sutton and is made up of pseudo-Lawrentian pronouncements on how spirituality and sensualism had long been misrepresented as antitheses. Maeve, however, treats the letter as confirmation of her sense that Larkin's irreligiousness was a temperamental shield against his deferred sense of an inner self. At one point she analyses the letter's imagery. 'Larkin begins by comparing man's life to a flower which, in its seminal stages, spends months in the ground, unseen and forgotten, until it blooms and has its moment of ecstasy. Unlike man, the flower does not seek to hasten its moment of glory' (*The Philip Larkin I Knew*, p. 74). Larkin is speculating upon sexuality, and for Maeve this strikes a very personal chord, particularly regarding the sense of patience and understanding that accompanied his confessed sexual desire for her. On the one hand, it reassured her of his basic qualities as a good man and, on the other, it indicated that, at a fundamental level, regarding a belief in something more than the tactile which Larkin had repressed since his early twenties, they were as one.

Larkin was living two lives, certainly, but it would be simplistic, even inaccurate, to describe his division of himself between Monica and Maeve as involving deceit or fabrication. He sometimes told lies for practical purposes, yet for each of them he was the real Philip Larkin, real in the sense that Amis, shrewd as ever, commented: 'He didn't half keep his life in compartments.' The contents of these compartments were only allowed access to each other for one purpose, as the impetus for poems.

In January 1960 he wrote but never published 'None of the books have time', a rumination upon the supposedly clear distinction between selflessness and selfishness. Books apparently make selflessness 'sound a superior way / Of getting what you want'. Larkin disagrees. 'It isn't at all.'

> Selflessness is like waiting in a hospital
> In a badly-fitting suit on a cold wet morning.
> Selfishness is like listening to good jazz
> With drinks for further orders and a huge fire.

This was written shortly after Monica first began to suspect that he was seeing someone else, and he appears to be advocating, or accepting, the victory of the inexorable over the self-determined. The similarities between this and his letter to Monica on how both of them seemed to have been overtaken by events beyond their control is stunning: they were written on the same day, 1 January 1961.

Almost two years later, when his double life was fully established, Larkin returned to the draft of the poem and rewrote it as 'Love', which is worth quoting in full.

> The difficult part of love
> Is being selfish enough,
> Is having the blind persistence
> To upset an existence
> Just for your own sake.
> What cheek it must take.
>
> And then the unselfish side –
> How can you be satisfied,
> Putting someone else first

> So that you come off worst?
> My life is for me.
> As well ignore gravity.
>
> Still, vicious or virtuous,
> Love suits most of us.
> Only the bleeder found
> Selfish this wrong way round
> Is ever wholly rebuffed,
> And he can get stuffed.

The most obvious change is that here selfish and unselfish inclinations demand action by the person doubly inclined, but the third stanza solidly maintains the first draft's mood of emotional indifference and adds a practical point – don't be found out. Four years after this, in autumn 1966, following one of their by then almost routine crises regarding the existence and status of Maeve, Larkin wrote Monica two letters which are effectively prose explorations of the cruelly specified instincts of both poems. The letters were prompted specifically by the fact that Larkin had told Maeve that she could write to him while he was staying with Monica. He apologizes for this, rather complacently, and then reflects, 'I suppose I am trapped by my personality, which of course is made by circumstances: I've never in my life felt I had a free will, have you?' which catches perfectly the poem's curious sense of inclination without choice or responsibility. As he puts it, 'My life is for me. / As well ignore gravity.' Significantly there is a particular exception to his general notion of there being no such thing as free will. 'Then you see people like Kingsley' (15 September 1966), who two years before had left his wife and family and begun a relationship with Elizabeth Jane Howard: and we are back again to 'Letter to a Friend About Girls'.

In another letter to Monica a month later he declares, 'I *am* at home with you and think you are delightful and irreplaceable: I hate it when you go, for the dreary failure and selfishness on my part it seems to symbolize – this is nothing to do with Maeve, you've always come before her: it's my own unwillingness to give myself to anyone else that's at fault – like promising to stand on one leg for the rest of one's life' (8 October 1966). In a twisted way he was being honest with Monica; twisted because while the actuality of betrayal could be disclosed, the true nature of the act should remain secret:

> Only the bleeder found
> Selfish this wrong way round,
> Is ever wholly rebuffed.

Six weeks before the letter to Monica he had written to Maeve that he 'thought a lot of you [though not] very decently for that matter. You know I'm never anything but happy to take you in my arms and enjoy that kind of kiss that seems to be your own speciality, or patent' (6 August 1966). As the poem concludes of the hypothetical, comprehensively honest man,

> And he can get stuffed

It was not that Larkin was declaring his affection for each of them menda-ciously; in his world, comprised exclusively of circumstance and fate, they were receiving what was necessary and appropriate. In early summer 1966 he and Monica had holidayed in Devon, and afterwards he felt it necessary to explain his failure to live up to her expectations. 'I'm sorry that our love-making fizzled out in Devon, as you rightly noticed . . . I am not a highly sexed person, or, if I am, it's not in a way that demands constant physical intercourse with other people . . . I think sex is a curious thing . . . A kind of double symbol that we aren't alone and that we aren't selfish whereas of course we are alone and we are selfish . . . Anyway, I'm sorry to have failed with you!' He is commendably frank – although how this openness would have registered for Monica is open to speculation. The letter discloses the man who enjoys pornography, who favours the private, inexpensive plea-sures of masturbation above the speculative demands of a sexual relationship, and links him with the speaker of the poem for whom 'selfishness' is a condi-tion rather than a choice.

His letters to Monica about Maeve are peculiar. For example, he begins, 'Cry all you need. It is not right to think you have to spare me the pain of remorse caused by injury to you is it?' and having dealt with their mutual distress, in the manner of one who had ruined his friend's dinner party, he moves on to a hypothesis, an endearingly honest admission of uncertainty. 'But then I wonder if there *is* a "situation" – do I *really* want an RC wedding with Maeve and a "reception somewhere in Hull" etc.' (10 August 1964), at which point one begins to wonder if he has experienced the epistolary equiv-alent of crossed lines, forgotten that he is writing to Monica and temporarily replaced her with Amis or his mother. No, of course not: 'Anyway, dear, I wish I were with you now, especially if you are wearing your mauve dress.' Monica became used to the peculiar indeterminacy of her status.

> Dear, don't, please be miserable over this Maeve business. You've been extremely tolerant all the time and I shall be glad to have your sympathy . . . she is more upset than I, because it is she who has been rebuffed . . . We are quite friendly, and have to see each other daily – the *real* break and dismay is yet to come. (14 September 1964)

Years later Monica returned to this letter and underlined in pencil the passages in which Larkin is guiltily candid and apparently oblivious to the pain that this will cause her. She even offered a comment in the margin: 'Note the style, the corny style and no intention of doing what is said, and both of you had my sympathy – what a good giggle for both of you . . . I learned a good deal more later.' At Leicester Monica's essay-marking technique was famously ruthless – she had a particular loathing for fake erudition – and her adaptation of this to a letter from her lover is ghoulishly appropriate. When she made the annotation Larkin was dead, but for her the sense of having shared him with Maeve and, more significantly, of having had only a proportion of his well-catalogued store of emotions lived on in his letters.

One feature of his relationship with Monica which did remain relatively consistent – although its association with the rest was customarily unusual – was their sex life.

> I wish I could be with you and we could plunge into bed – I wished it yesterday very much. Do you remember putting on your red belt and openwork stockings? I shall remember *that*, a cataclysmic spiritual experience . . . (20 May 1963)

This is not, one assumes, the same kind of cataclysmic spiritual experience for which, on reading his 'moment of ecstasy' letter, Maeve thought that he secretly yearned. Larkin was particularly attracted to and aroused by the decorative lewdness of sex. Monica acquired an impressively varied wardrobe of erotic underwear and, although encouraged in this by Larkin, she as much enjoyed the role-playing aspect of their sexual activities as he did. It was for her a private counterpart to the image that she regularly presented for colleagues and students at Leicester as the shamelessly alluring academic, the fishnet bluestocking. As with Patsy their sex life became the embodied version of Larkin's taste for pornography, and while he sometimes averred that pictorial fantasy was far less bothersome than the real thing Monica was willing to indulge his taste for both. She would send him photographs of herself, suitably semi-clad, and include commentaries on what they might well be doing if the photographic image were real and the words on the page replaced by their spoken form and accompanying inclinations. This, she knew, blurred the distinction between pornographic satisfaction – which for Larkin was agreeably selfish and non-committal – and the complications of sex with someone who would be inescapably present, before and after the act. It made the former something in which she might participate and erased from the latter Larkin's fear of drab permanence; and to an extent it worked. He wrote on 17 August 1963 to thank her profusely for the most recent 'pictures', which had very much aggravated his 'condition of randiness'.

Along with the images he was particularly impressed by her account of 'hair under the arms and bare breasts and nipples and the like'. He admits also that he becomes especially aroused by the mixing of the actual with the fantastic; 'it makes me think of *you* in these respects and I get *colossally* excited, almost unreally really – well really unreally, I suppose. As you said, I dwell in my own imagination. I spend too much time on . . . visions – and honestly 95 per cent are about you.' His 'visions' were extensive: 'you've been cavorting around in my mind dressed in pink shoes and pink pop-beads and nothing else. All to the detriment of my typing . . . You must look a wonderful sight in fur hat and boots – nothing else? Holding a rawhide whip? (You see how naturally my mind composes aesthetic montages for you.)' He confesses that particular visions, such as the one she verbally provoked 'about putting elastoplast over your nipples', 'send him into a sort of incapable trance all day', but while 'there's nothing I'd like more than photographs of you in your private clothes or no clothes at all . . . I can't feel right when it seems more exciting than the reality.' One suspects that it is the combination of the image and the reality and the attendant sense of unease, even guilt, that excites him most, and in this respect 'Sunny Prestatyn' is brought to mind. His description of the 'girl on the poster' in the opening stanza is an almost elegiac celebration of lust:

> Kneeling up on the sand
> In tautened white satin.
> Behind her, a hunk of coast, a
> Hotel with palms
> Seemed to expand from her thighs and
> Spread breast-lifting arms.

The poster existed, certainly, and Larkin's verbalization of it makes one wonder if its creator was attempting to transplant a jollier version of Edvard Munch's *The Madonna* to the Welsh seaside. Larkin is honest enough in his admiration for the way in which pure sexuality has blended so well with provincial cosiness, and in this respect the poster would have brought to mind his holidays with Monica, as they took their happily decadent sexual practices to nowhere more exotic than, say, Guernsey, and there on only one occasion.

Within 'a couple of weeks', however, the girl has been visited by graffiti artists who disfigure her face, embolden the rest of her with 'Huge tits and a fissured crotch', 'set fairly astride a tuberous cock and balls' and eventually ruin her completely with a knife stab through her already 'moustached lips'. 'She was', concludes Larkin with a pitiless irony that would have made Swift wince,

> too good for this life.
> Very soon, a great transverse tear
> Left only a hand and some blue.
> Now *Fight Cancer* is there.

The guilty excitement prompted by the pictures of Monica is reflected in the poem – his confession that 'it seems more exciting than reality' is echoed in 'She was too good for this life' – but there is no evidence that Larkin was ever inclined to visit disfigurement upon images of his girlfriend, at least not literally.

The poem was begun in early 1962 shortly after Monica had started to drop hints about a research student in English whose master's thesis she was supervising and who, she suggested, was making it clear that his interest in her was not strictly academic. They had started to go for drinks together and while all this was true there was a tactical element in her disclosures to Larkin. She was placing him in the equivalent of her position regarding Maeve and awaiting his response. Larkin at first seemed tolerant enough, but in a letter in which he suggests that to an extent the young man is entranced by her sophisticated maturity he cannot quite help also disclosing something resembling participatory lust. 'I imagine he *is* attracted to you . . . the tremendous physical attraction that you have . . . you know what I mean – legs and body . . .' (23 January 1962). There is just a hint here that the thrill of the pictures, partly attributable to their status as confidential pornography, the kind of material which other men would use for gratification, is being taken a stage further, to the real thing. Correspondingly the excitement is double-edged here, too, and later in 1962 he admits to 'a queer disagreeable feeling' when he thinks of her in the company of her young escort (29 September 1962). He wrote this approximately one week before he completed the poem, and one should note that the 'tuberous cock and balls' upon which the girl is astride is 'Autographed *Titch Thomas*' which, as any folklorist will confirm, is the traditional nickname for an inexperienced, over-confident young man with a penis much smaller than advertised.

Monica would have recognized an appropriately grotesque reflection of their relationship in the poem, but what of Maeve? In her memoirs she recalls her 'indignation' when Larkin began to show her poems that went beyond the quiet decorum of 'An Arundel Tomb' or 'Here'; such as 'Sunny Prestatyn'.

> His response was: 'That's exactly the reaction I want to provoke, shock, outrage at the defacement of the poster and what the girl stood for'. I was not convinced and dismissed the poem's subject matter . . . as unfitting for poetry. (*The Philip Larkin I Knew*, p. 60)

Touchingly, she does not indicate her feelings or suspicions about what really lay behind the gestation of the poem. During the summer of 1962 Larkin and Monica spent more than their routine amount of time together. In autumn 1961 Monica had used the money from her late parents' estate to buy a small cottage in Haydon Bridge, near Hexham, Northumberland, with views directly from the rear over the River Tyne and the ancient bridge. This was almost as far from Hull as Leicester, but it had the advantage, from Monica's perspective, of independence. Previously she had either visited him or when he went to visit her in Leicester the visit always seemed to involve some commitment to his mother who lived less than ten miles away in Loughborough. Now she had a house that was chosen by her and separate from all the compromises and entanglements of their past. At first Larkin seemed to disapprove – all change provoked suspicion in him – but by the spring vacation of 1962 he was full of praise for her choice, and it was during the periods that he spent there that summer in what almost amounted to a semi-rural idyll that they diverted themselves with an intriguing pastime.

Early in their relationship they had found an affinity in their tendency to cut out the diplomatic aspects of critical scrutiny. If they thought it was rubbish, irrespective of its canonical status, they said so. Both reserved a special loathing for Iris Murdoch (one of the few inclinations that Monica shared with Amis), and their emendations to her second novel, *The Flight from the Enchanter* (1956), begun during that summer involve the literary-critical equivalent of what happened to the girl in the poster; Murdoch's original 'Her lips were parted and he had never seen her eyes so wide open' became 'Her legs were parted and he had never seen her cunt so wide open'. It seems more than coincidental that at the same time that Larkin and Monica were amusing, even arousing, themselves with this game he was putting together a poem that includes 'a fissured crotch / Were scored well in, and the space / Between her legs held scrawls . . .'

13

Choreography

'Broadcast' was one piece which Maeve saw as involving material entirely fitting for the elevated genre of verse. Indeed it was addressed to her, but its apparent transparency is deceptive. It offers an account of an actual event in 1961. On 5 November that year Maeve attended a concert of various pieces by Elgar at Hull City Hall which was broadcast live on the radio, and the poem involves Larkin listening to the concert at home in Pearson Park and imagining Maeve in the audience. His decision to write the poem invites several questions; principally, did he intend it to be read by anyone other than Maeve? If he was at first uncertain of this, the decision was effectively taken out of his hands by someone who informed Monica of its existence. In a letter to Monica in February 1962 he apologizes for 'causing you embarrassment *vis-à-vis* old Charity Boots', the last being a nickname that for Monica summed up Maeve's humble piety. The poem itself he dismisses as a parody of his association with Maeve – 'just a shade ludicrous' – and compares it with 'Maiden Name' in which he took revenge upon Winifred Arnott.

At this point Monica had not read 'Broadcast', but she was less than pleased to find it in *The Whitsun Weddings* two years later, particularly when she became aware of what it actually said. Listening to concerts or other radio programmes simultaneously, imagining the other's response and then exchanging recollections, had become a trademark of their relationship, special because it indicated, particularly for Monica, that there would always be something they shared despite their lengthy separations. They began this when Larkin was in Belfast. He would offer her impressionistic sketches of the day, what he had done in the library, his lunch, maybe a drink in the senior common room, the weather, and gradually the letter would move towards the present. The wireless is on: 'Whoops just heard that Princess M [Margaret] isn't going to marry Group Captain Fiddlesticks – well, what a frost.' Evenually they agreed in advance on points of vicarious contact (including episodes of *The Archers*) which they would talk about later. Now she found that not only was he involving someone else in an idiosyncrasy she thought exclusive to them but he had made a poem out of it. He describes the preliminaries of the concert, the 'whispering and coughing', the 'drum roll', and then, 'I think of your face among all those faces / Beautiful and devout'; or as Monica would have read it, '*her* face'. He imagines 'One of your gloves unnoticed on the floor / Beside the new, slightly outmoded shoes', and the last lines have him 'desperate to pick out / Your hands, tiny in all that air, applauding'. Maeve recalled that the shoes 'were a private joke':

> I had bought them (and the gloves) that autumn . . . Philip raved about the shoes. He used to take them off my feet, hold them up, stroke them, put them down on the sofa and continue to admire them; not just once but every time I wore them. (*The Philip Larkin I Knew*, p. 57)

Involuntarily, and with an ingenuousness that provokes sympathy, Maeve discloses what is whispered at in the poem: her gloves, shoes, are for Larkin a chaste counterpart to Monica's erotic wardrobe and, perversely, just as exciting.

'Dockery and Son' was inspired by Larkin's visit to Oxford in March 1962 to attend the funeral of Agnes Cuming, his predecessor at Hull. While there he also visited St John's, and during the subsequent twelve months the poem grew out of an idiosyncratic blend of recollection and introspection. Dockery and his son are not so much inventions as distillations of the fact that many of his college contemporaries – Iles, Hughes, Wain and particularly Amis – now had children, and at the same time that he was preparing the poem he wrote the introduction to the 1963 reissue of *Jill* in which he recalled the harmlessly anarchic behaviour of 'The Seven'. In the poem, however, he chooses not to dwell upon this:

> I try the door of where I used to live:
> Locked.

His awareness that those days are now distant and irretrievable is supplemented by his sense that he, despite appearances, has changed very little.

> To have no son, no wife,
> No house or land still seemed quite natural.
> Only a numbness registered the shock
> Of finding out how much had gone of life,
> How widely from the others.

He goes on to consider why others want or need children – 'Why did he think adding meant increase?' – and why he, Larkin, did not and never would – 'To me it was dilution' – and the poem concludes with his particular vision of life, stripped as it is of those supports, such as children, which for others grant it significance.

> Life is first boredom, then fear.
> Whether or not we use it, it goes,
> And leaves what something hidden from us chose,
> And age, and then the only end of age.

These lines bring to mind Book X of *Paradise Lost* where Adam and Eve meditate upon the apparent hopelessness of their recently fallen state and contemplate childlessness and death almost as compensations. While Larkin matches Milton's hard elegance line for line Adam and Eve seem euphoric by comparison.

The most engrossing lines of the poem are hardly ever commented upon. He is changing trains at Sheffield, has eaten 'an awful pie' and walked to the end of the platform

> to see the ranged
> Joining and parting lines reflect a strong
> Unhindered moon.

No figurative import is apparent, but the tone indicates a moment when he is if not exactly content then at least without complaint. The contrast between the lines 'joining and parting' and the moon 'unhindered' by their different directions is a fitting depiction of Larkin's double life with Monica and Maeve and recalls his account to Sutton of how lines that are separate in life are caused in poetry to intersect. In the first draft of the poem in his workbook he had written, 'joining and parting lines and thought how . . .', only to cross out the last three words, replace them with the more opaque image of the moon and avoid what might have come too close to the wrong kind of disclosure.

In 'The Dance', however, he took this very direction, and the poem is at once uneven, unsettling and unfinished because of it. Larkin is too often and incorrectly presented as a costive, uncongenial figure, a myth fertilized by his verse and the public image he quietly cultivated. In truth his social habits were the result of a compromise between unbidden anxieties and dependable habit. His stammer had by his early forties all but disappeared, but its legacy involved a fear of speaking in public or even conversing among groups of people whom he did not regard as close friends. As a consequence his social life was lively but calculatedly so. He went out frequently and hosted regular parties in Pearson Park, but he did so only with the compensating foreknowledge that many of those present would be well known to him and vice versa.

Maeve Brennan stated that the background to 'The Dance' involved Larkin going 'against his better judgement in following me to a Senior

Common Room dance' (*The Philip Larkin I Knew*, p. 58) that took place in late spring 1963. His better judgement told him that on this occasion Maeve would be accompanied by her, as she put it, 'jolly, lively group' of friends, who are referred to in the poem as 'her sad set'. These people would have known about their relationship, and there was no evidence of potential antipathy to Larkin on their part. But the very fact that he would spend an evening among people he knew only by proxy, via Maeve, and more significantly cause his relationship with her to become part of a social fabric alien to him created immense anxiety which in the poem often transmutes into anger.

Poems habitually address themselves to conditions that seem ineffable, but rarely if ever have states such as equivocation, vicissitude, irresolution and sheer panic been so effectively replicated as in 'The Dance'. Throughout the poem Larkin is confronted with decisions he is reluctant to make and encounters with people that generate immediate feelings of envy, boredom and undisguised contempt. He offers each of these in an unnervingly direct manner, as if he is participating in the poem involuntarily and doing his best either to stay in control or find release. For example:

> Chuckles from the drains
> Decide me suddenly:
> *Ring for a car right now.* But doing so
>
> Needs pennies, and in making for the bar
> For change I see your lot are waving, till
> I have to cross and smile and stay and share
> Instead of walking out, and so from there
> The evening starts again . . .

The piece is informed by a blend of impressionism and determinism, as if the language of the poem is continually attempting to accommodate and mediate factors that the speaker cannot foresee. Larkin had never attempted anything like it before, and the opening stanza involves his self-conscious acknowledgement of this.

> 'Drink, sex and jazz – all sweet things, brother: far
> Too sweet to be diluted to "a dance",
> That muddled middle-class pretence at each
> No one who really . . .' But contemptuous speech
> Fades at my equally contemptuous glance,
> That in the darkening mirror sees
> The shame of evening trousers, evening tie.

The first three and a half lines carry inverted commas not as a disclaimer – quite the opposite. They incorporate the trademark tension between colloquial informality and arrogant control of the idiom that Larkin had perfected since the early 1950s. His surrender of verbal authority to circumstance testifies to Larkin's awareness that his life and his verse were interdependent. Maeve:

> The dance was equally unforgettable for me. Having enticed him to it against his will, I judged his coming as a measure of his feelings for me and recognised, with some surprise that I exercised considerable emotional sway over him . . . (*The Philip Larkin I Knew*, p. 59)

Her account is particularly fascinating because it is often impossible to make a clear distinction between her references to the poem and her recollections of the evening. For example: 'The events and emotions that followed [Larkin's late arrival] were every bit as intense as he describes them in the poem which, for the next year, not only arrested his poetic output but also created a significant watershed in his emotional life' (p. 58). In truth, the poem does not so much describe intense events and emotions as replicate Larkin's anxious anticipation of both. Why, one wonders, did it in her view create a significant watershed in his emotional life when, to judge the evening by the poem alone, nothing actually happened? The answer to this should be sought in Maeve's remarks on another poem written four years later which opens with one of Larkin's most frequently quoted passages.

> Sexual intercourse began
> In nineteen sixty-three
> (Which was rather late for me) –
> Between the end of the *Chatterley* ban
> And the Beatles' first LP.

It is the accepted wisdom that 'Annus Mirabilis' offers the cynic's view of an allegedly liberating decade, but Maeve states that it is also 'a thinly disguised account of our relationship'. Perceiving it as both does not diminish its quality as a public poem, and its private dimension further animates one's fascination with its author.

Larkin offers no particular date in 1963 for the beginning of sexual intercourse, but Maeve's comments on 'his turbulent emotions on that memorable evening' cause one to suspect that 'The Dance' commemorates something more than it actually contains. Why else would he write it, and, more pertinently, why was he unable to complete it? It is a brilliant blending of raging anxiety and circumspection; all manner of things, sex in particular, seem imminent but beset equally by innumerable obstacles. If sexual intercourse did begin on the night of 10 May 1963 then one can appreciate why Larkin thought an otherwise unremarkable series of events at a dance should become the impetus for potentially his longest and certainly one of his most complex poems.

Never again would he make himself so vulnerably central to a poem. By the late 1960s he had begun to produce pieces of which he, along with his disarming recipe of hatreds, fears and nihilistic predispositions, was the integral feature, but always there was a sense of his determination to wrest control of the text from its subject. Compare 'The Dance' with 'Vers de Société'. The circumstances are similar, and there is evidence that Larkin consulted the former when preparing the latter. The 'weed from Plant Psychology' who takes the floor with Maeve and later 'Unfolds some crazy scheme / He's got for making wine from beetroot' is in 'The Dance' the cause of tangible states of frustration and uncertainty. In 'Vers de Société', however, he or his close counterpart is treated with confident disdain as part of 'these routines', 'Something that bores us'; 'Asking that ass about his fool research'. Similarly the 'Which fed argument' in 'The Dance' betokens Larkin's unease at being drawn into Maeve's group of friends, while in 'Vers de Société' discomfort is replaced by pitiless contempt, as he stands,

> Holding a glass of washing sherry, canted
> Over to catch the drivel of some bitch
> Who's read nothing but Which;

Larkin worked on 'The Dance' for more than a year, hoping to finish it in time for the publication by Faber of The Whitsun Weddings in February 1964 but realizing after forty pages of revised drafts that he would not meet the deadline and that it was by its very nature destined to remain unfinished. A tough, reflective codicil of the type that concludes 'Dockery and Son' or something more opaque and elegiac of 'The Whitsun Weddings' kind would have been the equivalent of him returning the poem to the inverted commas sequence which opened it, and a continuation of the story to its actual conclusion was also out of the question.

The fact that Larkin attempted for so long to find a solution to this is puzzling enough and becomes engrossing when considered in relation to his ongoing preoccupations and activities. Little more than a month after the dance itself he set off with Monica for their annual holiday, this time in Sark, and it was this excursion of fourteen days, and nights, that inspired his subsequent letter in praise of her luscious body and in which he fantasizes about putting Elastoplast on her nipples. Following his return to Hull his relationship with Maeve appeared to have entered a new phase in that their presence as a couple at university social events no longer drew comment or caused for Larkin the various states of anxiety and indecision recorded in 'The Dance'. More and more Maeve seemed to be operating as Larkin's proper and durable partner. It was she, for example, who successfully encouraged him to take driving lessons – something he had attempted briefly, falteringly, in Belfast and given up. He passed his test first time and purchased a Singer Gazelle – admitting that the whole procedure had been prompted by his unease regarding the possibility of 'other men' driving Maeve to places which they might have visited together, as a couple. Marriage became a topic that they began to seriously discuss, although on Larkin's part the exchanges were manoeuvres where he switched between abstraction and prevarication. Monica became aware that despite their gratifying summer Maeve was again playing a major part in his life at Hull, and he found himself gainsaying her bitter enquiries with a curious species of honesty – that Maeve wanted permanence and he did not. He was telling them both a contingent version of the truth, and it should be remembered that throughout all of this he was returning to 'The Dance' virtually day by day; between the events which inspired it and its abandonment he worked on no other poetry. There was evidently a symbiotic relationship between 'The Dance' and his equally indeterminate, vacillating involvement with Maeve, and to answer the question of how he was able to abandon the former while continuing in the same manner with the latter one should look to factors that significantly crystallized Larkin's perception of who and what he was.

In the summer of 1962 Larkin had put together a provisional selection of the poems that would make up his third volume. By this time he had also made it clear to George Hartley that he was unhappy that the Marvell Press had, as Larkin saw it, failed to properly promote and market *The Less Deceived*. The generally approving reviews that had come with the first edition had fed an interest in Larkin which he sustained with occasional poems in journals and magazines and regular reviews of jazz in the *Daily Telegraph* and of books in the *Manchester Guardian*. The Marvell Press regularly received individual orders for Larkin's volume but, owing to Hartley's reluctance to invest or expand beyond himself as director and Jean as sole member of staff, was slow to respond; book wholesalers were treated as profit-takers and rarely if ever supplied. The *New Lines* volume of 1956 had restored among the reading public an interest in poetry that had been in gradual decline since the nineteenth century. Many critics and poets made clear that they disapproved of what they saw as stylistic recidivism allied with inward-looking provincialism, but the fact that such debates occupied the attention of the news media reflected what appears to be a kind of poetic renaissance, irrespective of its divisions. Larkin's name and his verse featured prominently in all of this. In 1962, for example, eight of his poems were included in A. Alvarez's volume for Penguin called *The New Poetry*. Alvarez's intention in both his selection and his prefatory essay was to juxtapose the poets who made up the first team of the Movement – particularly Larkin, Conquest, Davie and Wain – and whom he regarded as insufferably parochial in outlook and manner, with more radical, less predictable figures such as Geoffrey Hill, Charles Tomlinson, John Fuller, Ian Hamilton and, singularly, Ted Hughes. Aside from the validity or otherwise of polemics such as Alvarez's, Larkin found it bitterly ironic that while they were occurring eager readers were finding it difficult to obtain a volume of the poems that continued to fuel them.

Charles Monteith of Faber and Faber had since 1955 kept in regular touch with Larkin regarding his plans for another volume – shortly after Larkin had signed a contract with Hartley, Monteith had made a tentative offer for *The Less Deceived*. In March 1963 Larkin told Hartley that he would be placing his next collection elsewhere, sent it to Monteith in June and by the end of the month had negotiated and signed a contract with Faber. *The Whitsun Weddings* was published in February 1964 and established for Larkin a public presence at least comparable with the one enviably attained by Amis.

Alvarez in the *Observer* followed up his *New Poetry* diatribe and accused Larkin of dwelling upon the ordinariness of England in a way that suited the drab circumspection of his subject, but the doubters were outnumbered by the celebrants, most memorably John Betjeman. He had become, wrote Betjeman, 'the John Clare of the building estates'. More significantly he had 'closed the gap between poetry and the public which the experiments and obscurity of the last fifty years have done so much to widen' (*The Listener*, 19 March 1964). The claim that one man had in an instant put flight to the ogre of Modernism might seem close to hyperbole, but it echoed a consensus. Christopher Ricks in his *New York Review of Books* review of its US edition with Random House found a perfect 'refinement of self-consciousness, usually flawless in execution' and argued that at last poetry had become reconnected with the lives of its potential readers, 'the world of all of us, the place where, in the end, we find our happiness, or not at all'. The volume had, claimed Ricks, established Larkin as 'the best poet England now has' (15 January 1965).

The Whitsun Weddings sold almost 7,000 copies in its first year and up to the publication of *Collected Poems* never went out of print. In April 1964 Larkin was elected to a Fellowship of the Royal Society of Literature, and little more than three weeks after the publication date he received a letter from the TV film producer Patrick Garland asking if he would consider being the sole topic of a film for the new BBC *Monitor* series on the arts. At first Larkin was reluctant to cooperate, replying to Garland that while he was flattered by the enquiry he was temperamentally ill-disposed towards the kind of public exposure – including poetry readings or interviews involving potentially personal questions – that turned writers into celebrities; 'I've always believed that it is best to leave oneself to the reader's imagination' (24 March 1964). Garland reassured him that the *Monitor* series, whose previous subjects had included Pound, Graves and R.S. Thomas, was non-formulaic and would entirely respect the writer's wishes regarding its presentation of them. He also suggested, shrewdly, that much of the film would involve Larkin in conversation with another poet, John Betjeman. Larkin agreed to take part. The filming would take place exclusively in Hull and its environs over one week between 3 and 10 June.

Gradually and with some caution Larkin became aware during the filming that he could achieve a propitious reversal of what he most feared; that as well as simply leaving 'oneself to the reader's imagination' he could play a significant part in creating the image he would prefer the reader to imagine.

The film became for Larkin, albeit in its robustly understated way, the equivalent of the Lake District for Wordsworth. Although having met previously on only two occasions, he and Betjeman appear as old friends, their facial expressions and body language indicating mutual respect and amiability but with Larkin also balancing a subtle deference to Betjeman's seniority against a wily performance as the polite heir apparent. The film's greatest success was in its undermining of the school of thought advanced in Alvarez's introduction to *The New Poetry*. Alvarez had accused the Movement poets of a 'unity of flatness, [their] pieties . . . as predictable as the politics of the thirties poets'. They had, moreover, created an image to go with their manner, summed up in Larkin's 'Hatless, I take off / My cycle clips in awkward reverence'. This figure is the 'post Welfare State Englishman: shabby and not concerned with his appearance . . . he has a bike, not a car; gauche but full of agnostic piety'. This, contends Alvarez, might carry a whiff of radicalism, but in truth all that has happened is that the upper-middle-class gentility of the likes of Betjeman has dropped a class, 'but the concept of gentility still reigns supreme' and, with it, predictability: 'the idea that life in England goes on much as it always has, give or take a few minor changes in the class system'.

Alvarez's argument that reactionary predictability works like an infection, inhibiting equally a collective state of mind and a mode of writing, offered Garland and Larkin what would become the implicit agenda of the film. Larkin in one memorable sequence appears to have stepped out of Alvarez's article as the bald, slim, bespectacled man, clad in a very ordinary mackintosh who does indeed ride a bike and at one point enters a church and removes his bicycle clips. Alvarez's case might easily have been proven by this had Garland not cleverly altered the panorama, making sure that the church is derelict and sinister in aspect and that the entire landscape through which his camera follows Larkin is quite the opposite of, as Alvarez put it, 'Larkin's . . . elegant and unpretentious . . . nostalgic recreation of the English scene'. In the film the sheer ugliness of Hull and its suburbs is almost celebrated. The heavily industrialized landscape of the north of the city, bisected by open drains, gives way to the gloomy, untended Sculcoates Cemetery; via television the fish docks do not smell, but the expression on Larkin's face indicates their level of foulness. Throughout the film Larkin maintains a brilliant performance as someone caught between wry amusement and apathy. He takes Betjeman home to Pearson Park for tea, we are shown his working environment in the library, and at the end the viewer is left with anything but a feeling of predictability. The implied and often quoted subtext of the film is *The Whitsun Weddings*, and at its centre is an enigma, a figure apparently at home in a drab, unliterary landscape and capable of producing such poems as 'Sunny Prestatyn', 'An Arundel Tomb' and 'A Study of Reading Habits', superficially so dissimilar but each carrying an eerie echo of the other.

The *Monitor* film marked Larkin's arrival at a party that had been going on for about ten years. The Movement was one strand of a more diverse literary phenomenon comprised also of the so-called Angry Young Men and the regional, working-class-centred realism of Storey, Braine, Sillitoe and Barstow. Apart from a general distaste for Modernism the one characteristic shared by these individuals and alleged groupings was a new and unprecedented alliance with the popular press, film, television and radio. The film version of *Lucky Jim* was in production less than two years after its publication date; Terry-Thomas as Bertrand and Amis himself as Jim enacted part of the novel at the 1956 Edinburgh Festival as a promotion for the film. John Osborne's *Look Back in Anger* was transmitted live on BBC television a month after its first theatre performance and Braine's Joe Lampton of *Room at the Top* had metamorphosed into his screen version in Lawrence Harvey before the first imprint of the novel had sold out. The long-established interplay between authors and their created heroes now involved a far more complex blurring of presences, as books migrated into electronic and visual media and writers became celebrities. Mary Ure became fixed in the public imagination as the Alison of *Look Back in Anger* and shortly afterwards married Alison's creator, Osborne; next, her stage husband Jimmy would memorably be played by Richard Burton in the 1959 film. At the same time Osborne and Ure marched together in the first CND demonstrations while Amis and John Wain offered numerous articles and interviews on why they would not be taking part, irrespective of the political radicalism which had become attached to them, via their fictional personae.

During all of this Larkin had done a very brief 1956 BBC Third Programme piece on 'The New Poetry' and three other short appearances for regional programmes. Those with a particular interest in the voice behind the poems could purchase Hartley's LP version of *The Less Deceived*, but compared with many of his peers Larkin maintained a polite anonymity. The *Monitor* film was therefore all the more effective because the reading public and the vaguely interested viewer were suddenly introduced to a figure from the background, made up of disconcerting incongruities. *Contra* Alvarez's accusation that Larkin was a kind of below-stairs re-creation of Betjeman, in the film the latter gives off an air of puzzled fascination at Larkin's morbidity. When sitting among the dirty, collapsed gravestones of Sculcoates Cemetery Betjeman reads 'Ambulances'. His expression resembles Larkin's at the fish-dock: partly amused, partly unsettled by finding himself in what appears to be a nightmare version of his own *Summoned by Bells*.

The film also jarred against the ongoing fashion for the newsworthy author by concealing as much as it disclosed. In 1962 John Wain, aged thirty-seven, had published a warts-and-all autobiography; in the same year readers were enjoying, via the *Daily Express*, Hilly's comments on Amis's infidelities, their marital breakdown and thereafter a lurid panorama of accounts from various outlets of his new relationship with the beautiful novelist Elizabeth Jane Howard. Colin Wilson's interviews for newspaper and radio to accompany the publication of *The Outsider* – involving his views on and experiences of sex, his taste for sleeping on Hampstead Heath and so on – were standard fare. But what did Garland's film say about Larkin? The documentary style made him appear comfortable with the mannerisms, habits and settings on show but raised more questions than it answered. Did his life involve something other than cycling from derelict church to rancid fish-dock or loitering without obvious purpose in some industrial waste land? It might, but for those who watched the film the most strikingly unambiguous feature of Philip Larkin, and the one which corresponded with *The Whitsun Weddings*, was of calculated singularity; bachelordom not just as a transitional stage or a circumstantial condition but as an impregnable state of mind.

The night of the broadcast, 15 December, found North Yorkshire enshrouded in dense freezing fog. Larkin did not have a television so he, with Maeve, arranged to watch it in the company of his friends John and Angela Kenyon at their house on the moors. Larkin, anxious, got moderately drunk and found the journey home even more terrifying than the experience of himself on nationwide television; Maeve had to walk in front of the car with a torch. She later described Larkin on film as 'Wistful, speculative, sensitive . . . gentle and compassionate; albeit melancholy' (*The Philip Larkin I Knew*, p. 62), but in a more ingenuous, compelling account of the production itself she remembered 'just standing around or following the film crew' through various parts of Hull, 'off the Beverley Road', on to 'the west bank of the river', past 'murky waters and slimy banks'. To all involved it would have been evident that she and Larkin were a couple, of sorts, but neither she nor anyone else commented on the ironic contrast between her lonely presence behind the camera and the film's implicit claim to harsh transparency. Any other arrangement would of course have collapsed the complex network of emotions and attachments that surrounded Larkin but from which, when necessary, he kept his distance. Larkin inhabits the fabric of the *Monitor* film in much the same way that he does his best poems. His environment suits his presence not because it makes him contented or happy – sometimes quite the opposite – but because he has subtly appropriated it. The man on the television screen raises similar questions to the man in the railway carriage in 'The Whitsun Weddings': What does *he* do when not in his library or talking with Betjeman in the cemetery? Who does *he* meet after leaving the train in London? In 'The Dance' he had come close to letting the equivalent of Garland's camera run on, allowing Maeve into the shot and obliging Monica and everyone else to see it. The poem is brilliant but was by its nature destined to remain unfinished and, during his lifetime, unpublished.

Some evenings when on their way to a social event via the town centre Maeve and Larkin would call for a drink in the Royal Station Hotel. She recalls it as 'a more forbidding place than it is now', retaining even in the mid-1960s an air of late Victorian pomposity, with its 'formal, lofty lounge'. 'Friday Night at the Royal Station Hotel' was, she states, one of the few poems written during this period that he showed to her before publication, implying that their habitual use of the place had played some part in its composition. It had, but not quite in the way she imagined. In early March 1966 Larkin had hurried back from a visit to Eva to meet Monica who would be spending the night in Hull on her way from Haydon Bridge to Leicester. Her train was late. This was the Friday night of the poem, and Larkin had to sit for two hours in the lounge of the adjoining hotel.

The poem itself is quietly terrifying. The speaker – and one uses this term with caution – leads us through an apparently empty lounge and dining-room. The 'salesmen' have 'gone back to Leeds / Leaving ashtrays in the Conference Room'. Upstairs we pass along 'shoeless corridors', past vacant rooms containing 'headed paper, made for writing home / (If home existed) letters of exile'. The sense of the place itself as a kind of monument to absence is chilling enough, but just as unsettling is the sense of the witness to all this as a cipher, a condition of the pervasive emptiness. It is an impressive reproduction in a poem of an effect otherwise unique to film, in which the camera offers a record of objects or moods while remaining resolutely anonymous. There is no record that Stephen King or Stanley Kubrick ever read Larkin, but one is struck by the parallels between this eerie provincial hotel and the one looked after by Jack Nicholson in the film of *The Shining*. In both, vacancy is sinister enough to appear capable of extinguishing anyone who trespasses upon it.

It is unlikely that the Royal Station Hotel was completely empty that Friday night, but as he sat waiting for someone to arrive in a place he habitually visited with someone else, now absent, it would have seemed to Larkin as though it was.

'Friday Night at the Royal Station Hotel' was only the fifth poem that he had completed in five years, but within six months he would begin work on his three most frequently quoted pieces, 'Annus Mirabilis', 'High Windows' and 'This Be the Verse'. Their impact upon established perceptions of poetry itself, and indeed upon the public image of Larkin the poet, would not register until their appearance together in his final volume, *High Windows*, in 1974. Their provenance in the mid to late 1960s, however, and their correlative function as symptoms of Larkin's outlook and disposition tell us much about their apparent affinities.

Larkin had watched with a mixture of amusement and envy as Amis throughout the 1950s and early 1960s pursued his career of serial infidelity, but while this bespoke on his friend's part an outstanding level of energy and versatility it appears conventional when set against Larkin's affairs with Monica and Maeve. Amis, ever the novelist, practised all brands of fabrication and deceit, but Larkin evolved a fascinating if not entirely effective technique of oblique, misleading candour. He told Maeve and Monica the truth about each other, including just enough confessional material to create an authenticating blend of guilt on his part and hurt on theirs. When pressed he would also disclose to one characteristics of the other that were veracious – Monica's retentiveness and Maeve's unswerving religious commitment, for example – but in a double-edged way: he would subtly present them as features that despite himself he had to endure when in fact they made up the essential differences between the two women that fuelled his attraction to each. There is calculation here, certainly, but tinged with a scent of the ghoulish which strengthens when we consider the identity of the third woman involved in this clandestine fabric of truth-telling and evasion: Eva, Larkin's mother.

Maeve had got to know Larkin's mother on an irregular, informal basis as his junior colleague during Eva's occasional visits to Hull in the late 1950s. In 1960 it was Eva who introduced Maeve to Monica when all three were assembled to watch Philip officiate at the Queen Mother's opening of the new library. When exactly Eva was informed of Maeve's new status is not known, but she soon became her son's confidante in this, offering opinions to him on both of them while disclosing little or nothing to either of what she knew of Larkin's divided feelings.

When Eva first met Monica in the early 1950s they got on well enough, but the latter detected a reluctance to accept anyone into the Larkin clan who might not attend to its established conventions of how the women should behave with regard to the men; that is, as subservient. Eva's anxiety about Monica's confidence and independence was gradually dispersed by her recognition that while the relationship was serious and long term it would not actually involve marriage and its attendant expectations. Things were different with Maeve.

> I liked Mrs Larkin. Although initially she seemed of a somewhat nervous disposition, she was friendly and I found her easy to talk to. Philip told me she liked me – even to the extent that she hoped he would marry me. She talked a good deal about Kitty, her daughter, and Rosemary, her granddaughter, and was obviously immensely proud of Philip.
> (*The Philip Larkin I Knew*, p. 26)

Maeve's account tells us as much about her as it does about Eva. Philip and indeed Monica regarded Eva's commitment to family as inhibiting and stifling; Maeve's report on the same without comment, and seamlessly attached to her disclosure that Eva saw her as a suitable daughter-in-law, indicates a special degree of fellow feeling. But before one gives in to the onrush of that debilitating interpretive virus the Oedipus Complex one should note that, rather than treating Maeve as a substitute for something he may or may not have felt about Eva, he kept his mother informed in a rather dry, sometimes ironic way of their, Eva's and Maeve's, similarities. He reported on how Maeve in spring 1966 had persuaded him to donate a bottle of sherry and to attend an Oxfam party on the following Saturday, providing a detailed description of her dedication to the event and its charitable objectives and communicating a feeling of indulgent, genial boredom: 'You see how different she is from Monica – or from me, for that matter' (13 March 1966), and, there was no reason to add, how like you.

In 1965 Larkin had arranged for John Wain to visit the university to give a public reading or lecture – the format and subject were up to him – followed by an informal party at Pearson Park. Wain's performance was by all accounts idiosyncratic; he was obviously drunk and seemed regularly to lose track of what he was saying. Most of those present were veterans of such events and did not take offence, but somewhere between the lecture hall and Larkin's flat Wain disappeared, only to turn up later that evening and deliver an epilogue to his earlier performance with shattered plates as accompaniments to each leitmotif. Larkin's account of the evening for Eva is interesting. He edits out the worst aspects of Wain's behaviour and concentrates instead on how unappreciative in general people are of hospitality; all the cigarettes and food 'I put out vanished', and he had only protected the drink by keeping it in the kitchen and 'dol[ing] it out myself'. Maeve as co-organizer was there and features in the letter as would a suburban hostess/wife of some two decades' standing; a presence acknowledged but requiring no comment.

Eva, born and brought up in the reign of Victoria, was old-fashioned, but she was not naïvely credulous or incognizant of the world around her. She was aware that after staying in each other's flats and holidaying together for more than fifteen years Larkin and Monica were on more than platonic terms. Indeed, while she made demands upon Larkin's time and affections that he resented she indulged him in a way that no doubt deferred to the memory of Sydney. Larkin encouraged his mother to remain on friendly terms with two women with whom, simultaneously, he was having relationships, confident that his subtle games of deceit would not be disclosed by her to either of them and that she would talk with him confidentially about each – an unusual arrangement for middle-class, provincial England of the mid-twentieth century. Had it not been true it might have been written by Joe Orton, despite each character seeming superficially at least to have more in common with figures from the work of Barbara Pym.

Larkin's admiration for and eventual friendship with Pym is well recorded by Motion and in *The Selected Letters*. Her novels of the 1940s and 1950s were perhaps the only literary enthusiasm that he shared with his mother and sister Kitty. Monica enjoyed them, too, and in 1961 Maeve, following Larkin's advice, read *A Glass of Blessings* and *Less Than Angels* and became a convert. The feature of Pym's work that ensured interest among this otherwise disparate network of fans was her ability to blend realism with something that appeared anachronistically at odds with post-war British society. Her novels are generally set in the quiet backwaters of middle-class Englishness where spinsters, curates and junior academics pursue routines of professional and intellectual contentment shot through with celibate flirtation. Larkin spent almost two decades trying to persuade a publisher to take on her novel *A Suitable Attachment*, and in his 1965 letter to his Faber editor Charles Monteith he praises it as a 'sane novel about sane people doing ordinary sane things', much to be preferred to the ongoing fashion for 'spy rubbish, science fiction rubbish, Negro-homosexual rubbish, or dope-taking nervous breakdown rubbish'.

> I like to read about people who have done nothing spectacular, who aren't beautiful or lucky, who try to behave well in the limited field of activity they command, but who can see, in little autumnal moments of vision, that the so-called 'big' experiences of life are going to miss them; and I like to read about such things presented not with self-pity or despair or romanticism, but with realistic firmness and even humour, that is in fact what the critics would call the moral tone of the book. (23 August 1965)

There are of course parallels between this version of Barbara Pym's fictional world and Philip Larkin's poetic counterpart, but just as intriguing is the hint of personal empathy which underpins his praise for the former. In his letters to Pym Larkin created yet another hybrid reshaping of his various foibles and idiosyncrasies, but this one differed from the others because for most of its existence, from 1961 until they met in 1975, it was comprised only of words on the page. By 1963 Larkin in his letters to Pym was beginning to sound like a character from one of her novels. For example, he asks without a hint of self-caricature, 'Do you know any librarians who want to come north? They are in terribly short supply these days' (13 January 1967), and when telling of his recent 'pleasant few days in Shropshire and Herefordshire, looking at eccentric decaying churches', he informed her of how 'consoled' he had felt by 'passing Michael Cantuar in a narrow lane one day' (3 October 1967; this being Michael Ramsey, Archbishop of Canterbury). Significantly his mother features regularly – Larkin painting verbal pictures of the two of them on holiday in run-down East Anglian resorts, for example – but he cautiously avoids reference to anyone else. 'As a librarian I'm remote from teaching, examining and research; as a bachelor I'm remote from the Wives' Club or the Ups and Downs of Entertaining; as an introvert I hardly notice anything anyway' (18 July 1971). His claim to bachelordom was of course true but only in legal terms. Elsewhere he would report to Pym on his excursions through the picturesque regions of Britain without ever mentioning that he was accompanied by Monica. Along with his cultivated self-image as the retiring librarian his style of writing takes on the air of the cynical and certainly not unworldly Edwardian marooned six decades hence.

For some this might seem freakish, but it was consistent with Larkin's treatment of particular friendships and indeed relationships throughout his adult life. His sincerity was beyond question, yet all else was malleable to the extent that it could be shaped to accommodate another's apparent expectations of him. His concerns were as much for the other person as himself; he might argue, disagree, even appear obtuse, but within the controlling ground rules of a game played only by the two of them, if knowingly only by him. In his poetry, however, he was able to borrow features from the separate dimensions of his protean, real existence and reposition them as a hybrid, recognizably Larkin to all who knew him but not exactly the one they knew. Larkin addresses Maeve, Monica, Eva and Barbara Pym with confident foreknowledge of their responses. Their expectations of him are, albeit in different ways, conditioned by what he has caused each of them to expect. Sex is the predominant issue only for two of them, but all four have become part of a fabric, constructed by Larkin, where sex, even by its absence, is whisperingly apparent. His versatility is immense. He controls a web in which Edwardian hypocrisies, indeed locutions (Eva and Pym), exist alongside fetishism (Monica) and pietistic morality (Maeve). In the light of this 'High Windows', 'Annus Mirabilis' and 'This Be the Verse' should be seen as pure distillations of irony. Each addresses the theme of sex, and each ridicules its own candour. Larkin writes of 'kids . . . fucking', of 'sexual intercourse' as now being virtually an obligation and of being fucked up by his parents. But he does so as one who is contemplating a society in which the new opportunity to talk about all this seems to involve unprecedented release, hedonism without guilt. For him the inherent tensions between public morality and private inclination, lecherous predilection and conformity, libidinous excess and monogamy had been what made sex interesting. Now, apparently, little is forbidden and all can be said. He joined these exchanges, in his poems, as someone who could not quite make up his mind about whether he regretted the past, envied the present or was too disappointed by both to make up his mind.

Jean Hartley tells of how during the 1960s he would comment upon the apparent changes in the moral climate in a way that combined envy with cynicism. Frequently he 'would have a good moan about his sex life, and [then] . . . mention, enviously, how he had seen so-and-so coming out of a tutorial room with his arm round some toothsome undergraduate. "He's no doubt having it off with her. Lucky sod."' (p. 95), which could have been a rehearsal of the famous opening of 'High Windows':

> When I see a couple of kids
> And guess he's fucking her and she's
> Taking pills or wearing a diaphragm,
> I know this is paradise
> Everyone old has dreamed of all their lives –

Such facetious weariness brings to mind 'Sunny Prestatyn': 'She was too good for this world'; irony has rarely if ever been so crisply executed. He goes on to imagine himself as a teenager and wonders if anyone then imagined that he was having similarly libidinous experiences, and the meandering sentence carries its subtext like a banner: indifference.

Jean's shrewd depiction of him as caught between frustration and a kind of apathetic resignation corresponds closely with the voice of the poem, but in the poem he takes this a stage further to an image that is at once beautiful and outstandingly depressing. The 'deep blue' that is 'Nothing', 'nowhere', 'endless' is the most impersonal yet deeply felt conclusion to any English language poem about human relationships. The puzzle of how it can be offered 'Rather than words', given that it is comprised of words, provides a link between 'High Windows' and its twin 'Annus Mirabilis' because the latter demonstrates how words can cause candour and sanguine falsehood to coexist happily.

Larkin's declaration that sexual intercourse began in 1963 carries an absurdist echo of previous attempts to rewrite history and common sense – most obviously that of the French Revolutionaries who decided that nothing worth mentioning had happened before 1789. It is also a mercilessly jargon-free anticipation of the writings of cultural theorists who would come to perceive the 1960s as a kind of fantasy via public discourse; in his opening stanza he implies – and by implication ridicules – a symbiotic link between the legalization of Lawrence's allegedly corrupting novel, the unchaste potentiality of rock-and-roll now made socially acceptable and the sudden discovery of sex. Next he rehearses the 1960s' mantras on how, prior to 'sexual liberation', all human beings existed in a state of crippling self-denial beset by the twin evils of ritual and guilt.

> Up till then there'd only been
> A sort of bargaining,
> A wrangle for a ring,
> A shame that started at sixteen
> And spread to everything.

Larkin's cold glance upon contemporaneity should not be written off as that of the standard reactionary, because in this poem, as Maeve disclosed, generalities are interwoven with a very private resonance: it is 'a somewhat thinly disguised account of our relationship' (p. 63). This is what he had told her, but it was, typically, only half of the story. That Larkin should have begun a sexual relationship with Maeve in the year that, for many others, appeared to sanction sexual intercourse *per se* involved an irony that might have caused him to reconsider his agnosticism, if only to see God as a bitterly droll presence. He had begun having sex with someone whose standards of virtue, founded upon belief, resembled nothing that he had previously encountered, at least beyond the pages of Victorian fiction. He had, moreover, already been conducting a sexual relationship for fifteen years, with Monica, of the sort supposed to have been the invention of the newly liberated decade. One can almost see Larkin's smile forming behind 'Which was rather late for me'; by 'Though just too late for me' he is laughing aloud. Although the poem bears no obvious resemblance to 'Friday Night in the Royal Station Hotel', looked at in the context of Larkin's private life the two pieces are grumpily companionable. In both his voice exists in a kind of hinterland in which participation – in anything – is an obligation made bearable only by the masochistic accompaniment of contemplation.

'Annus Mirabilis' involves the same arch, ironic tone that Larkin employed when writing to his mother about Maeve and Monica, but in 'This Be the Verse' – a poem which maintains the theme of generations present and past – the parent is shifted from addressee to subject. Some critics have attempted to read a deeper, secondary significance into the words of this poem; foolishly, because it needs no explication. It is a witheringly transparent text. The idiom of the famous opening ('They fuck you up . . .') gives a slight nod towards fashionable contemporaneous ideas that respect for preceding generations should be replaced by radical contempt, but Larkin rapidly undermines this: we shall inherit the worst characteristics of our forebears, irrespective of us and them being guiltless in this spiral of decline. Procreation guarantees the perpetuation of the foulest aspects of humanity and the only way to prevent this is to remain childless.

One wonders if Larkin had a quiet regard for Milton because, as with 'Dockery and Son', *Paradise Lost,* Book X, is brought to mind. Eve suggests to Adam that their dreadful condition should not be visited upon their successors: 'Childless thou art; Childless remain'. True, Larkin's circumstances differed in that he was not the potential originator of the human race, but there were parallels. He had throughout his life regarded having children as a forbidding, menacing prospect. Now, alongside this inclination, he had the opportunity to reflect upon the long-term consequences of having parents. He was becoming more and more like Sydney; for both, their job and their shared inclination towards rigour and efficiency had become, in part, a release from other aspects of life, particularly those that involved emotional commitment. Eva had become retentive and demanding to the extent that Larkin had entered a cycle of finding it difficult to distinguish between regretful, tedious duty, genuine feeling and the kind of loathing in which one sees the other party as a mirror image of oneself.

While he would offer Eva a deadpan account of the state of play with Maeve and Monica, the latter received more complex reflections upon his feelings about his mother. In August 1968 he wrote Monica a long letter which strings anecdotes on his miserable times in Loughborough between more fundamental questions on why exactly he experiences such levels of contempt for Eva. Typically: 'I wish I could avoid being so cross and irritable at home. I wish I knew what caused it. It's probably a stock psychological trait . . . Or is it just that I resent the slightest demand on my self consciousness? . . . really my anger is a fight for emotional freedom against its enemy . . . I suppose it links with my unhappiness at ties of all sorts, or not so much at them, but at having to do anything to honour them.' He confesses to finding Eva 'irritating *and* boring' and then corrects himself: 'hasn't one a right to be boring at eighty?' (4 August 1968). In truth, what irritated Larkin most was the interdependencies that come with being alive. Parents were of course a necessary condition of existing at all, but the concomitant responsibility of giving up elements of one's own world to them seemed an unfair aspect of this arrangement. Or, as he put it in a more blunt report to Monica a week later, 'God, what hell . . . they [parents] *bugger you up*, then, then, *hang around your neck* and stop you ever curing yourself. To escape from home is a life's work . . .' (10 August 1968). He was working on 'This Be the Verse' at the same time that he wrote this, and the parallels are obvious, except that in the poem he takes the circle of questions and complaints of the letters to an unerring conclusion:

> Man hands on misery to man.
>   It deepens like a coastal shelf.
> Get out as early as you can,
>   And don't have any kids yourself.

At the end of April 1971 he sent Monica the typescript, calling it 'A Little Easter Poem' and commenting that 'I never remember my parents making a single spontaneous gesture of affection towards each other.'

In 1982, long after he had completed the poem, he wrote to Judy Egerton of the recent 'Larkin Fortnight', a festival on his life and work held mostly at the South Bank, 'there was rather too much of four-letter Larkin for my liking. "They fuck you up" will clearly be my Lake Isle of Inisfree. I fully expect to hear it recited by a thousand Girl Guides before I die' (6 June). Those with only a marginal interest in poetry have come habitually to associate Larkin's name with that first line, and their higher-minded counterparts treat the poem as symptomatic of his acerbity or complexity, depending upon their inclination. John Carey claims, shrewdly enough, to hear two voices in it: that of the moderately loutish cynic, the speaker of the Amis letters; and of the reluctant devotee of the poetic, capable of producing such a brilliant figure as 'misery' which 'deepens like a coastal shelf'. The problem with Carey's reading is that he treats the two voices as coexisting uneasily, irreconcilably, when in fact the poem opens the concluding stage in what had for two decades been an ongoing, incipient tendency. Larkin's various, sometimes irreconcilable states of mind and personal affiliations were finding a single voice in his poems, one that would eventually become unwelcome even to him.

Part 6

Suicide by Poetry

14

Calls from the Past

By early spring 1969 Stage 2 of the library at Hull was close to completion. Its official title was something of a misnomer; its sheer size and architectural presence made Stage 1 seem insignificant. It stood, indeed stands, as a seven-storey rebuke to the modest pseudo-Classical and Renaissance frontages of the original university buildings. Larkin, despite his loathing for Modernism, was proud of this statement in white tile, glass and provincialist Le Corbusier. He had been the intermediary between the different bodies, listened to the requests of the academic community, stood between what the Hull University management team said it wanted and what the University Grants Committee said it could have and balanced the sometimes impractical suggestions of the architects against his knowledge of what a library is and how it works. The building won the 1970 Civic Trust Award and in 1971 the Yorkshire Region Architecture Award from the Royal Institute of British Architects. For a year or so Larkin was content enough to be celebrated as major-domo in this claim by Hull to first division status among the red-brick universities, but it became gradually evident to him that involvement had been more satisfying than completion, that the strains and anxieties of work in progress brought pleasure of the endurably masochistic type and when one ceased so did the other.

'The Building' was written in early 1972, and in a letter to Brian Cox Larkin stated that it had been '"inspired" by a visit to the hospital here about a crick in the neck' (3 August 1972). His use of inverted commas is intriguing, because while the Hull Royal Infirmary certainly has a part to play in the making of the poem it is a peripheral one. That the building is indeed a hospital is more an inference than a statement. The vehicles that call at the entrance are 'not taxis'; 'a kind of nurse' turns up every few minutes to 'fetch someone away', and 'Someone's wheeled past in washed-to-rags ward clothes'. Throughout the poem each image carries a double focus, as if the idea – prompted by a recent memory – of being in the hospital has become inter-mingled with almost parallel and equally unsettling impressions from the rest of the world. It is significant that the Royal Infirmary was visible daily to Larkin from his new extension to the Brynmor Jones Library.

Architecturally the two buildings came from the same stable except that the Infirmary, ironically given their respective roles, made more concessions to the brutalist dimension of Modernism; it looked far more indifferent to humanity. Larkin's reluctance to allow the hospital to become the clear, unambiguous subject continually prompts the question of the cause of his distractedness, and as we read the poem with this in mind we become suspiciously aware of the similarities between the clinical environment depicted and the one in which Larkin spent his working days.

> There are paperbacks, and tea at so much a cup,
> Like an airport lounge, but those who tamely sit
> On rows of steel chairs turning the ripped mags
> Haven't come far.

In March 1972 he wrote to Barbara Pym of a student sit-in at the beginning of term, a protest against the university's holdings in a company with South African connections. 'The . . . Building stank for a week after the sitters in ("activists") had departed' (22 March 1972). They departed shortly before Larkin began 'The Building', whose first stanza closes with

> and in the hall
> As well as creepers hangs a frightening smell.

Throughout the poem Larkin will suggest the interior of a hospital but interweave the inference with an indication of somewhere else, the latter frequently bringing to mind a somewhat grotesque library. The two certainly have things in common, given that books and medicine often share a

> struggle to transcend
> The thought of dying, for unless [their] powers
> Outbuild cathedrals nothing contravenes
> The coming dark . . .

As early as 'Hospital Visits' (1953) and more conspicuously in 'Ambulances' (1961) Larkin had shown a tendency to treat the medical profession as an index to the dreadful nature of existence. He respected the pragmatics of its role in restoring good health or making the incurable biddable, but he saw it also as a microcosm and summation of life's only certainties – pain, suffering and death. It is fascinating to compare 'The Building' with 'Church Going' and 'An Arundel Tomb'. He treats churches with a kind of complacent respect; the rituals and tenets that they contain are for some an unconditional statement of belief and for others, Larkin included, worthy of sceptical interest.

Hospitals, however, seem far more ominous, given that they stand as monuments to something that is not an option.

> . . . the only coin
> This place accepts. All know they are going to die.
> Not yet, perhaps not here, but in the end,
> And somewhere like this.

For much of his life Larkin had been temperamentally inclined towards pessimism and discontent, usually leavened with dark humour, but as the age of fifty grew ever closer he began gradually to lose faith in anything that compensated for the worst aspects of existence. The principal cause of this was his sense of the future as at best a burdensome recycling of the routine and familiar and at worst a now obligatory accumulation of things once avoidable.

In August 1971 it was evident to Larkin and his sister that Eva, even with daily assistance, was incapable of living in her own house. Physically she found it difficult to walk from room to room, and her mental condition seemed in rapid decline, with her memory and frame of reference displaying unsettling levels of unreliability and arbitrariness. They found her a place in Abbeyfield House, an old people's home in Loughborough. In practical terms this appeared a reasonable, inevitable solution, although a year later it was decided by Larkin and Kitty to move Eva to the Berrystead Nursing Home, better equipped, private and consequently very expensive. Aside from the fact that Larkin experienced the standard levels of distress at watching his widowed elderly mother enter the final stages of existence, he pretended in all communications with Eva, by letter or in person, that little had changed. In 1975 when he won the Shakespeare Prize from the FVS Foundation in Hamburg, involving an award ceremony in Germany, he wrote to Eva with a detailed account of this, adding, with reference to dear old Sydney's embarrassing political affiliations, 'Wouldn't Daddy be pleased' (21 November 1975). He might well have been, but whether this registered for Eva, beset by Alzheimer's disease and due to die in her sleep four months hence, is doubtful. Eva was the embodiment of his past and her grim present presaged, potentially, his future, so he continued to address her as though the worst depredations of time were not taking their toll.

By the end of the 1960s Larkin was beginning to experience the past less as something recollected or replaced and more as a series of revisitations. In 1966 Patsy Strang came to stay with him in Hull. They had been in occasional contact since his departure from Belfast, but this was the first time since then that they had been exclusively in each other's company. The alluring bohemian with whom he had had an affair had returned as a depressive, volatile alcoholic. He remembered her as an amusing companion, a sexual fantasy made real, and now, selfishly perhaps, he could not wait to say goodbye to his nightmarish guest. She had brought 'with her an aura of death and madness in a general sort of way' (15 November 1966). Belfast was one of the happier periods of his earlier life, but the present seemed to be revenging itself upon nostalgia.

In August 1969 Larkin and Monica revised slightly their convention of not holidaying outside the British Isles and took the ferry to Dublin. In the early 1950s when he was in Belfast the border between the North and the Republic was a fact, begrudged by some but accepted by most on both sides as reciprocal *realpolitik*. In the late summer of 1969 the North appeared to be moving rapidly towards civil war. Larkin and Monica stayed south of the border, but by revisiting many of the agreeable sites of their holidays together in the early 1950s, particularly Wexford and Galway, their memories of those days were inevitably stained by daily reports on the incipient conflagration a few miles up the road. They stayed for two days with Richard Murphy in his house near Westport, which depressed Larkin even more. Murphy told of how his marriage to Patsy had gone into terminal decline, of her severe depressions, and Larkin was reminded again of how different from the woman of his recollections she seemed. She bore no more resemblance to the impetuous, convivial presence of 1955 than did Belfast to the content Victorian city of their affair; it was now the site of weekly gun battles involving the IRA, Official and Provisional, loyalist paramilitaries and the British army. The dreadfulness of all this prompted him secretly to write a letter to Maeve from Westport. It is rushed, almost desperate in its address to her as someone who would guarantee the present: 'I can't forget you, even if I had any inclination to . . . Accept a big kiss and some spectral maulings – are you wearing tights? Or stockings?' (4 September 1969).

During that same summer he had secured a one-year Visiting Fellowship at All Souls College, Oxford, which would begin in October 1970. Four years earlier he had been approached by Oxford University Press to become editor of a collection of twentieth-century English verse. It would, they informed him, supplant Yeats's *Oxford Book of Modern Verse* (1936) by covering the next third of the ongoing century. Yeats's editorship had reflected the general perception of him as guardian of the genre. Larkin was flattered and, although the contract had been signed in 1967, he had had little time to even think about the project. The All Souls Fellowship, secured with the assistance of his Faber editor Charles Monteith who was himself a Fellow, would enable him to spend two terms working in the Bodleian Library, which as a copyright institution contained editions of all poems published since 1900.

He had been back for short visits before, but this was the first time since the completion of his degree that he had lived in Oxford. The blackened stonework had mostly been cleaned up, but little else had changed. He had an office in All Souls, but he lived in a set of rooms in a college-owned house just off the Iffley Road overlooking the Thames. He would take lunch in the Kings Arms, next to the Bodleian, and most evenings dine in college. His companions, such as the eminent historian A.L. Rowse and Warden of the College John Sparrow, found his habits and demeanour unsettling. He drank enthusiastically and was unguarded in his opinions on the condition of the arts, academia and public life in general, to the extent that Rowse thought that he was 'Falling over backwards to be philistine . . . an undergraduate attitude perpetuated into adult life' (Motion, p. 404). The stern pomposity of Rowse's account is appropriate in that it was exactly the response that Larkin wanted to provoke. The one poem that he addressed directly to Monica ('Poem about Oxford') was written during his time in Oxford. It is the city 'we shared without knowing'.

> Till we left, and were glad to be going
> (Unlike the arselicker who stays),
> Does it stick in our minds as a touchstone
> Of learning and *la politesse*?
> For while the old place hadn't much tone,
> Two others we know have got less.

The ambivalent tone of the poem reflects mixed feelings of irritation and fascination regarding the place where three decades earlier he had begun his adult life. Now he was back and was expected to behave like the dons ('The arselicker who stays') that he, Amis and the rest of 'The Seven' had regarded with amused contempt; Larkin, to Rowse's humourless gall, was behaving as if he had never left, too. He wrote to Anthony Thwaite in April 1971, 'I'm through with All Souls now: Cinderella is back in the kitchen . . . Rowse and Sparrow as the ugly sisters.'

Disrespect, even bitterness might have informed his attitude to the city and the university, but he stuck diligently to the task that had placed him there. He set out from the beginning to remain undistracted by the established reputations and certainly the stylistic–aesthetic formations that already shaped most perceptions of twentieth-century verse. In twelve weeks he consulted – although sometimes did not in their totality read – every volume of poetry published since 1900. He did so chronologically, returned to those authors and poems he thought deserved special attention and made comparative evaluations. By the time he returned to Hull he had a short-list for the volume.

He wrote to Judy Egerton in 1971 that 'as I feared I'm drawing English poetry in my own image' (16 January), and his dealings with the work of Hugh MacDiarmid are illuminating in this respect. Dan Davin, Larkin's

Oxford editor, at first thought that the complete absence of MacDiarmid's work from the first draft was simply an oversight. No, answered Larkin, 'I am so averse from his work that I can hardly bring my eyes to the page, but I agree a lot of people will expect to find him there (assuming, of course, that he will consent to be included in a work whose title includes the word English)' (2 April 1971). Larkin regarded MacDiarmid's self-evolved synthesis of English and Scots dialect as much a concession to Modernist inaccessibility as an affirmation of national identity. In the end he yielded to Davin's request for inclusion, leaving an interesting clue for the vigilant reader. In the preface he attests to have 'not included' 'poems requiring a glossary for their full understanding'. The four by MacDiarmid are the only ones in the volume attended by footnotes, the inference being that even with a glossary they are largely incomprehensible.

MacDiarmid irritated him, certainly, but the rest of the collection appears to have been chosen according to a slightly idiosyncratic notion of gregariousness. The principal players all appear, of course, although even here there are surprises. The Hardy section (containing twenty-seven poems) outnumbers the runner-up, Yeats (with seventeen), by more than a third, and the likes of Robert Graves (thirteen), Rudyard Kipling (thirteen) and Larkin's personal favourite Betjeman (twelve) each seem to have produced more pieces worthy of public interest than that obscure old toiler T.S. Eliot (nine). Alongside the familiar names are a considerable number of poets who would otherwise, one suspects, have been forgotten because their work refuses to answer to the categorizations of academic criticism: F. Pratt Green's 'The Old Couple' or Christopher Hassall's 'Santa Claus' are worthily preserved moments of brilliance. Also Larkin is astute enough to include embarrassments which, despite their badness, offer a distinct sense of period; these are the McGonagalls of the twentieth century, including Philip Hobsbaum's 'A Lesson in Love' which ends with:

Truth lies between your legs, and so do I.

The most hostile reviewer was Donald Davie in the *Listener* who called it 'the perverse triumph of philistinism', a celebration of 'the amateur, the worst kind of post-modernism, the weakest kind of Englishry'. Although Larkin would have used different vocabulary ('accessibility' rather than 'philistinism') this is a reasonably accurate description of his objective, and it was praised as such by Auden in the *Guardian* and Betjeman in the *Sunday Times*.

Colin Gunner had been a friend of Larkin's at school in Coventry. They had not met or communicated for thirty years, but in summer 1971 he wrote to Larkin with an account of his multifarious life: war service with the Royal Irish Fusiliers, followed by various jobs in the oil and mining industry in

Britain, Africa and the Middle East and now postmaster and newsagent back in Coventry. He knew, of course, of Larkin's literary credentials and in this regard sought his assistance with a half-completed memoir of his wartime experiences which would eventually be published privately in 1975 as *Adventures with the Irish Brigade*. Gunner was the kind of eccentric Englishman one might expect to find in fiction but who frequently survives outside it: lower middle class, quixotic and reactionary, and almost endearingly self-destructive. In 1971 his was the voice that struck Larkin as the perfectly dissonant echo of several chords within his own.

They would exchange letters regularly until Larkin's death fourteen years later, and Larkin constructed for Gunner the last of his epistolary personae. Initially they simply shared reminiscences and anecdotes and discussed Gunner's projected book, but it became gradually evident to Larkin that his old friend involved an even more grotesque recycling of the past than did the pitiable Patsy. Gunner referred frequently and admiringly to Sydney, principally regarding his political allegiances. In Gunner's view these had been prophetic; hard, right-wing authoritarianism was the only solution to the problems of a once great country now at the prey of nefarious trade unions, a Moscow-sponsored Labour Party and hordes of immigrants. Larkin responded in kind and hardly any of his letters from 1972 onwards fails to include, apropos nothing in particular, some reference to the enduring presence of 'Pakis' or 'Niggers' in English society, such satanic figures as Arthur Scargill or the burden placed upon taxpayers like Gunner and himself by the growing mass of lazy, unwashed left-wing students.

The letters to Gunner are by far the most abundant source of evidence for Larkin's allegedly far-right, racist inclinations, a reputation, albeit posthumous, that he deliberately, perversely engineered. He gave Gunner the impression that he was working resolutely to find a publisher for the memoirs, but this was a half-truth. He wrote to Monteith, 'Have no fear: I am not going to ask you to publish it. I am not even asking you to read it: you will soon see what sort of thing it is' (29 October 1975): brutal, polemical, disorganized and displaying a good deal of sympathy with Gunner's combatants, principally the Germans of the Italian campaign. All Larkin requested was advice on how to find an acceptable, specialized publisher who would, with the help of Larkin's diplomatic foreword, take it with a subscription to cover a limited print run. Of the many unsolicited revisitations of his past Gunner was the most compulsive because he was the worst. In Coventry he had played the role that Amis would take on in Oxford and later – an escapist substitute for Larkin's sense of unease about himself. Now he was back, still wayward and non-conformist but in a way that reminded Larkin of his father.

Larkin's racism was by equal degrees specious and puzzling. His dislike of trade unions, the Labour Party and the welfare state and non-Oxbridge universities was a familiar Conservative recipe. He was, with middle age, simply finding more and more targets for his life-long temperamental inclinations, ones that he shared with many of his friends and peers, but his apparent obsession with race was extraordinary. Even those who regard figures such as Amis and Conquest as exemplars of some innate affinity between literary traditionalism and right-wing politics would accept that their intelligence enabled them to recognize racial stereotyping as an absurdity. They and Larkin held almost identical opinions on everything, with the apparent exception of race. Sydney's views did not become for his son a genetic inheritance. They transferred themselves in ways that can only be described as reciprocally accretive. Wordsworth advanced that 'the child is father of the man', but he did not explain what happened when the former grew up. In Larkin's case he began to find more and more similarities between himself and a figure who had died when he was only twenty-six: passionately modest, bitterly pragmatic, a realist as much by disappointment as conviction and one who regarded his nation as something to be treated with equal measures of attachment, unsentimentality and vigilance. At the same time, however, he could not forget that he carried through much of his life feelings about his father that were ambivalent to say the least, predominantly a mixture of grudging admiration and discomfort.

The one distinction between himself and his father which he knew was irrefutable was the fact that while Sydney was unapologetically the same for all comers Larkin was an honest dissimulator, able to reshape himself without resorting to untruths. For example, when he wrote to Amis and complained about 'PLUMBER bum, CAR bum, SOFA bum, TUNE-AMPLIFIER bum' (1 August 1978) the message was as usual swamped by self-parody. His additional comment that 'Also got a nigger for a neighbour' is consistent with the blimpish image of the rest of the piece and very different from the transparently bitter presentation of the same man in a letter to Gunner: 'Not many niggers round here I'm happy to say. Except the Paki doctor next door . . .' (2 August 1983); his inability to distinguish between forms of racist abuse might appear laughably incompetent were it not also repugnant. Some years earlier the same neighbour had appeared in a letter to Pym: 'I have *got a gardener* . . . the man next door kindly passed him on to me.' Abhorrence inclines us to regard his presentations to Pym and, less discreetly, to Amis as concealments of the real Larkin, a presence he felt more comfortable disclosing to the like-minded Gunner. But it could conversely be argued that the letters to Gunner show us just as inaccurate an image of the real Larkin as do those to his other correspondents. Motion contends that 'as he grew older he was more inclined to show each of his correspondents the face he knew would please them most' (p. 332). This verdict leaves unaddressed the possibility that alongside his contingent, diplomatic inclination to 'please' his various acquaintances his character-refashionings might also have satisfied more private predisposition to see his different selves as dimensions of a completeness that only he could really know. None were pure inventions, but through their various contrasts, exaggerations, abatements and expurgations they enabled him to compensate for his life-long conviction that existence is largely meaningless. During the 1940s Amis and Sutton had allowed him to balance the instinct of anarchic irresponsibility against a pseudo-Lawrentian idealism, until he found that he could have one without the other. By the time he reached his fifties each previously mutable disposition seemed to become all the more ineluctable; the maintenance of balance was sidelined by the contemplation of extremities, some of which, particularly through his letters to Gunner, gripped him with a compelling and morbid fascination.

We will never know the exact origin or extent of Larkin's feelings about non-white people. There is no record of him speaking of these matters. All that exist are the letters, and these give us cause to suspect that Larkin the racist was a self-willed grotesque, if no less execrable for that. It is evident that he felt something instinctive, a mixture of unease and resentment, at the arrival and integration in Britain of non-white people from what used to be the colonies. Such instincts can originate in temperament or background, and while they are not always possible to eradicate at source they can be recognized by the person involved as illogical, reprehensible, repulsive. In the few instances when he disclosed his racist inclinations to people, other than Gunner, who knew him well he did so in a way that indicated just as much fascinated self-disgust as ideological commitment. He sent Monica, Anthony Thwaite and Conquest versified lamentations on the decline of empire and patriotism, the vileness of Labour policies and the influx of non-whites, and in doing so he showed that he, one of the most celebrated stylists of his age, could use doggerel in a manner more usually associated with football hooligans. He knew that while these recipients would not be completely shocked by what they read they would feel a tremor of discomfited embarrassment. He reserved the most virulent, baleful outbursts for Gunner, his childhood friend, a figure of no significance who certainly did not need to be persuaded of the attractions of racist authoritarianism. Gunner was his worst *alter ego*, someone he could treat with equal degrees of insouciance and masochistic self-recognition.

In spring 1972 Larkin spent a week with Amis and Elizabeth Jane Howard at their impressive Georgian house, 'Lemmons', in Hadley, Hertfordshire. Amis and Larkin had now resumed more regular contact following the relative hiatus of the early 1960s when Amis seemed continually preoccupied with other matters – divorce, remarriage and regular trips abroad in particular. Jane Howard had not witnessed their friendship of the 1940s and 1950s and was consequently fascinated by their habit of shutting themselves away for hours in Amis's study, usually accompanied by generous amounts of alcohol; on other occasions Amis had seemed to treat everyone, apart from herself, with amiable aloofness.

Amis told him about his ideas for his next novel. Lemmons was occupied by Amis, Jane, Jane's brother Colin 'Monkey' Howard, Colin's friend the jazz musician Sargy Mann and later, until her death in 1975, Jane's mother Katherine. Amis was content enough with this arrangement, but at the same time it seemed rather dull compared with the clandestine, romantic mood of their early years, and there appeared to be no reason now why things should change. So he imagined what such a gathering would involve for a similar group of people twenty years hence, when they were in their seventies. Out of this would evolve the novel *Ending Up*, published in 1974. Larkin was intrigued, mainly because he and Amis had been born in the same year and had reached the point at which old age was still something to be contemplated but only just; its beginnings were imminent. A gloomy subtext to these exchanges was provided by C. Day Lewis, who was occupying an upstairs room. He had terminal cancer and would die within a week of Larkin's departure, aged sixty-eight.

Within a couple of months Larkin began drafts for a poem that he would complete in January 1973. A comparison of 'The Old Fools' with Amis's *Ending Up* provides us with an insight into the different ways in which the personal characteristics of each man inform their writings. Amis's narrative moves with alarming speed. The chapters are short, and in each one there is an almost manic, kaleidoscopic blending of different foci, all of which contrasts in a darkly amusing manner with the fact that in real terms the characters' lives are slowing down. Everyone dies in the concluding chapter, alone and in a variety of sordid, uncomfortable ways, each departure linked to the residue of practical jokes set in chain by the malicious central character, Bernard. Larkin had been amused by Amis's plan, particularly the modelling of Bernard around his, Amis's, role at Lemmons. It was also evident to Larkin that, although they were both contemplating the notion of ageing, Amis's projection of this into his writing reminded him of *Lucky Jim*; Amis had made fantasy seem realistic and now he was turning black comedy into a substitute for a very humourless prospect.

'The Old Fools' was Larkin's response to this. At first it appears to treat its apparent subjects in a brutally uncompassionate manner:

> Do they somehow suppose
> It's more grown-up when your mouth hangs open and drools,
> And you keep on pissing yourself, and can't remember
> Who called this morning?

but gradually it becomes clear that the dreadful states that accompany ageing are not so much reflections upon what Larkin has witnessed as a myriad contemplation of everything he fears. At one point he imagines

> being old is having lighted rooms
> Inside your head, and people in them, acting.
> People you know, yet can't quite name; each looms
> Like a deep loss restored . . .

There are projections here of his own recent experiences. Gunner had returned from his adolescence, and in August 1972 he received a birthday card from Winifred Arnott, now Bradshaw, prompted by a radio programme called *Larkin at Fifty* which included Roy Fuller reading, as Larkin put it in his reply, 'your poem', 'A Few Lines on a Young Lady's Photograph Album'. All of this might appear innocuous enough, even gratifying – for some – but in a letter to Amis he moves seamlessly from reporting on his renewed contact with Winifred to 'Funny being fifty isn't it . . . add ten years on, what's ten years? Compared with eternity . . . ah gets tuft. No doesn't bear think-ing about . . .' (11 August 1972). But in the poem he does force himself to think about it, of 'never perceiving / How near it is . . . how it will end'.

In November he received a letter from Patsy, not entirely coherent but informing him that she had been admitted to a nursing home that dealt with mental illness and specifically with the psychological effects of alcoholism. She would not have found his reply particularly cheering: 'I don't expect to write any more. As for being 50 that hasn't cheered me either – to think that even if I attain 3 score years and 10 I've only as long forwards as arriving in Belfast was backwards' (25 November 1972). Belfast, where everything had been so different for each of them. Patsy would be dead in less than four years. As in the poem the 'lighted rooms' of Larkin's own head were becoming crowded with presences from his past who in different ways insisted to him that memories carry a dreadful message that the past is irrecoverable.

> . . . they give
> An air of baffled absence, trying to be there
> Yet being here. For the rooms grow farther, leaving
> Incompetent cold . . .

As if by some conspiracy of fate he received, two days after his reply to Patsy, a letter from Barry Bloomfield asking if he would approve his editor-ship of a bibliography of all Larkin's writings and related published material. Bibliographies, while very flattering, were generally regarded as monuments to death and completion. After its publication in 1979 Larkin wrote that it felt 'like a tombstone being gently lowered over me' (to Winifred Bradshaw, 23 August 1979).

The fusillade continued when soon after Christmas 1972 D.J. Enright sent him a copy of his recent verse sequence, *The Terrible Shears*, on the childhood he had spent in the same part of the Midlands and during the same period as Larkin's; the latter thanked him and added, 'the things one tries to forget get bigger and bigger' (3 May 1973).

From 1970 onwards virtually all of Larkin's poems involve what can only be described as a reluctant presence. Read as a sequence they are informed by a mood which has no exact precedent. Literature is replete with figures beset by various conditions – mental, emotional and physical – from which they seek release, but none comes close to the effect created by Larkin in these pieces where a condition of claustrophobic unease seems to surround each word or phrase, irrespective of its meaning.

'Vers de Société' reads almost as their manifesto. He is pithily contemptuous of another evening with 'a crowd of craps', including the 'bitch / Who's read nothing but *Which*' and the 'ass' with his 'fool research', but the alternative involves something that he cannot quite bring himself to describe. He circles it, using such phrases as 'Funny how hard it is to be alone', and comes closest to disclosure with:

> sitting by a lamp more often brings
> Not peace, but other things.
> Beyond the light stand failure and remorse
> Whispering *Dear Warlock-Williams: Why, of course* –

He splits the semantics of the two words 'failure' and 'remorse' so that we are never certain if they refer to the grim social obligations that irritate him, but from which he cannot fully disengage, or whether they carry traces of those 'other things' that haunt his solitariness. One is reminded of the closing stanza of 'Best Society' (1952) where he locks his door, celebrates 'uncontradicting solitude' and savours what 'cautiously / Unfolds, emerges, what I am'. Now he is much less comfortable with this state.

Larkin had always been selectively gregarious, enjoying the company of particular friends, less so the kind of event described in the poem, but he had also put up with what he had to do, secure and comforted by the knowledge that having to be nice to people he did not know or care about was an interlude between times spent by himself or with people he liked. In the poem these compensatory balances have ceased to exist, and he finds himself accepting the invitation from Warlock-Williams as an escape from what he once craved. In life Larkin took this a stage further. He spent time in the Common Room Bar with a particular group of men who held opinions not dissimilar to Gunner's and became a member of a drinking club and a dining club in the university, both red-brick versions of the kind of Oxbridge society that Waugh presented with facetious accuracy in *Decline and Fall*; exclusively male, proudly impenetrable and unwittingly absurd. At the same time he joined the Cottingham Memorial Club, whose function seemed to involve the provision of an escape route for local small businessmen from the demands of family life. It hardly needs stating that men no longer immature who attach themselves to such groups are usually in retreat from something else, but Larkin was prompted by an element of self-loathing. He was doing something that ten, even five years earlier he would not even have considered, but then he had been more content with who and what he was.

In a letter to Monica in 1971 he suspends for a moment his standard retinue of complaints about his health, the unions, the unemployed and Harold Wilson and confesses that he cannot produce poems. This grievance appeared frequently enough in letters to friends and acquaintances, but for Monica he explains, 'I don't really want to write about myself, and everything else hardly seems worth bothering about' (26 September 1971). He does not say why exactly he feels so uncomfortable with writing about himself but the poems in which he forces himself to do so offer painfully eloquent testimony to his state of unease.

'Forget What Did' is, as he stated in a 1980 interview, 'about a time when I stopped keeping a diary because I couldn't bear to record what was going on' (*Further Requirements*, p. 60). His diary was his informal poem *manqué*, not simply a 'record' of things and feelings but a process by which words gave some shape to life. Now,

> Stopping the diary
> Was a stun to memory,
> Was a blank starting.
>
> One no longer cicatrized
> By such words, such actions
> As bleakened waking.

The syntax itself seems crippled by the pain of putting the words on the page, and while the ostensible subject is the cessation of his diary entries, his fear of 'words' as prolonging a 'bleakened' state of mind is brilliantly, grievously enacted in the poem itself. It was completed three weeks before he informed Monica that 'I don't really want to write [poems] about myself'.

Two poems, 'I have started to say' and 'The View', were written within a year of 'Forget What Did' and in both he gives voice to some of the thoughts about himself that distressed him:

> All that's left to happen
> Is some deaths (my own included).
> Their order, and their manner,
> Remain to be learnt.

As he put it in a letter to Amis, 'I keep seeing obits of chaps who've passed over "suddenly, aged 55", "after a short illness", "after a long illness bravely borne, and 57" . . . No it doesn't bear thinking about' (11 August 1972). Thinking about it was bad enough, but putting it into words was worse. In 'The View' he tried:

> Where has it gone, the lifetime?
> Search me. What's left is drear.
> Unchilded and unwifed, I'm
> Able to view that clear:
> So final. And so near.

In 'Dockery and Son' he had contemplated this same state of unwifed childlessness as a token of life without significance, and had done so with clinical indifference. Now fear seemed to play a part. He left both pieces out of *High Windows*, and they remained unpublished during his life. Stylistically they meet the standard set by other pieces in the volume, but Larkin's problem was that unlike 'Vers de Société' or 'Forget What Did', in which his depressive, nihilistic condition is made enigmatic, or even 'This Be the Verse' and 'Annus Mirabilis', where it is protected by a hint of self-caricature, they are unambiguously reflections of a state of mind that he loathed, could not escape from or even properly comprehend. They were the poems that he 'did not want to write about himself'.

He produced for *High Windows* a sequence of pieces which are versatile in their avoidance of matters connected directly with their author. 'The Explosion' is the most widely acclaimed. 'Livings' is intriguing in that it is comprised of three sections with no apparent thematic or tonal continuities, unless one regards them as demonstrations of the different ways in which a writer can remain aloof from the text. 'The Card Players' offers us a brief glimpse into the nocturnal activities of Jan van Hogspeuw, Dick Dogstoerd and Old Prijck who occupy the same grim quarters and seem to have exchanged communication for pissing, drinking, belching, gobbing and farting. It is a superbly protective poem, in that few poetry readers would expect its author to regard such a vision with anything resembling familiarity or approval, at least until the publication of the Larkin–Amis correspondence, which would be posthumous.

The most impressive exercise in self-abnegation is 'Show Saturday', based on the County Show, held in Bellingham, Northumberland, near to Monica's cottage, which they visited almost every summer from the late 1960s onwards. The poem is striking in its breathless, obsessive accumulation of detail. For fifty-six lines Larkin seems driven by a self-willed obligation to document everything – from the dogs and ponies, through egg and scone stalls to the haircuts of the farmers' sons – and miss nothing out before the show closes. It does, in the final stanza, and accordingly the pace of the poem slackens. The closing lines nod towards the show as sustaining the traditions of country life – 'Let it always be there' – but this is an act of courtesy. 'Show Saturday' is actually an ingenious demonstration of how to write about something that is part of your life while excluding yourself from the process. The crowding together of facts seems puzzling until one becomes aware that he is doing this as a means of smothering comment or reflection.

In the letter to Monica mentioned earlier, he complains that 'everything else [other than himself] hardly seems worth bothering about. I mean I can't write poems about Brenda [Moon, his assistant] or love's new food . . .' (26 September 1971). He did not offer further explanation because for Monica he did not need to. She would appreciate that he had built his reputation upon poems in which the most routine and commonplace features of 'everything else' took on a special quality but that to produce such poems he had also been writing about himself. 'The Whitsun Weddings' is captivating because the polite, almost inhibited presence of Larkin the observer informs every line, but now he seemed reluctant to allow himself to participate, even obliquely. 'Show Saturday' is important because it is a poem in which craftsmanship and obligation are forced to work together, irrespective of what the poet might have wanted to do. It is comprised of a vast amount of 'everything else', and by refusing to allow himself to interrupt this catalogue of data Larkin maintains a tragically eloquent silence.

It was completed at the end of 1973 when *High Windows* was at proof stage. He sent it to Anthony Thwaite for comments – Thwaite thought it was superb – and it was included as the final piece just as the collection was going to press in 1974. 'The Life with a Hole in It' was begun soon afterwards and is a vivid demonstration of what happens when he does write about himself and an indication of why he felt reluctant to do so. Its closest relative in *High Windows* is 'Money'. Both are bitterly autobiographical, but critics routinely treat them as self-parodic or as dramatizations of an unwelcome state of mind. Only Alan Bennett treated them as transparent, and he responded to 'The Life with a Hole in It' as if he had recently been obliged to endure the distasteful presence of Larkin at some social event. 'Larkin [is always] wanting his cake but not wanting to be thought he enjoys eating it . . . it's hard to go on sympathizing as Monica and Maeve . . . are expected to do, as well as any woman who would listen.' Bennett, writing in 1993, tells us, albeit inadvertently, a great deal about what lay behind the composition of the poem almost two decades before. In 1974 no one outside his closest circle of friends knew the real Larkin, but he was aware – as early as 'Posterity' – that eminence would eventually ensure disclosure. So when Bennett read the poem he found it difficult to concentrate on it as an artefact, given that every line seemed to offer a parallel with the Larkin he had come to know, and dislike, via Motion's biography and Thwaite's edition of the *Letters*. Larkin was reluctant to write about himself because, as he later put it, 'I suppose I always try to write the truth and I wouldn't want to write a poem which suggested I was different from what I am' (*Further Requirements*, p. 23). In 'The Life with a Hole in It' the truth is painfully evident:

> the shit in the shuttered château
> Who does his five hundred words
> Then parts out the rest of the day
> Between bathing and booze and birds
> Is far off as ever . . .

As far as 300 miles or so. Certainly, Amis did not live in a château, but, as he wrote to Larkin soon after moving to Lemmons, 'This is a bloody great mansion in the middle of the country' where he would live with the best-looking of the many 'birds' of his long, libidinous career. In 1970 Amis had been commissioned to do a series of articles called 'On Drink' for the *Daily Telegraph* magazine and asked Larkin to let him have 'some thoughts on drink [for an article on writers and alcohol] which I could work up into about 250 jolly spontaneous sounding words'. Amis had always seemed to him the one for whom fate reserved limitless generosity, and in his poems bursts of alliteration usually signalled impatience or ill temper.

He was not and would never be Amis, but neither was he saddled with such responsibilities as 'Six kids, and the wife in pod, / And her parents coming to stay', which might once have brought some relief – as it did so churlishly in 'Self's the Man' – but not now. All that is left now is the 'three handed struggle, between / Your wants, the world's for you, and . . . what you'll get', a struggle that is inescapable, endless and pointless, 'a hollow stasis / Of havings-to, fear, faces'.

Larkin, never the optimist, seems here to be exploring a special level of hopelessness. The poem begins:

> When I throw back my head and howl
> People (women mostly) say
> *But you've always done what you want,*
> *You always get your own way*

    – A perfectly vile and foul
    Inversion of all that's been.
    What the old ratbags mean
    Is I've never done what I don't.

It has long been a working truism of criticism that all poems are versions of the dramatic monologue, that the speaker and the poet can never be treated as the same person, regardless of the parallels. 'The Life with a Hole in It' goes some way to disproving this. The bitterness and anger of the opening passage are not reconstituted emotions; they are active, present in the poem itself, as if Larkin is using the formal features of the verse as restraints, inhibitors, and with only limited success. Compare this opening stanza with a less restrained instance of him throwing back his head and howling. 'Fuck the non-working classes . . . Fuck the students (fuck you students everywhere) fuck the Common Market e'en. Hurray for Ian Smith, Ian Paisley (fuck all branches of the IRA)' (letter to Conquest, 16 March 1971). Offered as Socialist Realist satire, as a speech delivered by some fictional embodiment of snarling bigotry, xenophobia and intolerance, this would be treated as laughably overwritten. It is scattergun polemics, a monosyllabic burst against the most obvious targets delivered with such unfocused bile that you almost expect him to go back and add, in his characteristically polite manner, 'Oh, sorry, yes I forgot: Fuck the unions, fuck Harold Wilson and several cheers for the Vietnam war and Enoch Powell.' There is no doubt that Larkin's views on most things were genuinely right wing, but one also gets the impression, particularly in statements like this, that such opinions also served as release valves for less easily defined moods, with his life-long inclinations towards cynicism and anticipated disappointment now no longer anchored to anything resembling sang-froid.

In a 1982 interview Larkin said that he had 'never tried to make poetry *do* things, never gone out to look for it. I waited for it to come to me' (*Required Writing*, p. 74). The contrast between 'Show Saturday' and 'The Life with a Hole in It' indicates that in 1973–4 his admirable commitment to the poem as a measure of his state of mind was becoming more and more intractable. The former was an impressive anomaly, something that he would not repeat – standing outside a poem went against his basic predilections – while the latter appeared to be the ultimate inversion of Dylan Thomas's advice to 'rage, rage against the dying of the light'. Larkin seemed full of rage and indifferent to whether the light died or not.

15

Last Moves

In January 1974 Hull University informed Larkin that it had decided to sell off a number of the non-academic and administrative properties that it owned in the city. Pearson Park would go on the market later that year and he would have to find somewhere else to live. Larkin had, since Oxford, been an obsessive upper-storey-flat renter. The notion of being physically detached from, while able to observe, the rest of the world, along with the welcome absence of responsibility – with someone else having to deal with repairs, upkeep and other burdens of ownership – suited his temperament perfectly.

The university's decision seemed to him another example of the activating power of cynicism. Many of his most pessimistic poems appeared able to set in train actual events and occurrences that had first been imagined illustrations of mood – the most obvious being 'Ambulances', written approximately six months prior to a seizure or black-out that caused him to spend lengthy periods being treated and speculatively diagnosed. 'Money' was completed less than a year before the university decided to sell his flat. In the poem he rehearses his standard double act of envious disappointment and bitter relief: money might have enabled him to have purchased more of the pleasurably disposable – particularly 'goods and sex' – if only he'd have had more of it, but then the man with the 'second house and car and wife' is the pitiable slave to what has to be paid for.

> I listen to money singing. It's like looking down
> > From long french windows at a provincial town,
> The slums, the canal, the churches ornate and mad
> > In the evening sun. It is intensely sad.

If there is a brand of Marxian ideology that incorporates glum insouciance, this must come close to it. In truth Larkin was given to anxious parsimony. He feared money, or rather what the absence of it might involve. ' . . . I was over fifty before I could have "lived by my writing" . . . and by that time you think, Well, I might as well get my pension, since I've gone so far'

(*Required Writing*, p. 62). By his early fifties he was drawing the administrative equivalent of a professorial salary, and the royalties on his two major poetry collections plus the immensely popular *Oxford Book of Twentieth-Century Verse* made him as much per year as a reasonably successful novelist could expect to earn. His outgoings were slight: apart from buying two relatively modest cars he had only ever spent money on food, drink, clothes and holidays; the rest he saved. An amusing anecdote from Martin Amis provides a channel between 'Money' and its poet. 'We thought we'd lay on a bit of a show for you since you don't come to London all that often...' wrote Kingsley to his friend on 28 October 1976, 'with some of your admirers', including Arnold Wesker, George Steiner, Ian Hamilton, Al Alvarez and A.L. Rowse. This retinue of Larkin's enemies was a transparent spoof, but a modest get-together did take place in Amis's and Jane Howard's new house in Flask Walk, Hampstead. At one point Martin, fascinated, watched from a distance as Larkin illustrated his discourse with impassioned hand gestures. Later he asked his father what the subject of this had been; clearly something he could himself, as an ambitious young man of letters, add to his stockpile of literary anecdotes. 'Oh yes,' said Kingsley, 'he went on about his electric bill, the rates, the inflated price of train tickets from Hull, the cost of new shirts, the usual stuff...'

Larkin found himself, in early 1974, with enough money to do much as he wished and obliged, via the university, to make a decision he would have elected to avoid. There was no reason why he could not have rented another flat, or purchased one for that matter, and although Hull did not have an abundance of charming, antiquated properties there was a sufficient number of Victorian and Edwardian houses on the market to have suited his politely reclusive sensibility. Instead, and for no obvious reason, he responded to the suggestion of a fellow member of one of his university dining clubs, went to see 105 Newland Park and then, with suicidal abruptness, decided to buy it. It was the kind of house owned by Arnold of 'Self's the Man' or similarly ensnared wife-and-two-kids characters who feature regularly in his verse, like demonic reminders of what he would always avoid.

By all accounts, his own included, Larkin hated virtually every minute that he spent in the house, where he would live until his death just over a decade later. Architecturally it was a perfect example of the kind of nullity-by-compromise that was only properly achieved in Britain in the 1950s and 1960s, in that while it disclaimed all reference to earlier styles it also cautiously avoided anything even mildly radical. Larkin soon made matters worse by redecorating with William Morris wallpaper, 1970s vintage, and sympathetically patterned carpets. His letters to his closest friends from June to August 1974 include an immense range of complaints about everything from the central heating to the size of the garden. To Pym, in the arch, parochial manner he reserved for her, he called it 'an ugly little house, fearfully dear . . . As near to its neighbour as a Council estate . . . a fearfully *graceless* house' (5 June). To Anthony Thwaite he was gloomily candid: 'I've been v. upset [since the move] in most senses: feel like a tortoise that has been taken out of one shell and put in another' (11 July). The question that must have occurred to these correspondents was 'Why, then, are you buying the place?', and for Judy Egerton he offers a clue. 'So Larkin's Pearson Park Period ends and his Newland Park Period commences' (17 February 1974). He was aware that moving from his flat and buying a charmless house would not by itself unblock the creative impasse to which 'The Life with a Hole in It' testified, but at the same time his so-called 'Newland Park Period' involved an elaborate, purposive exercise in which environment and circumstances would be altered and results awaited.

According to the poem the 'annus mirabilis' had been 1963, but in terms of Larkin's reputation as a poet it was 1974. In October of the previous year he had attended the memorial service for Auden in Oxford. Afterwards, at the wake in Christ Church, John Betjeman asked Larkin if he would be interested in taking on the Poet Laureateship when he, Betjeman, eventually resigned (in the end, he stayed in post until death). Larkin prevaricated and at the same time became aware that the enquiry was the equivalent of being suddenly woken and finding oneself become what before had only been imagined. Alongside Betjeman sat Cyril Connolly, giving full approval to the former's suggestion, and across the room was Stephen Spender.

Smaller indications of esteem began to form a queue for his agreeably bemused attention. In May 1973 St John's College, Oxford, made him an Honorary Fellow. Between June 1973 and July 1974 he received three honorary doctorates (from Warwick, St Andrews and Sussex), and in December 1973 he was asked to inaugurate 'The Philip Larkin Collection' which would, he was assured, eventually be worthy of its own room in the library he had assembled. In January 1974 he was sponsored by Ansell Egerton and Harold Pinter to become a member of the MCC, the equivalent for a devoted cricket follower of an elevation to the peerage.

During this period *High Windows* was being prepared for a projected publication date of June 1974 – 'but Joe Gormley may intervene', as Larkin put to Judy regarding the imminent miners' strike – and even without Faber's shrewd publicity machine there was a general and growing sense of anticipation. Along with Betjeman and Hughes he could claim to command equal measures of popularity and respect, and in earning this he had been tantalizingly unhurried. His two previous volumes had fascinated readers not simply in terms of their innate qualities but because *The Whitsun Weddings* had involved the poetic equivalent of someone you thought you had known for years disclosing new dimensions of their personality; now more than a decade later there was much speculation over how *High Windows* might further compound the paradox of this withdrawn, enigmatic figure who spoke so candidly to his readers.

The reviews were generally favourable, with the notable exception of Robert Nye in *The Times*, but each reflected the difficulty of writing a 500–1,000-word piece on a collection which, while short, compelled fascination and confusion. The admiration for the volume was genuine for most reviewers, but one also senses anxiety in their prose, particularly on how to describe the individual genius at work in poems such as 'Annus Mirabilis', 'The Explosion' and 'The Building' and at the same time explain why each is so radically different. Nye overcomes this problem by treating the differences as ineffective masks for a consistently nasty presence. Conversely John Bayley in the *Times Literary Supplement* offered a thumbnail monograph on Larkin's entire literary career, including comparisons with Shakespeare, Keats, Owen, Hardy and Yeats, which prompted Amis (whose own *Observer* piece was unreserved and unspecific in its praise) to comment, 'What does he *mean*? (Bayley) Throughout. Eh?' (Amis to Larkin, 31 July 1974).

It was the most popular volume of previously unpublished verse to go into print since the war, with over 20,000 copies sold in the twelve months following the publication date. Since *Lucky Jim* and as their friendship became interwoven with their literary careers Larkin had accepted the role of sanguine junior partner to Amis; gradually he had earned respect in his second-choice genre while Amis had rarely been out of the spotlight as the celebrity novelist. Now briefly their roles were reversed. *Ending Up*, published a few months after *High Windows*, was shortlisted for the Booker Prize, but it did not sell as many copies as its poetic counterpart, nor did its author attract so much popular fascination.

In his private life Larkin appeared similarly to have brought to an end the oscillations of his past. In the summer of 1971 Maeve had spent her holiday in County Kilkenny with an 'Irishman' then resident in Hull. She was candid with Larkin, informing him that at this stage they were simply friends, temperamentally compatible co-religionists with similar family backgrounds. He approved, for two reasons. He could now report to Monica that despite his previous dissemblings he was committed to an irrevocable, if gradual, process of separation from Maeve and, knowing that Maeve was not given to sudden visitations of capriciousness, he could be confident that for the time being not much between them would change. However, in August 1973 both of them recognized that some kind of decision had to be made, and, mostly at Larkin's prompting, they split up. With consummate timing and sensitivity he gave her a copy of 'The Dance', inscribed so as to dispel any doubts regarding its subject and, of course, tantalizingly unfinished.

Monica began to assume the role of his official permanent partner. She accompanied him to the Auden memorial service in Oxford. She sat next to him in church, and he made sure that her name was included beside his on the exclusive list for the lunch and wake at Christ Church. More significantly she was with him at the launch party for *High Windows* held at the Garrick Club, with Betjeman, Lady Elizabeth Cavendish, the Thwaites, Amis, Monteith and du Sautoy in attendance. By autumn 1974 his life seemed comprised of consciously executed points of transition and completion. He had even come to terms with the fact that Eva was now in an irreversible state of benign dementia. He still spoke to her and wrote her letters but more as marks of respect for their past communications than in any realistic expectation that she would properly understand, let alone respond to, his words. She was now permanently installed at Berrystead Nursing Home, and he was resigned to the fact that her 88-year-old body would soon follow her mind's retreat to oblivion.

John Haffenden asked him if in 'the practice of writing poetry . . . you predetermined what you felt about life, that you made up your mind once and for all', and he answered, '[you've] got it the wrong way round. I don't decide what I think about life: life decides that' (*Further Requirements*, p. 51). He knew that the decisions made for him by life had in *High Windows* reached an irrevocable set of conclusions. He could not change these; all he could do was shift perspectives and hope that something different, in poems, would emerge. There is cause to disagree with Motion's assessment that 'Buying Newland Park was a form of creative suicide' (p. 448). His decision to do so could, conversely, been seen as one element of a broader fabric of alterations, including his separation from Maeve and the elevation of Monica to a new status. He could not foresee the precise consequences, but they might, in accordance with his philosophy of 'life decides', offer ideas for poems that were not just extensions of work already done.

In March 1974, three months before the publication of *High Windows*, he began work on what would be his last major poem, and by the end of that year the first three stanzas of 'Aubade' were in draft form. Among the dozens of significant poems on death in English this one can claim uniqueness not entirely because of what it says but through its sinister emulation of its theme. From *The North Ship* onwards the image of time as a dreadful, threatening presence, forcing us to accompany it to an even more terrifying state of nothingness, seems never far from the core of Larkin's verse, while never quite the comprehensive, inescapable theme of the poem. In 'Aubade' it becomes just that. His choice of sub-genre, the poem that, traditionally, laments the dawn as the moment that lovers must separate, involves a dark inversion of expectations. He spends nights alone, 'half drunk' following the day's work, and 'waking at four' he stares past the 'curtain-edges',

Till then I see what's really always there:
Unresting death, a whole day nearer now,
Making all thought impossible but how
And where and when I shall myself die.

The sense of death as informing 'all thought' resonates through the poem. It is a brilliant, exquisitely crafted piece of work in that he proves able to write continuously about the same theme, never releasing the texture of the verse from a sense of dread and hopelessness, but at the same time lending this horrible process an equal dimension of beauty.

The experience of writing the poem would have involved for Larkin something close to Motion's notion of 'creative suicide'. After 'Aubade' it would have been impossible for him to write another poem that addressed itself to his particular conception of death, and while it would, hypothetically, have been possible to write about other things Larkin was aware that doing so involved at the very least the adoption of a false persona. Thoughts of death, as he made clear in 'Aubade', pervaded every element of his conscious existence. It had become evident to him that the changes in his lifestyle that had occurred during 1973–4 – specifically the purchase of Newland Park and the monogamous relationship with Monica – bespoke feelings of occlusion and cessation that were demonstrably counterproductive for his poetry: he was in the midst of writing a poem with an insistent subtext; 'beyond this there is little, if anything, to be said'. So in November 1974 he set the poem aside. He knew that eventually he would finish it, but for the time being its progress could be suspended because he had decided to alter yet again, and this time more radically, the mode of existence for which it seemed to be a self-composed obituary.

It was sixteen months since he had split up with Maeve. They saw each other regularly in the library and exchanged occasional letters of the friendly, uncomfortably reserved kind – 'I hope the book [High Windows] will receive as happy a reception with your reading public as its presentation means to me,' she had written in May 1974 – and in mid-November they found themselves at a Friday afternoon drinks party organized by a colleague in the Senior Common Room. Early that evening when other guests were dispersing Larkin suggested that she might come with him and look at his new residence in Newland Park, which she had never seen, and both knew that the invitation was politely spurious, that he wanted them to begin again. They did and with a more passionate intensity than before. Absence had made much grow stronger and her reservations regarding sex considerably less so.

Little more than three weeks later, in March 1975, he began an affair with his secretary, Betty Mackereth. They had worked together since 1959 and, while she respected his seniority, had developed the kind of day-to-day familiarity that was the stuff of a natural friendship. She was a local woman of solid although not impoverished working-class background and since leaving Newland High School and Hull Commercial College had held posts involving such practical skills as bookkeeping, typing and, briefly during the war, welding. In 1968 he wrote to his mother that 'alongside her stern secretary manner is a completely frivolous, almost skittish person, a kind of schoolgirl that giggles at the back of the class' (5 October 1969), adding that she was also a woman of 'boundless' energy and admirable efficiency in her work; 'I'd be lost without her.' She treated him with the kind of amused tolerance that unambitiously intelligent people reserve for intellectuals: his female-student-targeted spyglass, desk-mounted portrait of Guy the gorilla and taste in socks and shirts – 'a bit homosexy, the colours he wore,' as she put it – were the kind of things she expected of a poet, in the sense that the dockers and fishermen half a mile down the road similarly conformed to stereotype. But she was also aware that for Larkin dilettantism went with self-caricature.

Apart from Conquest and Amis no one knew more about the real Larkin than Betty. As his personal assistant she was fully acquainted with the pragmatics of deception that enabled him to conduct a dual affair with Monica and Maeve; on those rare occasions that he took the latter for holidays Betty would assist with his 'official business' cover stories. When his fame as a writer increased she devised a full recipe of responses to protect him from unwanted enquiries, and she was the one who knew which of the office cupboards contained his impressive collection of pornography. From the late 1960s onwards Larkin had become notorious for the ways in which he would indicate various levels of indifference and contempt for senior members of the university – academics and administrators alike – whose bickering and insistence on this or that policy for the library encroached on his way of doing things. At meetings of Senate he would often contrive to fall asleep in the chair only to revive himself miraculously and pour scorn on an outstandlingly pointless contribution from a fellow member. With mischievous skill he would make sure that the secretary of a professor to whom he was conveying a telephone message would have to edit out comments such as 'tell the old windbag' or 'inform the pompous arsehole', in the full knowledge that the windbag or arsehole concerned could hear him in the background. Through all of this Betty became the sanguine, pragmatic half of a kind of double act, and, when from the mid-1970s onwards his feigned periods of somnolence were frequently exchanged for more genuine drink-fuelled versions, Betty made sure that he would be able to sleep them off in his office without disturbance. 'I was like a wife really. I knew everything a wife knows, more than some wives know, probably' (Motion, p. 282).

After one of the final meetings with the library architects Larkin took those present out to dinner. He offered lifts home to Betty and another library colleague, Pauline Dennison, making sure that Betty's house was the last stop. She asked him in and commented later that 'he . . . told me that he had arranged the whole thing in his mind'.

What he did not tell her was that while his attraction was very real it involved a supplementary agenda of motives. He had restarted his affair with Maeve which, in terms of sex and his personal attachment to her, was fulfilling enough, but at the same time the blend of deception and uncertainty, even perhaps guilt, that accompanied it during the 1960s and helped infuse his poetry with its characteristic dimorphism had been replaced by a tiresome predictability. It was certain that Monica would find out, he knew that her response would be less than cordial, but he knew also that they were now too set in their ways for her to be bothered even with an implied threat of separation. With Betty there could be a brief period of treble deception, involving an exhausting but, for Larkin, perversely satisfying exercise in emotional gymnastics. Although Betty seemed to be the only one of his three lovers with comprehensive knowledge of what was happening, even she was sometimes obliged to play an involuntary, unwitting role, as the poem 'When first we faced, and touching showed' testifies. It was begun soon after the start of his affair with Betty and completed in December 1975.

It stops just short of the rhapsodic, hinting at the affected in its description of a first kiss. The moment itself compels a reflection upon how the past, with its private commitments and demands, will always compete against a moment of intimacy, raising the question of whether two people can ever really know each other, irrespective of the apparent depth of their immediate feelings.

> But when did love not try to change
> The world back to itself – no cost,
> No past, no people else at all –
> Only what meeting made us feel,
> So new, and gentle-sharp, and strange?

This question is rhetorical – love has always tried to reclaim everything for itself – but he leaves unresolved the attendant issue of whether it might ever succeed.

Maeve was not aware of the existence of the poem until Anthony Thwaite showed it to her when he was scrutinizing unpublished material in preparation for the *Collected Poems*. Her first response was recognition. The final stanza, quoted above, 'sharply resembled Philip's actual words to me on that February evening in 1961 when we embraced for the first time' (*The Philip Larkin I Knew*, p. 66), but taking into account its date of composition she conceded that it could have been written to 'celebrate his mature affair with Betty Mackereth' (p. 67). In truth it could only have been written because Larkin was having a relationship with both of them. He sent Betty a copy of 'When first we faced' ten days after completing it, knowing that she would experience the gratifying sensation of having been selected for special treatment in a poetic memento; she knew of course of his affair with Maeve, but the poem was hers. Or was it? On the same day that he sent the poem to Betty, 31 December 1975, he wrote to Maeve, 'I am very close to Monica and very fond of her . . . But it's you I *love*; you're the one I want.'

Poetic inspiration has through literary history laid claim to many grounding impulses – moments of spiritual revelation, opium, nightingales and so on – but Larkin is probably unique in his (albeit late) addiction to multiple infidelity. The moment in the poem where the sense of 'other meetings, other loves' seems to threaten their moment of togetherness is also that which enables Larkin to write it.

'Morning at last: there in the snow' was completed almost a month later, and Maeve was more confident regarding this one's affiliation: 'he told me how, first thing, he had looked out of an upstairs window and been mesmerised by "four small blunt footprints" imperceptibly dissolving in the melting snow' (*The Philip Larkin I Knew*, p. 67). But again, she did not become aware of the existence of the poem itself until after his death. He withheld this one for a number of reasons. He was confident enough that his affair with Betty would remain a secret. It was, with Betty's compliance, clandestine. She had since the early 1960s regularly visited him at the Pearson Park flat on library business, and she continued to do so at Newland Park. Even if she were seen leaving his home in the morning, before work began, it would be assumed that as usual Betty was collecting papers or reports well in advance of a meeting later that day. Her diligence and commitment to the job and her boss, even beyond 9–5, were legendary. But despite this unsolicited fabric of alibis he could not be certain that at some point Maeve would not find out about Betty. If she had, and had then read this poem in the knowledge that while the disappearing footprints were a 'sign / Of your life walking into mine' hers were not the only ones to have taken this same route, perhaps within weeks, even days, of that snowfall, the effect would have been distressing to say the least.

Also the poem was part of a curious dialogue that Larkin was conducting with himself. It is at once enlightening and disquieting to compare it with 'Aubade', the latter being stalled when it was written. The theme of morning pervades both, but far more striking is the difference between the levels of energy that compel and inform each piece. The three octosyllabic triplets of 'Morning at last' seem by their very nature to bespeak a need for brevity, the desire to capture the moment matched by an equal impulse to dispose of it without too much opportunity for potentially dangerous reflection. In 'Aubade', however, the horrible sense of pointlessness, of death being all that life has to offer, is dealt with in a pitilessly diffused, painfully conversational manner.

The third poem to be completed while 'Aubade' was still in progress was 'The little lives of earth and form'. It gives respectful consideration to the animal kingdom, something humans might envy:

> A kinship lingers nonetheless:
> We hanker for the homeliness
> Of den, and hole, and set.

This poem seems to be directed towards Monica. She was of course his 'Bun' and they had on holidays shared an enjoyment of the landscapes of Britain and their non-human inhabitants.

> I see the rock, the clay, the chalk,
> The flattened grass, the swaying stalk,
> And it is you I see.

Larkin appears to have written into these poems a kind of signature which attaches each of them to one of his lovers – with Betty he forwarded a copy, just to make sure – but at the same time none of them is entirely exclusive to that woman; each carries a trace of at least one other. 'When first we faced' seems by its closeness in time to his first physical, sexual contact with Betty to be hers, but Maeve recognized part of it as an almost verbatim quotation from her moment in 1961. 'Morning at last' must surely be Maeve's, yet as a gift it is cruelly fashioned, with the phrase implying that her departure is greeted with a hint of relief, an ambiguity returned to at the close; 'happiness or pain'. Monica's claim as the subject of 'The little lives of earth and form' would be secure were it not for the fact that Larkin remains coyly evasive regarding the species of 'little lives' referred to. Both rabbits and mice (Maeve being his 'Miss Mouse') could inhabit the 'den, and hole' of line six.

'Lines on a Young Lady's Photograph Album' and 'Maiden Name' (Winifred Arnott), 'Wild Oats' (Ruth Bowman) and 'Talking in Bed' (Monica) are all autobiographically aligned. But in each he succeeds in making the true identity of the woman largely irrelevant by virtue of the quality of the poem itself. In the three quixotic 'love' poems of 1975–7 he seems no longer possessed of the cautious intelligence that had once made good verse out of hoarded privacy. In each he operates as a ventriloquist or puppeteer; without Monica, Maeve and Betty the poems would not exist, but without knowledge of their background we would not grieve for their loss. They are curiosities of harmlessly prurient interest. When writing them he was attempting to recapture the voice, the presence that had informed the dull, sincere amatory verse of his past. This had provided a counterbalance to the more powerful poems in which he dwelt alone, simultaneously the addresser and correspondent for reflections on a life which year by year seemed further stripped of meaning or significance. This latter voice was still there, waiting for him in the as yet unfinished 'Aubade'.

It cannot be accidental that he returned to this poem at the same time that he decided to dismantle his tripartite love affair. In May 1977 Maeve's mother died. His letter to her of 25 May bears a close resemblance to the one that he had written to Monica following the deaths of her parents: unctuous words of condolence which seem to be causing as much pain to Larkin as he claims to intuit in Maeve, followed by an account of matters so mundane – the size of sandwiches in the SCR features prominently – as to make one almost sympathize with his obviously desperate attempts to change the subject. As usual he detected danger signs. Maeve had been closer to her mother than her father; the latter was in good health, could manage on his own, and Larkin suspected that Maeve might now, albeit late in life, feel more inclined towards independence from her family. He helped later that year with their move to a smaller house, but during the summer he set in train what would become his final ritual of disengagement.

In August Maeve was due to go into hospital for an operation that would leave her bedridden for at least a week. Her condition was not life-threatening, but following two months during which she had dealt with the practical and emotional consequences of her mother's death she was particularly unsettled by the prospect. Since May Larkin had, when required, offered support, but throughout this period he had known that his compassion, although not spurious, was cursory and provisional. Every summer he spent at least three weeks with Monica, and on this occasion he would extend this to include periods in London and Oxford and be absent from Hull for more than six weeks. He did not inform Maeve of this until two weeks before her operation, which was due shortly after his imminent departure. She wrote to him in the early hours of the morning following his announcement: 'our manner of parting upset me grievously . . . [I] beg you to think of some way of breaking this six week parting . . . Please don't fail me this time' (3 August 1977). He did, because without wishing to cause her gratuitous pain he expected that she might now be prompted to recognize that when such choices had to be made his commitment was and would always be to Monica. Maeve would, he hoped, spare him the task of ending things by doing so herself, but heroically she forgave him. For the next six months their relationship continued in much the way that it had for the previous sixteen years, except that now it was attended by a mutually sensed but never addressed air of precariousness. Both knew that a version of the August episode would recur, and it did in March 1978.

Larkinland, a celebration of his work and interests, first performed at the South Bank, London, in February 1978, was to be relaunched in Hull at the university on 16 March, with Larkin himself as guest of honour at a reception to be held afterwards. As Maeve put it, the evening 'ended in a serious misunderstanding and I considered Philip had gravely misled me about the subsequent reception' (*The Philip Larkin I Knew*, p. 228). If he had it had been a deliberate attempt to precipitate an exchange that he knew was inevitable. To have gone to the reception as a couple would have involved their as yet most explicit public disclosure of intimacy. Larkin was by his presence offering approval to an – albeit selective – account of who and what he was, and Maeve could not be seen to be his partner in this. She could, he told her, during the brief period between the performance and the reception, attend the latter but along with the other friends and colleagues; not with him. There were phone calls, a meeting and brief letters of apology and explanation, but within two days both knew that their relationship was over, irrevocably.

16

And Arrogant Eternity

The years between late 1974 and mid-1979 saw the decline and death of Larkin as a poet. The best explanation for this is offered, obliquely of course, by the man himself. As Chairman of the Booker Prize selection committee he gave an address in November 1977 on the award of that year's prize at a dinner held in Claridges. The winner was Paul Scott's *Staying On*, although Larkin had favoured Barbara Pym's *Quartet in Autumn*, also shortlisted. While giving respectful praise to Scott, Larkin used the speech as an opportunity to reflect upon fiction in general, comparing it with its most prominent and estranged companion, verse. He states that he considers 'the novel at its best to be the maturest of our literary forms' (*Required Writing*, p. 96).

> The poem . . . is a single emotional spear point, a concentrated effect that is achieved by leaving everything out but the emotion itself . . . In the novel, the emotion has to be attached to a human being, and the human being has to be attached to a particular time and a particular place, and has to do with other human beings and be involved with them. (*Required Writing*, p. 95)

This is a succinct, brutally candid description of how Larkin failed as a novelist and succeeded as a poet. His fiction, published and unpublished, was lyric verse in prose: narrative diversity, context and characterization would always be provisional elements, subsidiaries to the mindset of Philip Larkin, the latter sometimes disguised but continuously predominant. And it is clear whom he has in mind when he offers an illustration of the demands of the two genres. 'The poet says old age is sad; the novelist describes a group of old people.' He wrote 'The Old Fools' and Amis produced *Ending Up*.

> The novelist . . . has not only to feel emotion and devise a human situation to express it: he has to evaluate its causes and its objects in his reader's terms as well as in his own. Or, to put it in its simplest terms, if you tell a novelist 'Life's not like that,' he has to do something about it. The poet simply replies, 'No, but I am.' (*Required Writing*, p. 96)

If one leaves aside their ostensible topic of genre designation and read through these words to Larkin's state of creative inertia they provide a profoundly honest account of the latter. He affirms that poetry is coterminous with the life and immediate experience of the poet and the question prompted here is not addressed in the speech. If we accept his thesis, or even if we accept it as tenable for particular poets, then what happens if the poet reaches the point at which he feels that nothing unprecedented will ever happen to him and that everything else is already addressed in his writings? According to Larkin's model of poetic creativity the answer would be straightforward: he ceases to be able to write anything.

Larkin had reached that point. His experiment with Maeve and Betty was consistent with his conception of life and poetry. It was not that he was using these women as inspirational devices; not quite. His failure to produce anything but extensions of themes addressed in *High Windows* was symptomatic of his general condition of torpidity and stagnation. There might perhaps be uncharted emotional and indeed sexual territories to explore, an enterprise that would enrich the lives of those involved (assuming that Maeve remained ignorant of Betty, of course) and cause a concomitant reanimation of his verse. It did not work. Around the same time that he gave the Booker address he returned to and completed 'Aubade', fully aware that it was only a matter of time before his relationship with Maeve would end for good.

One other event drew him back to the unfinished poem: on 17 November Eva died in her sleep. Larkin's relationship with her was unusual, to say the least. After Sydney's death she became her husband's passive, and adhesive, replacement. Her personality was comprised of all that his was not: his drive and energy were matched by her enervating anxiety, his combative certainties equalled by her cloying vacuousness. But despite their differences she became a kind of living monument to him, her presence demanding surrogate respect and attention. Larkin obliged, gradually recognizing the bifurcation of his inherited personality. The more the memories of Sydney, good and bad, receded the more Larkin began to recognize those features of his mother that were now his own, particularly an inclination towards lethargic fatalism. His response to her death – somewhere between respect and supine quiescence – was thus appropriate. When her ashes were interred next to Sydney's he remarked to his sister Kitty that at last 'they are together again', which from a confirmed agnostic could have been faux-Christian sentiment displacing morbid humour, or the other way around. He had helped Kitty with the funeral arrangements and subsequent legal matters, but beyond that he remained for those who knew him best predictably saddened and no more. For someone like Larkin, however, such apparent insouciance was deceptive; death was part of life, its presence continually anticipated and pondered so that when it actually occurred it was as much a confirmation as a calamity. Or as he put it in 'Aubade',

> Death is no different whined at than withstood.

'Aubade' was his final statement, in poetry, on death. He knew there was no more to be said, and 'Love Again' took care of everything else.

He had completed the first stanza and the opening four lines of the second in August 1975, shortly after rekindling his relationship with Maeve. The same night he wrote a letter to her, declaring that he wished 'you hadn't gone away when you did', her departure causing him to have two 'losing dreams . . . you going off with someone else' (*The Philip Larkin I Knew*, p. 68), all of which seems rather histrionic given that she had 'gone off' with her sister and nephew for a brief holiday in Ireland. He might have experienced some subliminal conjunction of her destination with the 'Irishman' of her recent past, but Larkin was not generally disposed to turn tenuous links into states of anxiety. Maeve was puzzled by the fact that hours prior to writing delicately of his commitment to her he could hypothesize on

> Love again: wanking at ten past three
> (Surely he's taken her home by now?) . . .
>
> Someone else feeling her breasts and cunt,
> Someone else drowned in that lash-wide stare . . .

Motion proposed that the poem was evidence of his 'discovery that beneath the calm surface of his affair lurked feelings as turbulent as those he had known as a young man' (p. 454). This gives a false impression of the poem as a mixture of nostalgia and perplexity when in truth it was a meticulous, calculated exercise in masochism. In the letter there is a coda to his description of the dream of her 'going off with someone else': 'which was all very silly, for how can one lose what one does not possess?' This would, as intended, have registered for Maeve as a mature acknowledgement of her independence, but for Larkin it overlapped with 'Love Again'. In the poem the notion of 'losing what one does not possess' becomes perversely exciting; it fuels the image of 'someone else feeling her breasts and cunt . . . drowned in that lash-wide stare' and overrides the bogus spirit of regret. Also there are obtuse parallels between 'Love Again' and the contemporaneous 'love' poems, particularly 'When first we faced' and 'Morning at last'. Compare the following from 'Morning at last':

> Not the candle, half-drunk wine,
> Or touching joy; only this sign
> Of your life walking into mine . . .
> What morning woke to will remain,
> Whether as happiness or pain.

with these lines from 'Love Again':

> The drink gone dead, without showing how
> To meet tomorrow, and afterwards,
> And the usual pain . . .

The 'half-drunk wine' they had shared in the first becomes the 'dead' drink consumed alone in the second, and while her footprints were a 'sign' of 'her life walking into mine' there is in 'Love Again' nothing left but 'afterwards' and the 'usual pain'.

In 'When first we faced' the act of 'touching' is treated with equal measures of delicacy and sadness, the latter provisioned by a notion of 'other meetings, other loves', a 'different life' that altered their moment of intimacy. This becomes brutally literal in the other poem, with the image of 'someone else feeling her breasts and cunt'. While her 'inch-close eyes' in 'When first we faced' hint at a 'past' that 'Belonged to others' and make him want to 'hold you hard enough / To call my years of hunger-strife / Back for your mouth to colonise', in 'Love Again' we find

> Someone else drowned in that lash-wide stare,
> And me supposed to be ignorant . . .

The same images and circumstances, indeed the same phrases, migrate back and forth between the love poems and 'Love Again', and if these poems had followed the providential chronology of experience, of loving and losing, then their unflinching transparency – particularly the shift from thoughtful affection to prurient cuckoldry – might have invoked feelings of empathy, even compassion. But they did not. They were begun within months of each other during a period in which little, if anything, changed in his relationship with Maeve. Maeve concludes that Larkin's 'motivation for finishing it ["Love Again"] was . . . the new relationship I had formed in August 1979' (*The Philip Larkin I Knew*, p. 68) and involuntarily discloses a less palatable circumstance. Certainly he finished it in September 1979, but the passage in which he imagines her with someone else had been written four years earlier. The certain knowledge that the 'he' did not exist at the time of his appearance in the poem would have added a special thrill to his drafting an account of them about to have sex. The language is aggressively erotic, in the manner of Larkin's beloved pornography, and the similarity is deliberate. He takes a kind of revenge upon the grim certainty that he would never have in life what pornography offered upon the page by making a pornographic subject out of Maeve. He knew that their relationship would end, but until it did he left the poem unfinished. While they were together he could take depraved satisfaction from the verbalized image of 'Someone else feeling her breasts and cunt'. When they did part for good he returned to the poem, shifted the focus to himself and asked, 'but why put it into words?' The succeeding six lines, the last he would produce before becoming in verse a shadow of himself, have of course been subject to considerable scrutiny; attempts to explain the 'element' which 'spreads through others lives like a tree' but which 'never worked for me', and the latent, suggestive,

> Something to do with violence
> A long way back, and wrong rewards,
> And arrogant eternity.

Given a sufficient degree of application and cunning it is possible to fashion an ill-fitting biographical frame for those lines – a residual sense of envy for what others achieved and enjoyed and he did not, a memory of the fractious, bitter mood of the Larkin household – not literal 'violence', of course – and the arrogance of something that is at once limitless, pointless and unavoidable. But in doing so one also becomes aware of Larkin's dejected anticipation of such a procedure, his offering to the credulous reader of obvious clues, and then of a more pervasive condition which drains the lines of any significant meaning at all – a mixture of resignation and weariness that informs the tired syntax. The passage answers its prefatory question of 'why put it into words?' with a dispirited demonstration of what it is to be unwilling and unable to write the kind of poetry that was inimitably his own.

The poems that followed 'Love Again' are a small, desultory crew, each reflective of distracted quiescence. He had not completely given up verse, but he was no longer attempting to write poems that tested his virtuosity or said anything beyond their self-confirming subjects.

'The Mower' is a poeticized version of his account to Judy Egerton of finding 'a hedgehog cruising about my garden, clearly just woken up' (20 May 1979) and a couple of weeks later: 'killed a hedgehog when mowing the lawn, by accident of course. It's upset me rather' (10 June 1979). The poem clothes this in unmetrical pentameters which he cannot even be bothered to rhyme, and the reflective coda reminds one of a priest who no longer believes in God reciting a litany:

> we should be careful
> Of each other, we should be kind
> While there is still time.

Larkin still carried a special affection for animals, but it is revealing to compare 'The Mower' with 'Take One Home for the Kiddies', written two decades earlier. The latter creates an unnerving dynamic between two supposed states of innocence and vulnerability, in animals and children, and more than hints at the human version as a mask for innate malevolence. Larkin's feelings had not changed, but they no longer energized his verse.

His two pieces honouring, respectively, the birthdays of Gavin Ewart and Charles Causley are tortuously respectful and amiable, and while he certainly admired the work of both men and liked each of them the poems are shot through with the difficulty of writing about age and verse without lapsing into self-pity or offsetting this with cloying banality, or as he puts it in 'Dear CHARLES . . .':

> One of the sadder things, I think,
> Is how our birthdays slowly sink . . .
>
> Although I'm trying very hard
> To sound unlike a birthday card . . .

Larkin's lifetime was not comprised of events or experiences that even the most languorous person would treat as exciting, but after 1979 dullness acquired an almost rampant trajectory. Things happened, of course, but they did so either as an involuntary consequence of fame or because life in general becomes for those approaching and overtaking sixty beset by unwonted difficulties.

He greeted the election of Mrs Thatcher to the premiership in 1979 with something like enthusiasm. In 1975 after she became leader of the Conservative Party he had written to his mother, 'She has a pretty face hasn't she . . . I expect she's pretty tough' (12 February). Amis had been similarly impressed by her blend of power and aggressive flirtation. He had been introduced to her by Robert Conquest at her home in Flood Street before the 1979 election and, again encouraged by Conquest, had given a speech on government sponsorship of the arts at the first post-election Conservative conference. Conquest was concerned that the Tories, particularly during their rightward shift away from the consensual middle ground they shared with Labour during the 1960s and 1970s, should be seen to be carrying with them a respectable number of supporters of an artistic or intellectual stamp. Larkin, probably England's most popular living poet, would be a useful recruit, and he was invited to a Downing Street reception in May 1980. Mrs Thatcher quoted to him, incorrectly, a line from one of his poems, but he did not mind; 'I . . . kiss the ground she treads,' he wrote later. In August the same year at another gathering of right-wing *cognoscenti* he had engaged Mrs Thatcher in an exchange regarding the Berlin Wall. Thatcher, of course, looked forward to the dismantling of the Warsaw Pact and the wall that characterized it, but Larkin asked, 'Surely you don't want to see a united Germany?' The Prime Minister assumed that he must be referring either to a rebirth of pre-1945 Germany or a Communist takeover of the whole country and answered, confusedly, 'Well no . . . perhaps not.' 'Well then,' replied Larkin, 'what's all this hypocrisy about wanting the wall down?' At the same event Amis presented her with an inscribed copy of his latest novel, *Russian Hide and Seek*, an Orwellian story about life in Britain, and indeed the rest of Europe, under Soviet occupation. She was impressed. Clearly, to her at least, Amis's grasp of twentieth-century politics was more astute than his friend's, and it must have seemed to both men as though a very real, alluring version of Brunette from *Trouble at Willow Gables* had pursued them with a vengeance into their dotage.

It was clear to all involved that while Larkin was instinctively inclined towards a reactionary, conservative state of mind his perception of the *realpolitik* of all this was rather confused. There would only be one more invitation to Downing Street, in 1982; not that he appeared to mind. He enjoyed, from a distance, Thatcher's defeat of Argentina in the Falklands War and was even more gratified by her success against Arthur Scargill and the miners during the 1984 strike.

The year 1982 was one that he looked forward to with a mixture of dread and grim forbearance. Since twenty he had treated the decades of his life as unforgiving milestones on a route that he was obliged to take. The sixth was particularly forbidding. In 1979 Anthony Thwaite had volunteered himself as editor of a projected volume of essays on his life and work, which would be published in his sixtieth year. At first Larkin was horrified. Bloomfield's bibliography had brought to mind a 'tombstone', and this would be worse. It would be a celebration of a living poet who had produced four presentable poems in the previous eight years. His work would be scrutinized – he did not mind that – but there would be an implicit question raised by the lengthy period between the publication dates of the poems most likely to feature and the present day. But he trusted Thwaite as a cautious, circumspect critic and as a friend, and eventually gave his approval to Monteith at Faber; he knew that something like this would happen in 1982, and at least with his close acquaintance and his publisher involved he could maintain a degree of control.

All seemed to be going well enough – he particularly enjoyed Amis's reminiscences of their Oxford days – until he read the piece by the only contributor who had known him before Oxford, Noel Hughes. He complained to Thwaite and even claimed to have consulted Kitty regarding Hughes's comments on their father Sydney, specifically that he had been an avid supporter of Nazism and a member of the British Fascist group the Link, had caused a continual, almost sinister mood of gloom to enshroud the Larkin household and had been notorious in Coventry City Hall both as a bully and as a fondler of women employees. In the end Hughes left out his remarks on the home environment and distilled the rest into the relatively innocuous, 'he was noted for staffing his office with pretty girls', 'his cast of mind was authoritarian' and 'on his visits to Germany, qualities of decisiveness and vigour in German public administration . . . compelled his admiration' (p. 21).

In a letter to Hughes in May 1981 Larkin is clear enough about how unsettled he was even on reading the revised draft but seems incapable or unwilling to isolate the exact cause of this: 'your contribution struck me as different from the others by being non-friendly, and possibly at times unfriendly. While not a hatchet job, it read like a deflation job . . .' Significantly he refers to Hughes's earlier letter defending the probity of his comments on Sydney as concerning itself with 'whether they are true or not. I should have thought that *in a book of this kind* (and I underline that heavily) that was not the main point.' Larkin concedes implicitly that Hughes was telling the truth and goes further, stating that his piece 'read more like a posthumous article, to be published when I was no longer around to mind' (10 May 1981).

The prospect of having to deal with the public disclosure of his late father's 'cast of mind' was distressing, but at least Sydney could be treated as the long distant past. Imagine, however, how Larkin must have felt when he read the following, little more than a paragraph after the mini-biography of Sydney.

> There is in Philip much that is reminiscent of his father. I am sure that Sydney would have directed his early reading, and he left Philip with an abiding regard for Lawrence. He must have contributed something to that superb mastery of language that has characterised all Philip's verse. In common too there was fastidiousness in dress and a preference for bow ties . . . There was the urbanity verging on courtliness . . . Detached from his father's quirky involvement in politics Philip has remained instinctively rooted on the right. (p. 21)

The amiable, impartial tone of this carries with it a ruthlessly effective whisper. He does not state that a fascistic inclination is hereditary in the Larkins, but he plants a seed of suspicion. By 1982 potential parallels between D.H. Lawrence's ideas and fascism were spoken and written of. Perhaps by artfully respectable means Larkin senior had inculcated Philip with a tainted aesthetic, and although the son had not attached himself to a particular political creed Hughes seemed to be implying that the spirit of Sydney lived on and manifested itself in various aspects of Philip, his taste in clothes, his mannerisms, even his 'mastery of language' and his 'verse'.

Whatever one feels about Hughes's reasons for producing this essay one cannot but admire its unflinching guile. Larkin was distressed to the point of confusion in his letter to Hughes because the original had obliged him to look at what he was or, more specifically, what he had become. The parallels between himself and his father were stifling and unavoidable. Years earlier he had written in his notebook that 'By the time I knew it my father worked all day and shut himself away reading in the evening . . . [his] state of mind at that time cannot have been cheerful . . . I remember once saying to him that he had had a successful life. His humourless yap of laughter left no doubt as to what he thought on the subject.' He had also written that his father's state of unhappiness had made him determined to avoid the same by taking basic precautions. '[His] marriage had left me with two convictions: that human beings should not live together, and that children should be taken from their parents at an early age.' Fate, however, seemed to have other ideas. In March 1983 during their stay at the Haydon Bridge cottage Monica began suddenly to experience regular and unbearably painful headaches accompanied by blurred vision. She had developed shingles, a condition that could be moderated with drugs but whose sufferers could not be expected to endure without regular care. Within a month she moved permanently to Newland Park. Larkin's relationship with Monica bore no resemblance to that of Sydney and Eva, and Larkin did not resent having to share his house with the woman whose affection, presence and company he valued. At the same time the simple fact that what he had studiously avoided all his life – living together – had become a necessity pointed up something that Hughes had not mentioned: that not only did he and Sydney share temperamental affinities, both would be pursued to a standstill in later life by a condition of hopelessness. The following from a letter to Judy Egerton of 9 June 1983 could be a paraphrase of his notebook observations on the later years of Sydney's life except that now he was the subject: 'Life is depressing on all sorts of counts – *work*; well that one time refuge, I can see, is coming to a close . . . I positively dread retirement. I have no "inner resources", no interests, nothing to fall back on.' The 'nothing', he did not have to add, also involved writing.

The question of why he could no longer write had been addressed and implicitly answered in 'Aubade' and 'Love Again': if every attempt to form an imaginative, finely crafted structure out of your own thoughts and experiences drags you magnetically and inexorably to the topic of death, then quite soon there really is 'nothing to be said'. As early as 1975 when a state of creative inertia seemed more than a possibility, he had, as he put it to Conquest, taken to 'boiling down my diaries', meaning that he hoped to find enough in the voluminous notebooks and diaries of the early 1940s to the 1960s to provide the raw material for something autobiographical. What kind of generic shape would be given to this – poems, fiction, memoirs – was not clear, but his desperation was evident. His life and his writing were coterminous. The present offered nothing for either, so he attempted to ransack the past. Within a few months he gave up and for several reasons. Poems were impossible because the diaries recorded the candid, sometimes disturbing background from which his best verse had already been distilled. An autobiography would have been for the reader fascinating and for him unendurable: he had already offered up various profiles of himself which cautiously excluded the material that he did not want to have disclosed before his death.

The one feature of Larkin the writer that survived the death of his poetry was something that he might have put to use in a return to the genre, fiction, that had deserted him in the 1950s; he remained a magnificent practitioner of dry comedy. He could create discontinuities and sly juxtapositions that made prose representations of virtually anything, from the banal to the tragic, inescapably funny. It is possible to speculate on what a semi-autobiographical novel written in this manner would have been like because it exists in fragmentary, involuntary form and as such testifies to the impossibility of its proper realization. I refer to his letters to Amis. Amis said that late in his life when he had become bored with practically everything that was available to read his spirits would always be lifted by the sound of the mail coming through the letter box. There might be a letter from Philip. These were for Amis richly entertaining and for the same reason their author could never use the talents that so engaged his friend as anything other than something they shared privately. Their roles were ordained. A darkly comic novel shot through with recycled personal reminiscences would by the late 1970s and early 1980s have been seen as Larkin desperately treading ground already well occupied by his old friend: *Lucky Jim* revisited by its unacknowledged co-author.

So during the 1980s Larkin found himself in a variation upon the state of limbo. His ordinary life, incorporating roles of librarian, householder, occasional reviewer, partner to Monica, appeared to continue much as it had done, except that it and his life as a poet had once been more than interdependent. The fact that he could no longer write obliged him to examine again what had made his existence worth while in the first place, and the answer was starkly evident: without poetry, not much. A particularly grisly twist to this came in his recognition that while he had once been able to treat death as a subject, to savour and acknowledge its grim inevitability by writing about it, their roles were now reversed. He had run out of things to say about it, at least in poetry, but it seemed to be pursuing him with a vengeful assiduousness. Inevitably many of his friends and acquaintances had literary connections, but it is striking how their deaths seemed to suggest for him that oblivion was making amends for his poetic treatment of it. David Williams, one of 'The Seven', had died in March 1976. Larkin wrote to Amis, 'Bad news about David, Christ. The first of "The Seven" to go.' For Larkin there was an essential if illogical connection between being of an age when, for all seven, death was more than a hypothesis and another kind of loss. He continues, 'I am more or less all right except that I never put pen to paper' (13 April 1976). Two years later, following the death of their mutual friend Bruce Montgomery, he appears, again in a letter to Amis, unable to separate the man from the writer. 'Whatever one thought of his books, and his sense (sometimes) of what was funny or desirable, he was an original nobody else was the least like, don't you think . . . as well as introducing us to things like Dickson Carr and "At Swim Two Birds"' (19 September 1978). He had learned of Montgomery's demise when, returning from his summer holiday, he had found three familiar-looking envelopes with Devon postmarks on his mat. The first was from the man himself confirming that they would meet two weeks hence; the next, from Montgomery's wife, told him that this might have to be cancelled because of his illness; 'then another from Anne [his wife] saying you know what'. Amis did not need Larkin to comment on how much this resembled life in a gloomy epistolary novel.

'Last year I came back from holiday and found [via a letter] Patsy was dead,' he informed Amis on 19 September 1978. A week later, with briskly sinister timing, he was informed that the BBC planned to record that embodiment of mirth Harold Pinter reading 'Aubade'. The reading was screened on BBC2 on 30 October and prompted a flurry of letters to Larkin on its subject, death. The event had unlocked a cabinet of nationwide fascination, gainsaying the general belief that death was something only feared, lamented or bravely encountered – it now seemed impossible to stop people writing about it. Some letters were reflective, others anecdotal, informing him, for instance, of how one woman of seventy now found herself unshackled from the horrors addressed in the poem that she, too, had experienced in her fifties; 'now I don't bother'. W.G. Runciman, the eminent Cambridge sociologist, sent him copies of pieces by psychologists and anthropological theorists which attempted to isolate, by various empiricist strategies, the cause of our fear of death. Larkin wrote back to him, politely commentating upon these scientific modellings, but throughout the letter his subtext is clear enough: fear, the personal, irreducible fear of death cannot be allayed by cold logic. He concludes by recommending some books to Runciman, literary treatments of the topic, particularly 'Llywelyn Powys's *Love and Death* an autobiographical novel that ends with death in the first person, quite a *tour de force*'. Quite, given that as Larkin was well aware that Powys's experiment played a tantalizing game with the relationship between literature and life, his autobiographical first-person novel coming as close as was possible to death by writing. Larkin himself knew there were parallels with 'Aubade', and in reply to Runciman's rationalist comment on fear of death as a neurotic condition he replied that 'nothing really expunges the terror . . . something one is *always* afraid of . . . It certainly doesn't feel like egocentricity' (26 November 1978).

'Aubade', he felt, was becoming a combination of a creative suicide note and a fixation for patrons of the macabre. In the USA an Oregon bookseller paid copyright fees to assemble an elaborately illustrated special printing of the poem, as Larkin put it a 'luxury edition', bringing to mind that wonderful evocation of abundance and morbidity in Waugh's *The Loved One*.

More cheerlessly, he had received during the summer the typescript of a novel by Virginia Peace, the wife of Hull's Professor of Russian. It was semi-autobiographical and based upon her own experience following the death by accident of her son three years earlier. He wrote back to her that 'you have done amazingly well to describe what happened in so dispassionate and calm a way [but] the reader wants that impure thing, literature . . . Your narrative isn't a story, it's a frieze of misery; your characters are numb with unhappiness, there is no relief, no contrast' (23 December 1978). One has only to consult his Booker Prize speech to discern a subtext here; her work bears too close a resemblance to verse to be successful as fiction. Equally, his description is a near-perfect account of the mindset and execution of 'Aubade' and 'Love Again': a 'frieze of misery', without 'story', 'self' or 'contrast', reflecting a presence so 'numb with unhappiness' that he has no more to say on the matter.

In early 1983 the *Observer* sent him a pre-publication review copy of *The Oxford Book of Death*, implying that they regarded him as a scion of the various manifestations of the book's topic. His review is scathing, and with characteristic sleight of hand he at once accuses and absolves the editor D.J. Enright of turning the truly horrific into the user-friendly.

> What might be called the majority view, however – death is the end of everything, and thinking about it gives us a pain in the bowels – is poorly represented. This is no doubt due to Dr Enright's tact as an anthologist. Unlike the Fat Boy he doesn't want to make our flesh creep; slide after slide is whisked away, with no chance of making a lasting impression. (*Further Requirements*, p. 247)

Larkin's objection is to the proliferation of material that is dishonestly courageous – elephants seemingly united in mourning, Woody Allen's black humour, time travel as a remedy for fear of chronology, the endless poetic conceits and extravagances that replace dread with fascination. Writing the review he would have recalled such recent events as the funeral of Barbara Pym in January 1980, reflecting afterwards that 'I found myself looking forward to getting a letter from her describing it all', and a year later the tragic, early death of Lesley Dunn, wife of his ex-colleague, the poet Douglas. He would have compared the bleakness of these experiences with attempts by another Donne ('Death Be Not Proud'), by Shakespeare, Marvell and dozens of others to reflect upon the unspeakably terrible in verse:

> the intrusion of death into our lives is so ruthless, so irreversible, so rarely unaccompanied by pain, terror and remorse, that to 'anthologise' it, however calmly, quizzically and compassionately, seems at best irrelevant, at worst an error of taste. (*Further Requirements*, p. 347)

We can without significantly altering Larkin's premise here substitute 'write about' for 'anthologise'. He was uneasy with literary representations of death as something not quite as foul as he knew that it is and would be.

Two years earlier, during a visit to All Souls, he had begun a slightly opportunistic friendship with the novelist and literary journalist A.N. Wilson. Wilson was becoming well known through his books and articles for his self-styled 'fogeyness', his ability to combine controversial presentations of contemporaneity with an unflinching dedication to Anglo-Catholicism. Larkin's interest in this Evelyn Waugh of the 1980s was fuelled by a broader and for him painstakingly open-minded reconsideration of something that since his childhood he had taken for granted, the non-existence of God. Wilson was acquainted with a Father Bown, a high Anglican priest with a parish in Hull, to whom he vicariously introduced Larkin. Larkin, with Monica, attended Evensong on one occasion, enjoyed the litany and the music and was amused by the presence of only seven others in the congregation. He bought an elaborately footnoted Oxford University Press Bible and consulted key passages every day, usually while shaving. The whole procedure resembled the excursion of a genial mid-nineteenth-century anthropologist into tribal regions of Africa or South America; respect for quaint rituals was leavened with a certainty that that was all they were. As he commented to Motion on his consideration of the Bible, 'to think that anyone ever believed any of that. Really, it's absolute balls. Beautiful of course. But balls' (Motion, p. 486).

Larkin's final poems carry with them the kind of quirky austerity one might associate with a prison cell that has become a home. 'Long lion days' is economically beautiful, each line not more than five syllables in length, with all ten of them combining to leave an image of summertime and little else. He appears to have worked hard at excluding anything resembling comment, even impression, as if allowing himself to discourse upon a summer's day might lead him along a track towards reflections upon time, transience, evanescence.

'Party Politics', his last written and published piece, is a conceit of the fastidiously reclusive kind. The half-full glass, never topped up, the guest continually ignored by 'mine host' might have something to do with Larkin's habitual sense of life as a catalogue of failures, or they might be a complaint about there never being sufficient booze at parties. In the end it is impossible to decide whether it is a figurative recasting of insignificance or simply a poem about insignificance. Like 'Long lion days' it evinces a reluctance to say anything more than is absolutely necessary.

In July 1984 he and Monica attended John Betjeman's memorial service in Westminster Abbey. Larkin was photographed by several newspapers, principally because it was thought that he would soon be asked to become Poet Laureate. Much amused speculation centred upon how the man whose most famous line was 'They fuck you up, your mum and dad' would deal with votive pieces on royal births, marriages and deaths, but irrespective of this Mrs Thatcher offered him the post. He turned it down, but not because he was incapable of fulfilling its slightly farcical, anachronistic duties. He had proved in his poem defending the English countryside, 'Going, Going', his elegy to the Humber Bridge and most recently (October 1983) his quatrain-blazon for the university library that he could write occasional poems that were neither trite nor affected. He did not want the job because he knew that the routine, obligatory production of such pieces would remind him that they were now all that he could do.

Larkin had never enjoyed particularly good health, with various ailments of the peripheral, mysterious and self-inflicted kind attending him from his thirties onwards. Some had been standard irritations. His failing eyesight required him to be tested for new and thicker lenses virtually every year, and since the mid-1960s he had endured a progressive condition of deafness. By the end of the 1970s he had attained a weight of $17\frac{1}{2}$ stone which, even for a man of his height, brought with it high blood pressure and breathless exhaustion when more than standard physical effort was necessary. In March 1985 his weight and excessive drinking appeared to be taking their toll in the form of 'cardio-spasms', with his heartbeat making percipient hesitations before resuming at a compensatory but no less terrifying high speed. Despite his bulk his appetite was poor, he had difficulty swallowing, he could sleep no more than three to four hours per night and he was plagued by a regular pain in his lower abdomen. He had a number of preliminary tests of which the only clear diagnosis was an enlarged liver, but in April the results of a barium meal disclosed a potentially cancerous tumour in his oesophagus. On 11 June he was operated upon. The cancer was confirmed and his oesophagus removed, but it was found that cancerous growths had spread to other parts of his upper body.

Monica was informed that the cancer was inoperable. She decided not to tell him that his condition was terminal, but because no one was prepared to offer him guidance on the length of his recuperation period or what this would involve he knew by implication that he was going to die.

Even before the operation he had begun to make small preparations for the worst. The night before his admission he had telephoned Maeve to ask if she along with his friends from the university, Michael Bowen, Virginia Peace and Betty would be prepared to give regular lifts to Monica to and from the hospital. This setting up of a rota of lifts was on the face of things an indication of pragmatic concern for his partner, but his choice of participants indicates something else. He knew that, regardless of the success of the operation, he would be in hospital for some time and that along with Monica the car drivers would also see him during visiting hours. Maeve gives an account of how on one occasion she was 'surprised' at the 'emotional intensity of his response as he exclaimed: "You look absolutely lovely." It reminded me of the occasion when I had visited him in hospital in 1961 when our friendship ignited into love.' More uncomfortably, she visited him a few days later at the same time as Monica: 'Philip reached out to me in a passionate embrace. Deeply embarrassed I froze under the hostile stare of Monica, who was sitting on the opposite side of the bed' (*The Philip Larkin I Knew*, p. 92). Maeve might be forgiven for a certain degree of emotional licence, but her account none the less raises the question of whether Larkin was recreating in miniature a version of his emotional life of the previous two decades. Betty, too, was regularly at his bedside.

He left hospital after two weeks and spent the next three months in Newland Park doing little more than drafting letters to his regular correspondents and those who had written to him on literary or professional matters. Not once in the letters or in his exchanges with Monica or friends who called did he mention what most if not all knew. On 28 November he collapsed at home and was rushed to hospital, where he died in the early hours of 2 December.

The funeral was a curious affair. It was explained to all present that Monica, his partner of thirty-five years, was too ill to be there, although it was assumed and accepted that she was simply unable to face the prospect. Betty and Maeve attended, as colleagues. Kitty and his niece Rosemary represented the family. Amis and Hilly travelled up from London by train with Andrew Motion and his wife, Charles Monteith and Blake Morrison.

Amis gave the funeral address, by equal degrees unflinchingly honest and moving, a tribute to 'the most private of men, one who found the universe a bleak and hostile place and recognised very clearly the disagreeable realities of human life . . . But there was no malice in it, no venom. If he regarded the world severely or astringently, it was a jovial astringency.' For those present, 'We are lucky enough to have known him', and the 'thousands who didn't and more thousands in the future will be able to share those poems with us. They offer comfort and not cold comfort either. They are not dismal or pessimistic, but invigorating.' Privately, he confided in Conquest:

> I don't know; presence? Keep forgetting he's dead for a millisecond at a time: I must tell/ask etc. Philip – oh Christ I can't. I still read a few pages of the works before going to bed. (1 January 1986)

Amis had known him as well as anyone, which, as he was soon to learn, did not guarantee that he knew the same person as others did. Numerous accounts of Larkin have accumulated since his death, but one, by Amis, remains largely unrecognized. Amis's penultimate novel, *You Can't Do Both* (1994), is unashamedly autobiographical, but while his parents and first wife Hilly are transparently evident, Larkin, as Andrew Carpenter, is an ambiguous, spectral figure. Carpenter and Robin Davies attend different universities, but their parents are neighbours. Carpenter becomes Robin's mentor, a reasonably accurate version of how Amis felt about Larkin in Oxford. He introduces Robin to the best jazz – like Larkin's, Carpenter's father has encouraged his interest – and the novels of Aldous Huxley and explains to him the related attractions of Homer Lane and D.H. Lawrence. Like their real-life counterparts, Carpenter and Robin entertain each other with imitations of people they know, and Robin reflects that Carpenter 'was just about the most marvellous and amusing companion that anyone could ever have wished for', perhaps an oblique note of gratitude for the fact that without the irreverent dynamics of their times together and their letters *Lucky Jim* would never have been written.

But with characteristic slyness Amis presents Robin as a figure whose knowledge of his friend is self-deceiving. In their maturity Robin exchanges respect for irritated tolerance and even comes to believe that he has succeeded in convincing Carpenter that Lawrence and Lane are self-indulgent pretenders, but for the reader his certainty is, by its arrogance, suspect. Amis gradually has us recognize that Carpenter is as much the product of Robin's perceptions of him as a figure in his own right, someone whose presence is blurred by our growing awareness that we see him exclusively via the lens of his friend's over-confident scrutiny. Alongside the game that Amis plays with the reader is one in which he privately engages, deliberately exchanging what he knows to be the truth about Larkin for its exact opposite. Carpenter, for example, is a homosexual who briefly and unenthusiastically experimented with heterosexuality at university.

Amis began the novel shortly after the publication of Larkin's *Selected Letters*, and having seen Motion's first draft for the biography he had come to recognize that while Larkin had never actually deceived him he had been tactically selective in his transparency. Thwaite and Motion confirmed what had begun to be evident shortly after Larkin's death. On 7 June 1986 he wrote to Conquest expressing his shock at having learned that Larkin had instructed Monica to destroy his diaries. It is clear from the mood of the letter that Larkin's decision itself was less significant than its contribution to Amis's growing perception of another man with other lives, particularly the one he shared with Monica.

> His chosen companion, what? Makes you think of Mr. Bleaney '. . . having no more to show Than that grim old bag should make him pretty sure He warranted no better'. As Martin [Amis] said, Christ, what a *life*.

There is bitterness here certainly, and in December following a Radio 4 documentary on the anniversary of his death Amis continued:

> Everybody talked on the level of 'he perhaps had a forbidding exterior but really he was very warm with a word for everyone.' So that was the cosy little nest that he had up there. The only point of interest was that P had a telescope on his windowsill to get a better view of passing tits. (Letter to Conquest, 6 December 1986)

Maeve Brennan irritated him most of all. She wrote to ask for a draft of Amis's funeral address to quote in her own contribution to a forthcoming *festschrift* while arguing, *contra* Amis, that Larkin had indeed shown signs of an albeit vague acceptance of God and an afterlife. Amis was outraged. His image of his friend as faithless cynic until death was the more accurate version, but what unsettled him most was the apparently incessant disclosure of new dimensions of the man he thought he knew. He wrote to Conquest, 'I never heard a word about her except that solitary "Maeve wants to marry me" blurting; you too I think,' and added, 'He didn't half keep his life in compartments' (17 November 1986). The reshaping of his friendship as Robin's with Carpenter six years later hovers between acceptance, apology and discontent, but what Amis eventually recognized was the essential characteristic of Larkin the poet. Only he had access to all of the compartments of his life, and only he could so skilfully knit their various contents into the twentieth century's most outstanding body of English verse.

Select Bibliography

Works by Philip Larkin
All What Jazz: A Record Diary, 1961–68, Faber and Faber, London, 1970
A Girl in Winter, Faber and Faber, London, 1947; 1975
Jill, Fortune Press, 1946; Faber and Faber, London, 1975
Collected Poems (ed. A. Thwaite), Marvell Press and Faber and Faber, London, 1988
Required Writing: Miscellaneous Pieces, 1955–82, Faber and Faber, London, 1983
Further Requirements: Interviews, Broadcasts, Statements and Book Reviews (ed. A. Thwaite), Faber and Faber, London, 2001
Trouble at Willow Gables and Other Fictions (ed. James Booth), Faber and Faber, London, 2002

Secondary material
Ackroyd, Peter, 'Poet Hands on Misery to Man', *The Times*, 1 April 1993
Alvarez, A., *The New Poetry*, Penguin, Harmondsworth, 1962
Amis, Kingsley, *Memoirs*, Hutchinson, London, 1991
Appleyard, Bryan, 'The Dreary Laureate of Our Provincialism', *Independent*, 18 March 1993
Bennett, Alan, 'Alas! Deceived', *London Review of Books*, 25 March 1993
Bloomfield, B.C., *Philip Larkin: A Bibliography 1933–76*, Faber and Faber, London, 1979
Bradford, Richard, *Lucky Him: The Life of Kingsley Amis*, Peter Owen, London, 2001
Brennan, Maeve, *The Philip Larkin I Knew*, Manchester University Press, Manchester, 2002
Brett, R.L., 'Philip Larkin in Hull', in Jean Hartley, *Philip Larkin: The Marvell Press and Me*, Carcanet, Manchester, 1989
Conquest, Robert, *New Lines*, Macmillan, London, 1956
Corcoran, Neil, *English Poetry Since 1940*, Longman, London, 1993
Hartley, George (ed.), *Philip Larkin 1922–1985: A Tribute*, Marvell Press, London, 1988
Hartley, Jean, *Philip Larkin: The Marvell Press and Me*, Carcanet, Manchester, 1989
Heaney, Seamus, 'Englands of the Mind', in *Preoccupations: Selected Prose, 1968–78*, Faber and Faber, London, 1980

Hughes, Noel, 'The Young Mr Larkin', in Anthony Thwaite, *Larkin at Sixty*, Faber and Faber, London, 1982

Jacobs, Eric, *Kingsley Amis: A Biography*, Hodder and Stoughton, London, 1995

Jardine Lisa, 'Saxon Violence', *Guardian*, 8 December 1992

Leader, Zachary (ed.), *The Letters of Kingsley Amis*, HarperCollins, London, 2000

Morrison, Blake, *The Movement: English Poetry and Fiction of the 1950s*, Methuen, London, 1986

Motion, Andrew, *Philip Larkin: A Writer's Life*, Faber and Faber, London, 1993

Paulin, Tom, 'Into the Heart of Englishness', *Times Literary Supplement*, July 1990 (reprinted in Tom Paulin, *Minotaur Poetry and the Nation State*, Faber and Faber, London, 1992)

Thwaite, Anthony (ed.), *Larkin at Sixty*, Faber and Faber, London, 1982

Thwaite, Anthony (ed.), *Selected Letters of Philip Larkin, 1940–1985*, Faber and Faber, London, 1992

Tomlinson, Charles, 'The Middlebrow Muse', *Essays in Criticism*, 7, 1957, pp. 208–17

Wood, James, 'Want Not, Write Not', *Guardian*, 30 March 1993

Page references for *Trouble at Willow Gables*, *Michaelmas Term at St Bride's*, 'What Are We Writing For? An Essay', 'Ante Meridian: The Autobiography of Brunette Coleman', *No for an Answer* and *A New World Symphony* are all from Philip Larkin, *Trouble at Willow Gables and Other Fictions* (ed. James Booth), Faber and Faber, London, 2002.

Index

and form', 244; 'This Be the Verse', 207, 212–14; 'Toads', 117–19, 125; 'To My Wife', 30; 'To the Sea', 27; 'Ultimatum', 40–1; 'Vers de Société', 18, 200, 228–9, 230; 'View, The', 229–30; 'When first we faced, and touching showed', 242–3, 249; 'Whitsun Weddings, The', 157–60, 231; *Whitsun Weddings, The*, 202–3, 204, 207; 'Wild Oats', 71, 244; 'Within the dream you said', 68; *XX Poems*, 118, 143

Prose fiction
'Ante Meridian: The Autobiography of Brunette Coleman', 52, 53–4; *Girl in Winter, A*, 66–7, 73–6, 77–8; 'I Would Do Anything for You' (co-authored with Kingsley Amis), 45; *Jill*, 46, 54, 55–64, 65, 66, 71, 73, 77, 78, 95; 'Jolly Prince and the Distempered Ghost, The' (co-authored with Kingsley Amis), 45; *Michaelmas Term at St Bride's*, 51–2, 55; *New World Symphony, A*, 87–8, 103, 109–15, 119; *No for an Answer*, 84–7; *Trouble at Willow Gables*, 51–2, 87; 'What Are We Writing For? An Essay', 52, 54

Larkin, Catherine 'Kitty' (sister), 28–31, 76, 209, 248, 261
Larkin, Rosemary (niece), 261
Larkin, Sydney (father), 23, 24–31, 34–8, 53–4, 62–4, 76, 77, 83–4, 127–8, 170–1, 172, 212–14, 223–4, 248, 251, 254–5
Laurel, Stan, 100
Lawrence, D.H., 16, 23, 26, 32, 46, 59, 60, 62, 63, 64, 69, 70, 76, 77, 112, 127, 212, 225, 254, 262
Layard, John, 46, 53, 59
Leavis, F.R., 109, 111
Lewis, C. Day, 226

Listener, 40–1

MacDiarmid, Hugh, 221–2
Mackereth, Betty, 96, 171, 240–5, 248, 261
Macmillan, Harold, 160
Mann, Sargy, 226
Manning, Norman, 62
Mansfield, Katherine, 26
Marston, Doreen, 86
Marvell, Andrew, 123, 152–3, 259
Maugham, W. Somerset, 118, 146
Milton, John, 33, 197, 213
Monteith, Charles, 67, 146, 202, 220, 239
Montgomery, Bruce, 46–7, 54, 55, 66–7, 121, 130–1, 177, 257
Moon, Brenda, 231
Morrison, Blake, 14–15, 136, 261
Motion, Andrew, 15, 17, 30, 68, 70, 111, 221, 232, 239, 240, 259, 261, 263
Movement, the, 14–15, 135–42, 261
Munch, Edvard, 191
Murdoch, Iris, 137, 193
Murphy, Richard, 96, 123, 145, 220

Nicholson, Jack, 206
Nye, Robert, 238

O'Brien, Flann, 44
O'Connor, William Van, 136–7
Olivier, Laurence, 159
Orwell, George, 150
Osborne, John, 204
Owen, Wilfred, 183

Paisley, Ian, 233
Paulin, Tom, 13–14
Peace, Virginia, 258
Pinter, Harold, 98, 237, 257
Pope, Alexander, 135
Pound, Ezra, 26, 35, 136, 203
Powell, Anthony, 114